Praise for
Dirk Hayhurst

OUT OF MY LEAGUE

"A rare gem of a baseball book. *Out of My League* captures both the joy and the toll of becoming a big leaguer."
—**Tom Verducci,** *Sports Illustrated*

"Hayhurst's vivid, deeply felt account of his rookie season in the Majors blends a humorous, candid, and insightful memoir with an appealing love story. Grade: Home Run."
—*Cleveland Plain Dealer*

"Dirk Hayhurst writes about baseball in a unique way. Observant, insightful, human, and hilarious."
—**Bob Costas**

"The best writer in a baseball uniform."
—**Tyler Kepner,** *The New York Times*

"This book shows why baseball is so often used as a metaphor for life."
—**Keith Olbermann**

"The most candid portrayal of life as a professional athlete I've ever seen."
—**Michael Dolan, editor-in-chief,** *Athletes Quarterly*

"Dirk Hayhurst has done it again . . . Turns out he's a starter and a closer."
—**Tim Kurkjian, senior writer,** *ESPN The Magazine,* **and analyst/reporter ESPN television**

"Hayhurst writes an engaging tale . . . Hayhurst's story is authentic baseball . . . this is a humorous, heartfelt, but gritty tale of the nomadic baseball life."
—**Library Journal**

"Hayhurst has done it again . . . If only I could pitch as well as he can write, I might have more Cy Youngs than Greg Maddux."
—**Jayson Stark, ESPN.com**

"Extraordinary experiences, plenty of 'dirty laundry' . . . Hayhurst creates forward momentum and we want him to succeed."
—*Kirkus Reviews*

"Memorable . . . Hayhurst delivers an entertaining story for more than just sports fans."
—**Jordan Bastian, MLB.com**

"I find his writing both entertaining and thought provoking . . . unlike his fastball."
—**Ben Zobrist, Tampa Bay Rays All-Star**

"Hilarious, illuminating and poignant . . . This is more than a baseball book. It's the story of a man learning that it's possible to grip a baseball without it gripping him."
—**Craig Calcaterra, NBC Sports.com**

"Funny, earthy, touching."
—**King Kaufman,** *Bleacher Report*

"Brutally honest . . . I laughed, I cried, I even learned how to doctor a baseball."
—**Jonah Keri, author of** *The Extra 2%*

"A stirring, revealing tale of humanity."
—**Ken Rosenthal, Fox Sports**

"It's never too inside baseball, even though it is literally from inside baseball."
—**John Manuel, editor,** *Baseball America*

"Fascinating, compelling . . . Hayhurst explains life in the minors and the major leagues like you've never read it before."
—**J. J. Cooper,** *Baseball America*

"As they say in baseball, he does have enough hops as a writer to keep him in print for years to come . . . Entertaining and engaging . . . Reminiscent of Jim Bouton's *Ball Four*."
—*Booklist*

"His soul-baring narrative reveals baseball as a lottery ticket job with few winners and lots of losers that keeps you hooked through hope, and strung out on chances."
—*Publishers Weekly*

"Insight and humor from the pitcher's mound. . . . An insider's story of the day-to-day life of a baseball player striving to make the Bigs and then, for a very short time, making it big."
—*Businessweek*

"Like *The Bullpen Gospels*, *Out of My League* is fast, funny, and unsparing."
—*San Diego Union-Tribune*

"An insider's story of the day-to-day life of a baseball player . . . written with insight and humor from Hayhurst's position on the pitcher's mound."
—*Newsday*

THE BULLPEN GOSPELS

"A true picture of baseball."
—**Tim McCarver**

"One of the best baseball books ever written."
—**Keith Olbermann**

"A bit of Jim Bouton, a bit of Jim Brosnan, a bit of Pat Jordan, a bit of Crash Davis, and a whole lot of Dirk Hayhurst. Often hilarious, sometimes poignant. This is a really enjoyable baseball read."
—**Bob Costas**

"Fascinating . . . a perspective that fans rarely see."
—**Trevor Hoffman**

"A rollicking good bus ride of a book. Hayhurst illuminates a baseball life not only with wit and humor, but also with thought-provoking introspection."
—**Tom Verducci,** *Sports Illustrated*

BIGGER THAN THE GAME

Restitching a Major League Life

DIRK HAYHURST

CITADEL PRESS
Kensington Publishing Corp.
www.kensingtonbooks.com

CITADEL PRESS BOOKS are published by

Kensington Publishing Corp.
119 West 40th Street
New York, NY 10018

All Kensington titles, imprints, and distributed lines are available at special quantity discounts for bulk purchases for sales promotions, premiums, fund-raising, educational, or institutional use. Special book excerpts or customized printings can also be created to fit specific needs. For details, write or phone the office of the Kensington special sales manager: Kensington Publishing Corp., 119 West 40th Street, New York, NY 10018, attn: Special Sales Department; phone 1-800-221-2647.

CITADEL PRESS and the Citadel logo are Reg. U.S. Pat. & TM Off.

First trade paperback printing: March 2014

ISBN-13: 978-0-8065-3487-9
ISBN-10: 0-8065-3487-7

Printed in the United States of America

10 9 8 7 6 5 4 3 2

First electronic edition: March 2014

ISBN-13: 978-0-8065-3671-2
ISBN-10: 0-8065-3671-3

Library of Congress Cataloging-in-Publication data is available.

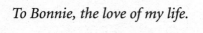

To Bonnie, the love of my life.

A NOTE FROM THE AUTHOR

When I was putting my first book together, more than a few teammates asked me what on God's green earth made me think I was allowed to break the code of the game and write about life as a player from inside.

Honest answer: because baseball was killing me.

I just didn't know it yet.

Let it be known that this book's purpose is to entertain. It is not intended to name names; pull the cover off the bare ass of drug use; show cheaters, adulterers, or tax dodgers; or do any other whistle-blowing. If you are looking for someone's dirty laundry, you won't find it here. Names have been changed at the request of some players and at my discretion, to give them more of a character feel as well as to protect identity. Some characters are composites created for ease of reading. While everything I relate is based on actual occurrences, I have attempted to conceal identities for the benefit of those who don't want to deal with any extra drama this book may bring their way. I was a teammate before I tried my hand at writing, and I hope to be one long after this book is published.

The mind is its own place, and in itself
Can make a heaven of hell, a hell of heaven.
—John Milton, *Paradise Lost*

Chapter 1

"Five!" I screeched. *"Five!* Sweet mother of God, are you trying to kill me?" I turned away and kicked a Plyoball across the weight room's sports turf floor and off a glass wall, hands extended skyward, as if asking The Almighty to intervene.

"Only five," corrected Mondo, clobbering me with a giant, sausage-fingered hand. "I'm not trying to kill you, I'm trying to make you into a beast!"

Mondo was the beast—a thick-necked, bald-headed behemoth of muscle; a former professional football player turned power lifter turned private trainer, and at six foot six and three hundred pounds he dwarfed me like a skyscraper over a hot dog stand. On more than one occasion, his "beast-making routine" worked me to complete muscle failure. Every time I found myself squirming for dear life under some crushing load he'd shoved on me, he'd laugh. And when I swore at him to shut up and get the weight off me, the big bastard would heft it with one effortless hand, saying, "It's not that heavy," as if I were being crushed by a kitten, or a butterfly.

Mondo did not understand his own strength. What was normal for him was abnormal for anyone who didn't grow up next to a nuclear power plant. I've seen him overhead-press three hundred pounds, which is more than I can squat. I've seen him dead lift more than eight hundred pounds, more than four of me. I've seen him pick a man off the floor and carry him to the bathroom so he could vomit. Okay, he picked *me* off the floor and carried *me* to the bathroom so *I* could vomit. But that was only because his workouts were the hardest I'd been through in all my years as an athlete.

Oh, and I was paying him for the privilege.

The previous off-season, 2009, I was claimed off waivers from the San Diego Padres and added to the Toronto Blue Jays. With this claim I received my first invitation to big league spring training. It was a major opportunity. I wanted to be ready. More than ready. I wanted to destroy the competition. You never know how many chances you'll get to impress the guys writing the big checks, and I aimed to blow them away. That's why I hired Mondo to give me that extra push and unlock my inner beast.

Instead of a push, I got punted by Mondo's size 17 boot. His workouts were nightmares, more crucible than training. Afterward, I crawled out of the place. Sometimes I crawled out before we finished, but Mondo would grab my foot and pull me back in. The gym was a state-of-the-art workout palace with sleek, polished glass, flat screens, fleets of cutting edge cardio equipment, a tanning salon, a day care, and a smoothie bar. But in Mondo's section—the section I was always in—it was nothing more than a glorified cage made from thick, scream-muting glass. Patrons routinely lurked against the panels, sipping their berry burst smoothies with protein boost, watching Mondo heap weights on me.

In the end it was worth every agony-filled second because Mondo got uncontestable results. I arrived at that 2009 big league training camp at a svelte 13 percent body fat, throwing mid-season heat, all cylinders firing. When a baseball entered my hand it became a deadly weapon.

It wasn't good enough.

I pitched well. Management confirmed that I put together one of the best spring trainings they'd ever seen and I'd more than earned a spot of the roster at the break of camp, but their hands were tied. They placed a bet on another player before the start of camp, bumping me off the forty-man roster to make room for him. The move made me ineligible for a big league roster until after the first month of the season.

I understood why they did it. Baseball is a what-have-you-done-lately job. The player they moved me for had a 96 mph fastball and an 88 mph slider. I had a 10 ERA in the big leagues. How could the Jays have known I'd show up as a well-oiled killing machine?

I made it up the majors eventually, and pitched myself into a 2.78 ERA when I did. That meant this spring, 2010, I was a front-runner to make the team, and I was not going to waste my shot.

My plan of attack was simple: work harder, go all out, leave nothing to chance. Whatever I did to get ready for last year's spring training, I'd do more of. However, as I looked over Mondo's planned workout—a circuit training course consisting of single and double leg squats, box jumps, hurdle jumps, bounding leaps, forward and lateral lunges, sled pull, RDLs, step-ups, crawler pushes, slide boards, kettle bell hops, rope slams, Vertimax jumps, abs, abs, and more abs, and all of it timed, with jump rope in between—repeating last year suddenly didn't seem like such a bad thing.

"Turn it over," said Mondo.

"Jesus Christ! There's more?"

"You're going to be a beast!" said Mondo, beaming, as if training ourselves into athlete pudding was not just healthy, but orgasmic. "You said that your boy Halladay does stuff like this all the time. You said you wanted to be like him."

"I know what I said, thank you," I said, waving at him in

hopes he wouldn't bring up any more of my foolish boasts. Roy Halladay's workouts are legendary. They made other players want to quit baseball, because mimicking them was hopeless unless you were built by a company that sent Terminators back in time. But, since I'd bragged about how I wanted to work out like Halladay, better even, Mondo invented a workout that would inevitably end with my final lift being the one where I pull my head out of a toilet bowl.

"You said you had the best year of your life after my workouts last off-season. Next year you're going to run laps around Halladay!"

I thought about how preposterous this was. How, right now, in some other gym in some other town, Roy "Doc" Halladay was probably looking at the same list I was. Except instead of whining, he was saying, "This is not enough! I pay you to challenge me."

"I'm fine with running behind Doc," I said.

"No backing out now," roared Mondo. "We're doing this!"

My shoulders slumped, and my head followed. "I'm going to need a real doctor after this," I said. Then, under my breath, "I hope I don't get any vomit in my hair."

"You won't need a doctor!" said Mondo. "You'll need a permit, because you'll be a dangerous weapon."

Looking over the list again, I asked, "Where are all the chest exercises?"

"You don't need a big chest to be a pitcher."

"But I want one. I mean, what's the point of all this self-abuse if I can't look in the mirror and feel sexy? I'm a damn big leaguer!"

"Who are you trying to impress with looks, your teammates? Hitters? Pssssh."

"Does it matter? It's my workout."

"Pitchers need glutes, quads, hips, and trunk." Mondo

pointed to all the respective body parts like he was singing the meathead version of "Head, Shoulders, Knees, and Toes."

"You'll feel sexy when you see all the zeros in that big league contract, Beast!" He slapped me again. Then, pumping a fist on each name, he shouted, "Dangerous weapon! Animal! Beast!" The recitation of the phrases really got him amped up, as if someone were yelling "bite, bite, bite" at an attack dog.

"Come on, just a few chest lifts?"

"You can do girl push-ups," said Mondo.

I threw my hands up. "I'm paying you to make workouts I want!"

"You are paying me to turn you into someone who gets paid tons of money. You're paying me to get that new house paid off for you. You're paying me to turn you into someone who can whip the ass of those bastards who made your life hell last year. I'm going to turn you into a monster that makes all the rules!"

I stopped my tantrum and eyed Mondo. He'd struck a nerve. Two, actually.

My wife, Bonnie, and I had just bought our first home. We financed it from the big league earnings I pulled down in my 2009 season. The place was historic, cozy, full of charm, with just enough grass for a dog to poop—nothing too fancy. It was totally within our means, in a good area with excellent schools and hardly any sex offenders. It was the type of thing we could resell should I get traded, even in a shipwrecked economy, not like some of the ten thousand-square-foot Mc-Mansions a few of the other guys I played with. However, despite Obama's handing out home-purchasing incentives like parade candy, I still had a sizeable mortgage to pay off. I could either (a) make it back to the big leagues and pay it off in record time, or (b) go back to Triple-A and take the loan to its soul-siphoning term. After plugging Mondo's weight routine into an equation for paying down compounding interest, I felt the will to get stronger coursing through my veins once again.

Getting stronger was one thing; the inner fire to endure Mondo's latest workout came from a different location: somewhere deep in an angry place. Yes, I'd made it back to the big leagues after a terrible debut in 2008. Yes, I'd done well for myself and was on the verge of a breakout season. And yes, I was living the big league dream life with beautiful wife and a lovely house with a chunk of sod for a dog to crap on, but I still had a chip on my shoulder. Something I wanted to prove to a certain group of bastards. That's the thing about baseball: there is a lot of competition to make it to the top, the most ruthless of which comes from within your own team.

"I'm a beast," I said it with a weak snarl.

"That's it, you're an animal!" shouted Mondo.

"I'm a monster," I said, more intensely this time.

"You're a machine!"

"I'm an interest-paying, fiscally responsible barbarian!" I shouted back at him.

"You're a . . . a . . ." Mondo hesitated.

"Never mind, meathead, let's just get this over with."

He clapped his hands together. "You're a beast!"

"Just don't injure me, okay?"

"Never!" he said. And slapped me on the back so hard my ribs popped.

Chapter 2

Mondo didn't kill me, but he damn sure tried. Exiting my car post-workout required me to hoist my legs through the driver's-side door as if I was paralyzed from the waist down.

Ignoring the pain in my legs and butt, I hobbled to the stairs at the front of my little gray, snow-dusted house, stopped, and stared at the three small steps leading up to my door as if they were Mt. Everest. I might have laid down and curled into the fetal position right there if not for the brown box perched at the top of the stairs. I fought my way up the steps, collected the box, pushed into the house, and collapsed onto my couch a spent man.

My stink was palpable. My workout clothes clung to me like wet newspaper. I needed a shower and a protein shake, but lying down just felt so good. I hated Mondo during the workouts, but afterward, when I knew I'd pushed myself to the limit, I loved him for not letting me quit. The confidence a hard workout builds is less tangible than the muscle but just as important, and this year I knew I'd need it.

I slid the box from the coffee table, placed it on my chest, and ripped off its tape packaging seal. Inside, along with a congratulatory note from my editor, was a trio of advance reading copies of my first book, *The Bullpen Gospels*. I'd spent all of last season writing it, and now the final product was almost ready. The book would hit shelves on April 1, opening day of the coming season, and when it did my life would be forever changed.

On April 1, I would join an elite company of player authors. Elite, but unfortunately not beloved, at least not by their teammates. From some, I would take hell for violating the code of the locker room. From others, I would be praised for letting people inside. But to all, I would represent a polarizing force—a bold move for a guy who hadn't yet accrued even one full year of big league service time. I was voluntarily breaking the code of the baseball locker room and I had to believe I was strong enough to handle what would happen as a result. I had my reasons, but they would be of little value if everyone felt I was guilty until proven innocent. And there was only one way I knew to be proven innocent.

I had to come into camp in shape and ready to dominate. If there was one thing the game had taught me, it's that success on the field covers a multitude of sins. I'd watched enough players get away with terrible behavior thanks to gifted on-field performances to know that playing results are the real judge and jury. Just the simple act of keeping a journal with the intent to write a book had earned me a few enemies. The finished book would surely earn more. But, if I pitched well enough, my success would go a long way toward absolving me of my many transgressions. If I didn't, it would be a long, hard season on and off the field.

As I lay on my black faux-leather couch with the book sitting on my chest and the coming season on my mind, my cell rang. Normally, considering how my legs throbbed with every heartbeat, I would have let the call go to voice mail. But it was the *Perfect Strangers* ringtone, a tone that demanded attention. I frantically rolled off the couch and crawled across the living room carpet to answer. Adopting my finest ass-kissing voice just before picking up, I greeted the caller with, "Alex, always *so* good to hear from you."

It was Alex Anthopoulos calling. The Blue Jays' general manager, and my boss. He had recently replaced J. P. Ricciardi, and was calling all his players and chatting about the state of the Blue Jay union. It was an attempt at transparency, a love language all players find seductive, including me. Alex was actually the first person I talked to when I became a Blue Jay. He was just the assistant general manager then, but he seemed happy to welcome me aboard and tell me how much the program liked me, or at least my "upside."

The GM's job is a real balancing act, and double-talk is an easy habit for them to fall into. On the one hand, Alex has to have friendly relationships with his players in order to coax the best out of their talent. On the other, he's charged with the responsibility of winning, even if it means reducing a friend into a pile of numbers and erasing them from the face of the game. This is probably why most players end up hating their GMs, because, statistically speaking, more players end their career released than with the GM's arm over their shoulder.

Alex knew this, and was honest and up front with his players, even if it wasn't good news. I liked that about him. And the way I figured it, the least I could do was shoot Alex straight in return. Sure, I was as sweet to him as a morning kiss when we talked, but that's because he was my boss. I never tried to put anything past him. I understood that the game was cruel, his job was hard, and that keeping things professional was best for both of us. When he called last year around this time to tell me my chance to make the big squad was gone after an entire off-season of Mondo kicking my ass to get ready for it, instead of uncorking a stream of cuss words and promising I'd make him regret it, I calmly told him that I understood, thanked him for the opportunity, and wished him the best.

I'll admit that getting sent to Triple-A Las Vegas to watch my ERA balloon in the hot desert air did leave me feeling a little angry. Then I got called up, Alex became the general manager, and I looked like a genius. In fact, after his promotion, Alex told me that in a business of egos and posturing, my calm acceptance of bad luck left an impression on him. It's always good to hear that you've made a good impression on your boss. What that meant for my future, I wasn't sure, but I kept my fingers crossed that it would be good, and if a little butt-kissing helped me stay in his good graces, so be it.

"Hey, Dirk. How are you?" inquired Alex.

"Better now." Smooch.

"Good, good." He went straight to the point. "I just wanted to reach out and touch base with all our guys, let everyone know where they stand going into this off-season."

"Okay."

"We're pleased with your performance last season. You pitched well. You could have cut down on the walks." He stopped. "You know what, I'm not going to knock it. You had a good season."

"Thank you." I smiled proudly.

"As for next year, we're thinking about using you in the same capacity. Looking at things as they stand right now, you could get some Triple-A time next year, like you did this year, but anything can change before camp. We have some guys that are going to get more expensive to keep, and we think you could be one of the guys that fills their roles when they do."

"I understand," I said.

"I'll be honest with you, because you've always been honest with me," continued Alex. "You never know how the future is going to work out, but we see you playing a role for us.

Come in dealing like you did last year and you'll make a strong case."

"That's great to hear, Alex, thank you. I appreciate your transparent communication." I sounded natural as I said it; he couldn't know I was vigorously fist-pumping as I spoke. Then I added, for good measure, "You know, I think your openness is the mark of a true leader. It's a gift I think the world has lost sight off in its constant quest for power and recognition. I'm so thankful you still have it, though I'm sure *my* humble opinion doesn't count for much."

"It counts, Dirk. I've always appreciated your insight and your candor. Don't be afraid to contact me for any reason. I want to have open dialogues with my players. I'd rather talk to you than your agents. Do you have any questions for me?"

"No, sir," I said. "You've made everything crystal clear, as usual."

"How's the book coming?"

I choked and sat up. I knew he knew I was a writer; everyone in the organization knew by now. It's just that I'd never been asked about it by the brass before, by Alex. "Good," I said, looking over to the advance reading copies on the coffee table, suddenly feeling like I'd just been caught red-handed. "It's all done and going out to reviewers now."

"Great. Can't wait to read it. It doesn't say anything bad about me, does it?" He added a playful chuckle, but he didn't know how many times I'd gotten that question without the chuckle.

"It doesn't say anything bad about anyone," I said.

"Sure, sure." The phone went silent for a moment before Alex followed up. "Alright then, stay in shape, there's a lot of opportunity this year." Then he added, "Just remember, anything can happen in the off-season."

"Sure, but the one thing you can count on is my being ready for any chance you give me, boss."

We said our good-byes and hung up. I set the phone down next to the books and thought about the conversation. What Alex said about me being a future role player stuck in my head. I'd always seen myself as an average right-handed minor league reliever. There were times I'd given up on the idea that I would ever make it at all. I had to scratch and claw my way to the big leagues through luck and attrition. Now I was in a position to be a role player with a big league team. In the no-guarantees world of baseball, this was about as good as it gets.

I picked up a copy of the book again. Turned it in my hands. Felt the weight of it. When I started writing, I hoped it would add something to my life. Now, with so much going for me, I sincerely hoped I hadn't created my undoing.

Chapter 3

"I think I need to go back to the gym," I said to Bonnie as she emerged from the bathroom in her giraffe-print pajamas.

It was late now, bedtime for my beautiful wife. I generally went to sleep later, after spending a couple of hours "unwinding" by splattering digital blood and guts in some PS3 video game world. I'd be knee-deep right about now, but I couldn't stop thinking about my talk with Alex, the future, books, chances, and guarantees.

"But you went to the gym once already today, didn't you?" asked Bonnie. "Remember, you said your ass was throbbing more than usual?"

"Yeah, but ass or no ass, this year is a big one. And, well, I really didn't get in any upper body," I said, while poking the soft mass that posed as my biceps.

"I like your upper body just fine," said Bonnie, sliding her hands over my shoulders.

"You're obligated to say that because we're married. Besides, we're still in the honeymoon phase. I just bought you a house, then there are the appliances . . ." I began counting off a list on my fingers. I bought our house as sort of a first-year anniversary present a little over a month ago. We were still getting used to it. Some might say I set the bar for our future anniversaries a little too high, but I was confident the best was yet to come.

"After all I've spent on us, you'd better like me for at least a few more years," I said.

"Shut up," she said, pushing me back onto the bed. "I'd love you even if you ended up in your grandma's basement. Now, forget the gym, I'll give you a workout."

Bonnie is smaller than me, but she pushed me around easily, as only a woman can. She had warm brown eyes and light brown hair, a genuine smile, and an unflinchingly positive personality. And she looked great in giraffe print. I loved her more than anything the game or its riches could ever give me, and I rarely skipped a chance to be in our bedroom with her. But I was now the head of a family, always thinking about our future happiness. I understood that it required present sacrifice.

"I have no time for your devilish tricks, temptress!" I declared, turning my face from her flurry of kisses. "I must train for the sake of our future well being. I must—" She connected her lips to mine, shutting me up. We kissed for a bit until Bonnie pulled back, revolted.

"You"—she tried to wipe the taste from her mouth— "have changed your protein-shake flavor."

"I did," I said with a tense frown. "I get a deal on EAS products through Major League Baseball. It also makes me a little gassy, which, uh, you're probably going to notice in a few seconds."

Bonnie stopped wiping and rolled off me to the far corner of the bed, where she scrunched up her nose before covering her face with a pillow. "Oh God, that's terrible," she said from behind the fabric. "Go to the gym. The moment is dead. You killed it."

"Hey, you were on top of me! Besides, I never say anything to you when you fart during our intimate moments."

"Because my farts don't smell like rotten vanilla protein."

"Banana cream!" I corrected.

"Whatever." She waved me toward the door. "My farts don't smell like yours."

"Well, they certainly don't smell like cotton candy."

"Go to the gym."

"Alright, I am, but when I get back I'm gonna rock you like a hurricane."

"Not unless you wipe your butt first," Bonnie said.

"*Romance!*" I said, and shut the bedroom door behind me.

I pulled back into the gym around ten p.m. By this time of night, the usual crowd of turbo moms and douchebags in V-necks with their hats turned backward was gone. A gym is an athlete's office during the off-season, and it's always nice to find your office free of calorie-burners playing for the tie in the never-ending battle between weekend binges and midriff management.

I've worked out in a lot of gyms in my professional career, but this was by far the nicest. Affording it was another perk of my big league paycheck. Before this, I could only afford to go to my old high school, or a YMCA, or wherever else there was something heavy that needed lifting. This place had personal trainers, like Mondo, who really knew athletes, and not just chunky mommies trying to work off baby weight. It had an area where you could throw med balls and jump hurdles and pull weighted sleds and run agility courses. But tonight wasn't about athleticism; tonight was about the gun show.

"You wanna whine about me writing something?" I said after a couple sets of biceps curls. "Boom—answer to these puppies." I flexed in the mirror as hard as I could; still not enough to fill my shirt sleeve. I frowned and decided I was more a pecs guy anyway. I scooped up a pair of fifty-pound dumbbells and carted them to a nearby weight bench. I lay back and pumped out ten presses, then sat up again and rested, balancing the weights on the thick of my thighs.

Between sets, while I waited for my chest to recharge, I glanced at one of the gym's "cardio theater" televisions hanging above. The aftermath of the Phillies' trade for Roy Halladay was still being sifted by the media. Talking heads offered insight, analysis, and prophecy. The general consensus was that it was a great fit for Roy, since he'd finally have a team behind him that could get into the postseason, where he deserved to be after his great years with the impotent Blue Jays.

It's not as if we, his old teammates, didn't know he deserved better with the quality of work he turned in every year. We'd even joke that if we made it to the postseason, Doc would probably pitch every single game. He was so good, the bullpen treated every game he pitched like a day off. There was no question that the Phillies would get their money's worth out of Doc. Big contracts don't always equate to on-field production, but he was as close to a sure thing as it got.

Doc's departure left colossal shoes to fill. He was the shining face of the Jays, significant beyond the level of a normal franchise player. The Jays don't receive a lot of attention in the land where hockey is king. It took talent like his to carve out a place among the steady stream of on-ice related highlights. Plus, because there is no ESPN in Canada, and no Rogers Sports Network in the United States, the Blue Jays were, for the most part, an afterthought unless playing one of the MLB's top-tier publicity mongers, like the Red Sox or the Yankees. Replacing Doc's arm in the rotation would be challenging; replacing his presence in the country was an entirely different issue.

The question the talking heads did not ask, but that

brought players like me to weight rooms at odd hours, was, who would take Doc's place? Someone would have to. A franchise needs a face. Baseball, after all, is not the only thing that the industry of baseball sells. It's not even the flagship product. It's greatness. And greatness can be manufactured around a player like a team must manufacture runs in place of a genuine offense. The Jays needed a new hero to put on advertising banners and gift-shop jerseys. Someone new would be chosen to play the role of team icon.

And I had just as much a chance becoming that icon as anyone else.

Sure, there were front-running candidates like Aaron Hill, Ricky Romero, and Adam Lind. But Alex Anthopoulos just told me the club liked me. That *he* liked me. That I'd get *my* shot. And if I hit my mark, with my book coming out at the same time, it could change my world forever. A little on-field success with a little off-field success could create the kind of synergy that could change my everything. I could go from being some non-prospect right-hander who never thought he'd make it out of the minors, to a name. A brand. A known commodity. A certified, nothing-to-prove, bona fide big leaguer. And no one, player or fan, would be able to tell me otherwise.

Excited, I traded in my current dumbbells for more weight. Fifty pounds—more than enough for a pitcher—became seventy. I carted dumbbells back to the bench and fell back into a supine position. I precariously moved the weight into place to press it. After getting the weight up five times, on the sixth attempt I felt a pop in my right shoulder.

I dropped the weights to the floor, where they rumbled across the rubber mats like boulders. Sitting up, I grabbed my shoulder with my left hand. No pain via touch, but when I wound my arm over my head, I felt a bite at the top of the circuit like an electric shock.

Spooked, I stood clutching my shoulder. This is the off-season, I reminded myself; this is the weight room. I've come out of here several times feeling bumped and battered, muscles I never knew I had aching. Just this morning, Mondo worked me so hard I could barely walk. There was no reason to assume this was anything more.

But it was also my throwing shoulder, my bread and butter. I stood up and ran my arm through a series of tests, poking and prodding and digging. I pushed against the weight-room wall, hung from the side of weight racks, and traced letters of the alphabet with my arm extended straight out before me like some fascist dictator. Nothing, or at least nothing consistent. According to the athlete's handbook, if the pain isn't consistent it isn't worth worrying about.

I breathed a sigh of relief. Looking at myself in the weight-room mirror, I said to the person staring back at me with his dreams of grandeur, "Remember your place, average righty. Leave the big weights to the big boys." Then I laughed at myself, and at the irony. To get hurt now with so much at stake would be catastrophic. I decided Mondo was one of the wisest men I knew, and called it a night. Big pecs could wait until I was retired.

Home, showered, the smell of protein shake fumigated from my mouth, I slipped into bed next to Bonnie. She wasn't asleep yet; she had stayed up watching gay men decorate houses while I was out.

"Mmm, you smell clean," she said.

"I showered, just for you," I said.

Bonnie shut the lid on her laptop, set it aside, and scooted toward me. "Breath check," she said. I exhaled. Minty freshness. "Butt check," she said. I lifted the covers and dropped them, billowing out nothing but crisp, clean air. "You pass," she said, and resumed putting her hands on me.

"I know why you are so frisky," I said, taking hold of her. "It's all those gay designers you watch. They leave you yearning for a real man in your life."

"No, it's that I have to make good use of the few times you don't stink."

"You'd better hurry up then, I drank another shake before I came up here."

Spurred by the threat of more banana-scented ass, Bonnie pushed me down on the bed, pinning my arms over my head.

"Oww!" I shouted, wincing in pain.

"What?" Bonnie said, recoiling. "Did I knee you in one of your man parts again?"

"No," I said, grabbing my right shoulder.

"What is it?"

I rolled to my side, cradling my shoulder as best I could. "I don't knnn—" I stopped myself. "It's nothing. I'll be fine . . . I think."

Chapter 4

They could release me, I thought, as I stood staring out the window of the Kent State field house. Winter had struck early and snow was blitzing the area with a surprise attack. *That would be their most efficient move. Maybe, if they're feeling merciful, I'll go back to Triple-A.* I took a deep breath and held it—*But they'll probably release me. That's what I'd do*—then exhaled.

A week had passed since the pop in my shoulder. In my eight professional years I've had plenty of random, unexplained pains show up only to disappear, in similarly random and unexplained ways, without a trace. Sometimes all it takes is a night off, a bag of ice, and a couple of Advils. Sometimes it takes several. But this pain was different. None of my remedies seemed to help. Each day that it lingered, my fear grew. The only medicine I had left was denial, and I applied it liberally.

It's masculine, even heroic, to deny pain. Athletes learn to do it from a young age as a way of earning respect. Honor is bestowed to those who soldier on while injured. Disgust is reserved for those who don't. Consequently, we learn to cut the language of weakness out of our vocabulary, and by the time we reach the pro level, it's second nature to pretend pain isn't there.

But denial as a survival skill is also useful for the business dynamics of the game. A player can pitch bad, slump, or commit a string of errors and still find a job. If he can play, he's got a chance. If he gets injured, however, he becomes dead weight—and dead weight doesn't keep a job for long.

This was why I made myself go to workouts with Mondo after the pop, why I soldiered through the shoulder pain, and why I refused to let on anything was wrong around Bonnie. And the absolute worst thing I could do was let the organization know I had pain. Not before I knew beyond a shadow of a doubt that I couldn't work through it. Once I told the powers that be I had pain in my arm, things would get a whole lot more complicated, and there would be no turning back.

As soon as a player says he's experiencing pain, a paper trail begins. Every step from ouch to operation is documented, and factored into the team's potential cost to payout. It's the economics of baseball. A player is a commodity at the professional level and injuries factor into their risk-versus-reward value. When players break, it costs the organization to fix them. If a player gets hurt in the minors, the fix is relatively cheap. If the player gets hurt in the majors, it can cost a fortune. The clout of the players' union means that when big leaguers get hurt, the organization spares no expense making them better, including all the peripheral expenses like medication, housing, rental cars, flights, meal money, and contracted salary—all on top of what it will cost to replace that player's talent on the field. Furthermore, each day a player spends on the big league disabled list counts toward his major league service time, the main gauge of a player's retirement benefits package, which the organization also pays for. Finally, the organization can't demote a player if he was injured as an active major league player (which, since this was the off-season, I technically wasn't).

If you stop to think about it, the big league disabled list actually provides incentives to get hurt, especially if you're a fringe talent promoted only to cover someone else's injury. In fact, being injured in the big leagues is so profitable that players routinely joke about getting to the Show just to pull up lame and check into what players call "Club Med" for a paid vacation. Some players fake injuries just to stay in Club Med and continue to draw service time and big checks. Some even fake it as a way of getting back at the organization for sending them down—or trying to send them down anyway, because once you say you're hurt in the bigs, you can't be sent down.

Organizations aren't stupid, which is why they track medical issues so fervently. Yes, the info is used to keep players healthy, but a wonderful side effect is that it saves a bit of money, too. If given the choice between two equal talents, the organization will go with the one least likely to break. Since the only way they can gauge who might snap is by keeping track of those who have a history of breaking down, players have learned to cover their tracks. They self-treat, they buy their own meds, they see their own doctors in private and pay them in cash. Some even leave the country to get treatment. If they must confess they're broken, they do it when they stand to gain, not during the off-season when the organization has all the power.

Today I was going to play catch, probably the most important game of catch in my entire life. I could push through off-season workouts by denying the pain and self-treating. But if I couldn't throw, the singular act that defines life as a pitcher, my hand would be forced and I'd be at the organization's mercy.

For the last seven years I did my long tossing at the Kent

State field house, which played refuge to several pro arms looking for a place to throw during the winter. I had a friend in the area I played catch with, a fellow pro named Jason Stephens. Like me, he was a 2003 draftee with seven years of professional experience. The difference was I signed as a senior in college while Jason signed as a senior in high school. He was four years younger, selected in a higher round, and for *way* more money. He was going to be the next big thing.

Then his elbow blew up.

Tommy John surgery and fourteen months of rehab put him off the radar and looking for work. The Phillies had just offered him an invite to minor league camp, but the injury had set him back substantially, maybe permanently.

Jason pushed through the doors while I weighed possibilities on the scales of doom in my head. He looked like a baseball-playing gingerbread cookie covered with powdered-sugar snow. He wore his workout gear into the facility: microfiber T-shirt, mesh shorts, his glove in one hand, a pair of sneakers pinched in the other. The only thing shielding him from the elements was a ridiculous hand-woven scarf.

"You're late," I barked at him, unconsciously digging in my right shoulder.

"Whoa." Jason held up his arms as if to say *don't shoot.* "Have you looked outside? I'm risking my life coming here at all. Most guys don't start throwing this early anyway. Don't know why you're in such a big hurry. Don't waste your bullets."

"Sorry," I said. "Normally I wouldn't waste any bullets, but . . ." I took my hand off my shoulder. "Well, it's been a long week."

Jason eyed me curiously. I looked back at him the same way. "Nice scarf," I said. "What's next, Skinny Jeans, 'Team Edward' stitched on your mitt?"

Jason shook his head and started walking toward the

doors of the field house. "Does it make you feel more like a big leaguer to pick on people lower than you?" He stomped the packed snow from his shoes.

"Yes, you know it does," I said. "That's the whole point of being a big leaguer—rubbing it in the face of minor leaguers."

"You've changed," he joked. "I thought you'd be one of the humble ones, but I was wrong. 'Big League Dirk.' Why are you having a bad week? One of your elitist big league friends threaten you for writing about them again?"

I frowned at him for bringing up such a sour memory.

"Sorry," he said. "Too soon?"

"It's fine. And it has nothing to do with the book."

"Did they take you off the roster?"

"Not yet."

Jason stopped walking and studied me. Then, as if someone let all the air out of him, his shoulders slumped and he asked, "You're injured?"

I looked away. "I dunno. Maybe," I said as nonchalantly as I could.

"Elbow?" asked Jason, turning out his arm to show the "zipper" scar left by the stitches of his Tommy John surgery.

"No, my shoulder," I said.

"Uh-oh," he said, stealing a glance back at the bleak weather. Then, just as you'd expect from a fellow professional player and friend, he helped me prop up my denial with a little of his own. "Well, it's still early in the off-season, so don't let it rattle you. It's probably just the weather. You'll feel better in a week or two."

I smiled gratefully and agreed.

We walked to the doors separating the lobby from the field house. The sound of metal college bats clanging in batting practice rang like hammers on anvils, echoing across the hollow expanse. The Kent State Golden Flash baseball team was working out, and we planned to act as parasites in the background of their operation.

"How's your literary masterpiece coming?" asked Jason. "The *Bull. Pen. Gospels*," he said, like he was reading a grand marquee. He looked back to me. "Did you leave in the part where you crapped in the mascot's head? That should win you a Pulitzer for sure."

I knew he was trying to change the subject, but, as I was learning, there were no subjects not related to my arm. The success of the book was connected to my career, my career was connected to my arm and, just like that, I was back to anxiously digging my shoulder again.

"The publishers let me keep it," I said.

"Wow. I still can't believe you did that."

"Yeah, neither can I, really. But that's baseball."

"I dunno; I never crapped in a mascot's head."

"And that's why you're not in the big leagues."

We ran a few light sprints, did jumping jacks, lunged in place. We spread out on the floor and flipped our legs over our heads and did some poor man's yoga. We pulled our fingers back and tweaked our elbows and spun our arms like propeller blades. Finally we stood up from the green field-house turf, backed twenty yards away from one another, and put our gloves on.

"You ready?" I asked Jason.

"Sure. You?"

I shrugged. "Guess we'll find out."

Glove on, ball in hand, I went into my throwing motion. The windup, the step, the release: pain, fresh and heavy ripping through the inside of my shoulder. Jason caught the ball, stopped, and looked me over.

"I'm fine," I said, and waved for him to throw it back.

He wound and returned it, just as easy as you please.

Back and forth we volleyed, the pain repeating each time,

though I refused to let on. Then, by the time we had backed up to about forty yards, I had to stop to take a Lamaze-like breather.

"What's up?" called Jason.

"I'm fine," and I waved at him to shut up and throw.

"Your arm bothering you?"

"It's just a little cranky," I said.

"It's early."

"Damn right," I said, clutching my shoulder like it might fall off at any moment. It only seemed to really hurt when I threw, but it throbbed from the aftershock long after I'd let go of the ball. I waited for it to dissipate before I tried again.

There was really no use denying it anymore. Something was wrong. It was now a question of how much pain I could take and still do my job. If this was as bad as it got, I could fight it. I could medicate it. I could make it to the first bullpen session of spring training and *then* fall off the mound screaming and clutching my arm, pointing the finger at everyone by me. But if this light-catch pain was just the beginning . . .

There was only one way to test it. On my next toss, I wound up and threw the ball much harder than I had before. With the increase of effort came an exponential increase of pain. As soon as the ball was out of my hand, I doubled over and cursed.

Jason caught the ball and froze, watching me with concern. The metal clanging of bats stopped as a few Kent State players ceased practicing to see what was the matter. I had grabbed my shoulder, not to dig, but to make sure it stayed attached. Then, under the weight of the truth, the pain, and the onslaught of repercussions, I dropped to one knee and began violently beating my glove into the ground with the arm I was still able to lift.

Chapter 5

A month later I sat on an examining table, shirt off, head drooped in what was becoming my customary posture. This was the third examination since the incident at Kent State, except this one was in Florida, by the Blue Jays' team doctor and head trainer.

The team flew me down to the Jays spring-training-and-rehab facility for a full inspection, including X-rays, an arthogram, and an MRI. They said this was the best way they could get a look at what was going on inside my shoulder. That is, without opening it up. Which, after two cortisone shots, a couple of high-powered bottles of anti-inflammatory pills, Hybresis patches, and dozens of rehab hours, was looking more and more like a possibility.

George Poulis, the Blue Jays' head trainer, stood in the corner of the small examination room checking his email on his BlackBerry while we waited for the doctor to arrive. Maybe it was because George dealt with the mortal part of the game so frequently that he had such a steady look on his face, like this was just another day.

I did not share his calmness.

I'd never been injured before. I didn't realize how arm pain could make your whole life hurt. I had always assumed that prosperity would flow uninterrupted from my right arm. Now visions of loss played in a continuous loop of excruciating detail in my head. *I'm not really here,* I kept thinking. *I can't be. Just a month ago, the GM was telling me I was part of the team's future.*

The team doctor entered the room, greeted George like a friend, then said hello to me. He had me get up, stick my arms out wide as if I were an airplane, then resist while he pressed my wings down. He moved my arms and tried it again, then another position, and another. These were all standard shoulder stress tests designed to engage different members of the throwing-muscle group. None of them hurt, so far.

"How about this?" asked the doc, pulling my arm over my head into the throwing position. That's when I felt it. Like someone crossed two hot wires somewhere in my shoulder. The doctor relented when I squirmed. "A little there, huh?"

"Yeah, just a little."

George watched with his arms crossed, a look of concern breaking on his face. The doc continued to find mines buried in my shoulder by pressing, pulling, and twisting it. I felt like someone was holding a voodoo-doll version of me and was driving pins into its shoulder and tying its arm into knots.

The doctor stopped experimenting on me and conjectured with George. They stood side by side, staring at me, muttering softly back and forth about the possibilities as if I was some math problem scrawled across a blackboard. I stared back at them, my eyes darting back and forth to follow their muffled comments, trying to piece together the gravity of the situation. Nothing came of it. When they finished, the only clear answer they had was that more tests were in order.

The arthogram was first. Forget the voodoo doll, since this test involved a foot-long needle getting pounded into my

shoulder capsule while I watched via continuous X-ray footage. Once it was in, dye was injected. It spread through my
shoulder joint like ink forming a cloud in a glass of water.
This dye, I was told, would help the MRI be more thorough.
"It had better," I said, staring at the needle as it dangled from
my shoulder like a flagpole.

After the needle was yanked out, I spent the next hour
jammed in a tube while an MRI machine painted the dye-
assisted picture. Then it was back to the doctor's examination room, where he and George stared at screens full of
images of my arm, looking for clues. It all looked like ab-
stract art to me: blues, blacks, and whites. I thought the tests
would show something clearer, something like the aftermath
of an explosion. Instead the pair pointed to little pockets of
white and made comments. They mentioned words like im-
pingements, fray, and tear. However, at the end of their conversation, they agreed there was no real way to be sure unless
they could get inside and take a look—the worst-case scenario.

"Here's the plan," said the doc, scooting his wheeled stool
near me on the examination table. "We're going to give you
another cortisone shot, this time in the back of your shoulder capsule, where I think most of your pain generators are.
See if we can't get it to calm down."

"Yeah, more needles," I said.

"We'll shut you down for about two more weeks and see if
it gets any better."

"Which would still give you time to get up and throwing
for spring training," inserted George.

"If that doesn't work," continued the doc, "I think our
only other option would be to go in and see what the problem is." AKA surgery.

"Give me some scenarios for what would happen," I said,
looking to George. "You know, depending on what you could

find in there." I nodded to my shoulder as if it were some place on a map and not my body.

"Well," George started, "if we find a serious tear and you need something anchored down, you'll miss all of next season, no question about it."

I took that like a punch in the face. I had known this was a real possibility, but I thought they'd at least warm up to it. Jab me a couple times with minor issues, then swing hard with the year-out-of-commission stuff. I guess we were past that now.

"I don't think that's what this looks like, though," George quickly added when he noticed me wilt on the table. "But you don't know what they'll find. I mean, every pitcher who gets an MRI is going to show an abnormal result. That comes with being a pitcher. It's an unnatural motion and we don't expect everything to be normal in there."

"And what is 'normal'?" added the doctor. "We could go in there and find everything torn up, and what would we be repairing it back to? Normal for a non-pitcher's arm is vastly different from normal for a professional player with a lot of mileage on his arm. For example, your humerus bone is actually twisted"—he acted like he was ringing water from an invisible towel as he spoke—"from all the years of you torquing on it via your throwing motion. When a surgeon goes in, he'd have to evaluate what he finds based on what changes are normal compared to the amount of damage. That's why these tests are so limited." He gestured back to the screen with all the scans. "Some guys have more damage than others, and that's *normal* for them."

"But if we go in at all," said George, "we're looking at you getting back to the mound by halfway through the season, best case. That's why we're going to try another shot with rest and see how you do."

A half season!—another punch in the head. Sure, if this

were a perfect world I'd be back with the big team as soon as I was healthy. But the baseball world is not perfect, nor is it fair. I got to the bigs with the Jays because someone else got hurt. Someone would replace me if I went under the knife— it's the natural order of the baseball kingdom. At my age, with my average stuff, if I came back from this less than 100 percent, it could mean the end of my big league career.

"Hey," George said, "if you weren't a player, we wouldn't be having this discussion. Even my grandmother, if left to recover, would get better from something like this. You'd eventually heal up if you didn't throw anymore. But because you're a baseball player and you've only got so many years to make use of that skill, time is a factor. We could rest you for a few months and see how you do, but if the pain is still there and we have to have surgery, you'll miss at least all of this coming season, and possibly some of next."

"Then is our best interest in doing the surgery ASAP?" I asked, hoping to take some comfort from the fact that if my hands were tied, I could at least commit myself to the best course of action from here on.

"Well," said George sadly, probably because he was going to have to punch me in the head again, "you never know how the body will react once you cut it open. You might not recover according to any of these plans. It's a possibility."

It was a lot of bad news in one sitting, but there was one thing I hadn't been told. One thing I needed to hear, just to get it all out there.

"Can the Blue Jays release me?"

"They would probably still pay for your surgery and rehab," he offered.

"But, they could release me?" I just wanted to hear George say it.

"You got hurt training to play for us, so, I don't *think* they would."

"But they could?"

"Yes," he said, finally. "Yes, it's in their right to release you."

I fell back on the training table—knockout.

"Soooo," said the doc, clearing his throat as I lay on the table with my eyes closed, "we'll give you the shot, see how you do with it, and then reevaluate you in another couple weeks. If you're still manifesting the symptoms, we'll decide how to move forward." Then, cheerily, he added, "Sound good?"

"Not really," I said.

Chapter 6

Two weeks later, the shot had run its course and I found myself sitting in bed with a shoulder that still hurt. The cortisone shot masked the symptoms for a while, but they came back, same as always. I had a long, hard talk with George about the next step. He said he'd inform Alex, and the next day they would call and tell me the organization's next move. I would have surgery; that was now guaranteed. What was yet to be decided was if I'd have it as a major leaguer, a minor leaguer, or a freshly unemployed free agent.

It was surreal how much life had changed in just a couple of months. I'd gone from fantasizing over how far I could fly with baseball under my wings to how hard the coming crash was going to be. I couldn't stop thinking about it, the way it happened, what could happen, and the bitter irony of it all.

"This could ruin everything," I said to Bonnie while hugging a pillow. It was late, but I couldn't sleep.

"We're going to be alright," said Bonnie, rubbing my back. "Relax, sweetie. We can handle whatever happens, together. You were smart with the money you made and put us in a good situation." She scooted behind me, wrapping her arms around my waist while resting her head on the back of my uninjured shoulder. "Even if you lose your job, I can handle things until we regroup. Remember the plan: 'You hit for power, I hit for average,'" she said, quoting our financial strategy.

I cupped her hand in mine and smiled. She had mastered the art of speaking to a baseball player in just over a year of marriage. "You're a great hitter," I said. "But it's not just the money. This is all I know. What if it's all over tomorrow? What if I never come back?"

"We'll cross that bridge when we come to it."

"We have come to it. We're on the bridge right now. Hell, we're trying to get across before it collapses. And"—I turned to face her—"this career is tied to so many things. It's been a part of everything I've ever done as far back as I can remember. I can say it's not a big deal, that it's a kid's game, that we'll find a way without it. But it's how I make my living. It's how we bought this house. It's how I became popular enough for someone to let me write a book and it's what that book is about. It's what I am." I was hyperventilating now. My heart pounding like I was about to run out of the bullpen. I didn't understand it, and I couldn't seem to stop it either.

"You're more than a baseball player," said Bonnie.

"Maybe, but it's a theory I've never had to test. This could be a long fall, honey, a *long* fall, and I don't know where the bottom is. I'm, well . . . I'm scared." I squeezed Bonnie's hand.

"I know you want to plan out how this is going to go," said Bonnie, "but you won't know what's going to happen until tomorrow. Don't torture yourself tonight."

"I don't want to, believe me. But sometimes what I want and what my mind does are very different things."

"I know the last two months have been hard for you."

"Will you still love me even if I'm not a player anymore?" I asked.

"Of course! My goodness, why would you even ask me that?"

"I don't know." I dropped my head. "The stuff going through my head lately . . . I don't know where some of it comes from. God, I never should have gone back to the gym." I grabbed my head with the one arm that could go up without pain.

"Don't look at the past," said Bonnie. "Concentrate on the positives. Just think, now you'll have more time to promote your book."

I smiled at her knowing full well it was an untrue statement. You don't need *time* to sell a book; you need connections, a platform, and a built-in advertising hook. Not being a professional player would hurt the book more than free time would help it. Even if I was in the lowest level of the minors, a dark and obscure world when compared to the frenetically over-covered majors, the novelty of a player/author was still an interesting story for a local beat writer. On the Disabled List however, I would be a ghost. Released, I would be nothing.

I decided it was best not to tell that to Bonnie. I knew she was trying to make me feel better, and I wanted her to succeed, for me and for her. I'd been married long enough to know how important it was to let her believe she could make me feel better.

I smiled and kissed her forehead. "You're right."

"See, always a bright side."

"Do you know why I started writing?" I asked.

"Because you want people to see the other side of the uniform."

"That's why I wrote the book. But did I tell you why I started writing?"

"No, honey," she said in her *tell me if it will make you feel better* way.

I smiled again and strummed my fingers through her brown hair, calming slightly. "Some people say the beauty of the game is in a kid's smile, or fresh-cut grass, or the crack of the bat. For me the beauty of baseball has always been that you don't have to face yourself as long as you get results on the field.

"Before I met you, when I was floundering in the minors, I was forced to face myself. I hit a long rough patch on the field and was failing far more than I was succeeding. It was the first time in my career it had ever happened and I couldn't run away from it. Beyond discovering that I wasn't as good at baseball as I thought, I also realized that a lot of people only liked me because I played it. Worse, I realized that *I* only liked me because I played it."

I stared across the room as I spoke, at the big league jersey I had framed, hanging on the wall. It was the Padres' away jersey, the first one I ever wore, blue and white and gold. It hung over the dresser, like some sacramental relic always watching over us. It made possible the bed and the dresser and everything in my charming little gray house. But I felt unworthy of it. Always unworthy of it.

"I'd stay up at night, wrestling with fear, torturing myself with the thought of losing it all, just like I am now. It followed me everywhere, even to the pitcher's mound. I'd talk to the guys on my team about it and they'd tell me to stop thinking, or quit worrying, or let it go. I hate that, when people say stop thinking about something when you obviously can't.

"I learned to keep my mouth shut. Confessing my fears to the team was a sign of weakness so I started writing them instead of talking. Over time, it became how I kept track of where the game ended and I began. Writing helped me balance the things I was supposed to believe as a player, the things I want to believe as a person, and the results I get being both."

"Good for you," Bonnie said.

"But, I was a minor leaguer then," I said, losing myself in the stitches on the back of the big league jersey. The soft light from the nightstands seemed to make the gold piping glow like real metal. "My ideals and hobbies were novel. I could have them and keep my jersey because I was only earning a thousand bucks a month. What did a guy writing from inside the game really matter?

"You know, it's funny." I lay back on the bed and looked up at our ceiling. "When you get to the big leagues, they say you should keep doing whatever you did in the minors to get yourself to the majors. For me, that was writing about the game. I guess I could have just kept writing for myself, in private, but it wasn't enough. I wanted people to read what I was writing. I wanted people to hear what was going on in my head and not tell me I think too much. I wanted to connect with people without having to act strong all the time. I hated feeling like I couldn't relate to anyone. I'm just not built that way.

"I thought if I explained it to my teammates, they would get why I wanted to share my experiences. But you remember how that went over." I laughed at myself after I said it, the way some older wiser man might laugh at the foolishness of his youth. But my mirth subsided as reality returned and my arm twinged in protest as I pushed myself over to face Bonnie once more.

"But now" —I nodded to my right arm—"well, you know how this game is: No one cares about you unless you're helping the team win. If I can't play, I have no value. If they keep me, not only am I not helping the team win, I'll be actively pissing it off by writing from the inside. Maybe it would be better it they did just release me."

"You're not actively pissing everyone off," Bonnie said.

"It's just a few jerks who are choosing to get upset over something that doesn't even concern them. Who cares what they think?"

"I do," I said.

"Why?"

"I just do. I want to belong to the team."

"But you have to be yourself, too."

"I know."

"Then don't worry about what they think."

"I'm not a good enough player to have that luxury," I said. "I had a chance to be, to be a contributor, an icon, and now it's gone." I looked at my right shoulder like it had betrayed me. Then I wondered if the Baseball Gods did it, if they were getting me back for breaking the codes of the locker room.

"You act like you did something criminal, like they have the power to convict you. All you did was write. The real criminals here are that jackass Brice who went out of his way to stir up trouble. The guys who were afraid that you were bringing a recorder to the bullpen. TJ, for threatening to kill you over it. The whole thing was a crazy, juvenile situation, and you're above that. And look, they kept you and got rid of TJ. Think about that. They paid him millions and he acted like he was the judge and jury and they released him and kept you."

I gritted my teeth at the names, but I said nothing.

"What, do you wish they hadn't?" asked Bonnie.

I looked back at the jersey. I felt like it knew I was unworthy of it now and wished it could be put in another room, in another house.

"I just wish I wasn't me sometimes," I said.

"Why, honey?" Bonnie touched my face.

"TJ's gone. But I remain, the team traitor. And Brice and a lot of the other guys that feel that way are still around."

"You're not the team traitor."

"I hear you, honey, but . . ." I let the words slip away into silence. We lay there, neither of us talking. The inner workings of baseball were crazy to those who looked in from the outside. As long as I wanted to be a part of it, I had to be crazy too.

"Look," I said, "I'm proud of the fact I did it, the book I mean, and the big leagues too, but what good is pride if you turn your world into shit trying to attain it? There are days I would give all that stuff back to wake up and not feel like I do now. I'd just wake up confident in who I was and where I fit in this world. You know, to feel like I had it right."

"Had what right?"

"This," I said, as if I could lasso together all of my life as a whole. "This."

I rolled onto my back once again and stared at the ceiling. Bonnie did the same.

"I think there are a lot of people who wish that," she said. Then, gently, "If writing helps you cope, maybe you should write about what you're feeling now."

"I've thought of that," I said, and turned back to kiss her on the forehead before continuing. "But I don't really have the words right now, which is probably for the best since I don't think seeing what's happened to me in cold black and white is going to make me feel any better."

An hour later Bonnie slept peacefully. Wide awake, I lay next to her, wondering if this would be my last night as a professional baseball player. All I wanted was the wheels in my head to stop turning long enough for me to rest.

I slipped out of bed and went into the bathroom. In a drawer under the sink I had stowed the travel toiletry bag I used during the season. Inside, was a container of small blue pills players referred to as "Blue Bombers." They were sleeping pills, fast acting and prescription strength. Teams use them to combat the sleep cycle wrecking caused by cross-country flights. That's how I was introduced to them, anyway. But it's not how I used them. Being a rookie in the bigs was stressful. Being a rookie author was even worse. I used the Bombers to help manage my anxiety. The pills made me so delirious I couldn't concentrate, and I fell asleep nearly as quickly as my head hit the pillow. It was system shutdown in a pill form.

I shook one out of the bottle and swallowed it with a scoop of water from the faucet. Then I stood in the twilight of the bathroom light spilling into the master bedroom and stared at the big league jersey on my wall, waiting for the effect of the pills to hit me. Fifteen minutes later, my thoughts started to scramble and, as if filled with helium, I floated to my bed. I pulled the covers tight and sank into darkness, the jersey watching me.

Chapter 7

The next day, middle of the morning, my cell rang with the *Perfect Stranger* theme. I choked on my coffee and reached for it. Bonnie, sitting across from me on the living room couch, shut her laptop and tucked herself into a defensive ball. I looked over to her with a reassuring mask of strength and answered.

"Hello, Alex."

"Hey, Dirk, how are you doing?"

"That depends on what you're about to say to me."

"I understand, and you can relax. We're going to keep you on the roster and move you to the sixty-day DL."

I let my head fall back into the couch cushions, relieved, though poor Bonnie contorted at what she thought my body movement meant.

"We don't have to, as you know," continued Alex. "We're allowed to send a player in your situation to the minors, or release you because this happened in the off-season. But we don't believe, as an organization, that that's the right or responsible thing to do. You got hurt training to help us, to make our club better, and we're going to honor that. We're going to fix you. You'll have this whole year to get better."

Then, like any good GM, he added, "After that, I can't make any guarantees."

He didn't have to. Giving me this whole year was more than enough. I gave a great sigh of relief. The game was cruel and Alex was right, he didn't have to keep me. In the fiscal battle constantly being waged between the players' union and the front office, Alex was doing me more than a favor; it was a blessing. My thankfulness came pouring out as if a dam had been broken inside me.

"Alex, *oh my god*, this means so much. Thank you *so* much. I can't even begin to tell you what this means for me and my family." Bonnie deduced what was happening and fell sideways on the couch in relief. "Thank you," I continued. "I want you to know I won't abuse this, either. I want to get better as fast as I can. I don't want to take advantage of the organization's generosity. I know some guys—"

"Dirk," Alex stopped me, "we don't think you're that kind of guy. We know what your character is like. I've known it since we first started talking, and by the way you handled that roster move last spring. Integrity matters to this organization."

Now I felt guilty. I had expected the organization to opt for the sterile, logical move. Now I was going to get paid to heal, which was a lot like getting paid to do nothing. I had an overwhelming urge to hug him, which was probably why I said, "I have an overwhelming urge to hug you right now."

"Uh . . ." Alex gave a strained laugh.

"I'm sorry, I'm sorry," I amended. "This just really means a lot, is all. And thanks so much for this news. This is huge. I don't know what to say."

"You're welcome, Dirk," Alex said with a finalizing tone. "You'll come to camp on the DL this year and we'll go from there. George will call you and set up your surgery. You can discuss the details with him. If you have any issues, contact George, okay?"

"I understand. Thank you."

"Okay. Get better. We'll be in touch."

Alex hung up. I dropped the phone. Bonnie stared at me, anxious for details. "I'll be on the roster all year," I said. "The house will get paid for, all the loans, all the medical bills . . ." I shook my head, stunned. "I can't believe it."

"Believe it!" squealed Bonnie. She leapt from the couch and scampered to me for an embrace. "You can't hug Alex, but you can hug me."

George called later in the day. He explained that the Jays would release the decision to the press as "exploratory surgery." He said this was the best way to describe it since it sounded less critical, and they didn't know what was actually wrong inside. Next he asked me where I wanted to get my surgery done, and if I had a particular surgeon I was partial to. I said I didn't know much about surgeons because I'd never had to pick one before. He suggested a few, like the Jays' team doctor in Florida, the Indians' doctor Mark Schickendantz (who worked close to where I lived), and the world-renowned Dr. James Andrews in Birmingham. George said they were all very good, so I decided to work with the one closest to me: Schickendantz. He'd already evaluated me, plus, if there were any complications during the surgery, I'd be close to home and my caring wife. George said he'd set it up and get back to me. Then, one hour later, like destiny on a tight schedule, I received a phone call confirming my date with a very sharp knife.

Lying on the surgery prep table made me rethink things. I wondered if Dr. Schickendantz was good enough to work on me, or if I should have gone someplace better. I'd heard there was a guy in California who'd resurrected dozens of pro careers. Rumor had it that Dr. Andrews, who had a clinic in Birmingham named after him, could heal me with a single look. What had the Cleveland Clinic ever done for baseball players? Who was the last major league pitcher to come off one of their tables? Would I even have an arm when I woke up from this?

The night before the surgery, I had to take two Blue Bombers to get some sleep. I wasn't supposed to. The clinic said no drugs before the surgery, not even fish oil or a multivitamin. I'm pretty sure it was out of my system by the time they wheeled me into the surgery prep room and slimed me with iodine and antibacterial goo. And if it wasn't, screw it: They were just going to knock me out again anyway.

An Asian doctor came in holding some syringes. Her being Asian made me feel better. I equated that with intelligence. She asked me if I wanted a nerve block for the surgery, or just standard sedation.

"What's the block do?"

"It will make your entire arm go numb for about twelve hours."

"Awesome, give me that."

"I have to tell you the risks first." She explained how the needle had to go into my neck—deep into my neck—and, while in my neck, it could over-penetrate and hit an important nerve, or my spine, or a large, life-giving vein. I thought she was just telling me this to make her job sound important because, in my mind, she was just going to give me a shot. Now it sounded like she was doing her best not to paralyze me for life. I went with the block anyway. Like I said, she was Asian.

Coupled with the nerve-block injection, she also gave me my first dose of sedation. I felt the effects instantly, and was tumbling over clouds when the surgeon came in to talk to me about what was going to happen. I can't remember the specifics of what he said, something about a quick in-and-out of my shoulder, taking care of trouble he found in there like he was the head of a SEAL team. Then he switched to a soothing tone, explaining how I could die during this, but, statistically speaking, probably wouldn't. I gave him two *Top Gun*–style thumbs up, and things went black.

My first memory upon waking was the nurse telling my wife I was taking more time than usual to come to. Yeah, I was, because I wanted to stay asleep, lady. I knew that once I returned to consciousness I'd have to deal with what had been done to me.

As promised by the anesthesiologist, my arm was completely paralyzed. It was just dead weight hanging from my right side. Ironic, I thought, since even when the feeling returned, it would still be just dead weight. It would be dead weight until I could pitch again.

The doctor gave me a set of internal body photographs showing how chewed up my arm was. It looked grisly, like a crab had fallen into a blender. There were all these dangling meat fingers floating in the fluid injected into my shoulder capsule. It reminded me of undersea footage, as though clown fish should be swimming around in my rotator cuff and labrum.

"It wasn't *that* bad," said my surgeon. "No serious tears, or rips. Just fray, though your labrum has taken some significant abuse. It could have been worse, though. I think you'll be back to the game soon." Then, as he finished his *Thanks for flying the friendly skies* postsurgical spiel, he handed me something way better than a lollipop: a prescription for some heavy-duty painkillers. "Take them as you need them," he said.

I read the prescription: oxycodone. I knew the pill based

on its effect: a warm and fuzzy feeling that didn't exactly take the pain away, but made you care less about it. As well as everything else. I'd never taken the pill before, but I learned about it and several others from playing ball for a living. Lots of guys used them to deal with, or recover from, injuries. Some, and these were the guys who told me what the pills did, just took them because they liked the way they made them feel. After seven years of playing, I knew these oxycodone could fetch me about twenty bucks a pop in Triple-A.

I first learned pain pills had value when I was in the low minors. I took a line drive in the junk without a cup on. I was laid up in the hospital for a night while the doctors discussed whether they were going to have to amputate. I was put on a morphine drip because the pain was astronomical. Then, after the swelling subsided and I was able to escape the place with my nuggets still attached, they gave me some high-milligram Vicodin for the road. I didn't use the pills much after the initial incident, but guys on the team made multiple offers for my leftovers. I even had a bonus baby offer me a thousand dollars for the remainder of the bottle and its refills. Unfortunately for him (and my wallet), one of my coaches threw his back out before I could become a drug dealer. He demanded I give him my leftovers, and finished the bottle in three days.

There is a market for pain relief in baseball. In the minors, getting relief is harder to come by because the cost versus the reward of treatment is different. Anti-inflammatories are still given out liberally, but anything more requires a lot of disclosure that could, in the end, be the difference between major league call-up and minor league backup.

Besides, anti-inflammatories aren't any fun. They do nothing to fight the off-field pains of minor league life, like bus trips, red-eyes, and all the other crap you endure. Two oxycodones and one stiff drink makes that long bus ride a lot smoother. Can't get comfortable in an economy plane seat? Wash a twofer of Percocet down with a double of Jack and there is no seat. Starting on a travel day? A Blue Bomber could mean the difference between a call-up-worthy outing and another month in the minors. When results are the difference between a check with two zeros and a check with five, you don't want to manage the pain; you want to kill it.

It's an entirely different equation in the bigs. You don't need to buy a couple of extra happy pills from a teammate because you can get just about everything you need by asking for it. I was introduced to my first sleeping pill through a teammate, but once I decided I liked it, all I had to do was tell a trainer I was having trouble sleeping and, hours later, I had a prescription in hand. In the minors, if I told a trainer I couldn't sleep, he'd say, "Sorry man, it's a rough league, hang with 'em." This is one of the reasons major league players often become clubhouse dealers to guys in the minors.

Furthermore, as long as it was something you couldn't test positive for, it wasn't wrong. It's not cheating the system if the system made the loophole. If a player is producing under the influence of legal drugs, the system doesn't ask questions. Test positive for illegal drugs, however, and we have an issue. This makes greenies and steroids wrong, amphetamines and hormones wrong. Sleeping is natural. Managing pain is normal. Discomfort-free play is something we want our athletes to have. The bottom line is, as long as there is money at stake, production to be lost, and championships to be won, players will find ways to get an edge within the parameters of what is "allowed."

Some might say that turning into a prescription drug dealer inside the game is immoral, and I can see that. But in baseball, morality is bought and sold by results. A guy that can help you find an edge or beat back your body legally isn't seen as a villain, he's seen as a good teammate. And twenty bucks for a legal fix was dirt cheap.

"Thanks," I said, looking from the prescription to the doctor. "I'm sure these will help a lot."

Chapter 8

I got the use of my arm back about eight hours later. It throbbed with a deep, dull ache connected to the rhythm of my heart. I couldn't do much with it other than lift the steady stream of Bonnie's grilled cheese sandwiches to my mouth. It was her special medicine.

Eight days later, I took off the bandages covering the surgeon's entry points. There were three holes in my shoulder, one in the front, one in the back, and one in the side: little slits about the width of a staple, just big enough for the surgeon's tools to get in and shave off all the fray. The scars were big enough to be noticed, but not big enough to be cool. I'd never get to point at them and brag, "Yeah kid, see this one? Got it back in 2010, my first shoulder surgery. Play as long as I do and you might have one yourself." I guess I should be thankful that medical science has advanced far enough that surgeons don't have to make a hole the size of a shark bite to fix a guy. But if scars say something about a man, mine said, "Quit whining."

Two days after I removed the bandages, I could use my arm from my elbow to my hand just fine. I could carry most things, had no problems driving, could brush my teeth and wipe my rear, but I couldn't push anything or extend my arm over my head. Sadly, I also couldn't fully embrace my wife good-bye.

The surgery had taken place about ten days before the start of the 2010 spring training, and it was once again time for me to trade her loving arms for the sweaty embrace of another season. We stood outside our new house, holding on to one another while my car idled a steamy exhaust into the cold winter air.

"Come with me," I said into her hair, her face pressed into my chest. It was pointless to ask. I knew she couldn't. She had a real job and we needed her to keep it because of Alex Anthopoulos's "I can't guarantee anything after this year." But I also knew how jealous I was of players whose wives joined them all season.

Bonnie squeezed me. "I would if you really wanted me to, but one of us has to keep a steady job if you're going to keep getting hurt all the time."

"You married a delicate flower, what can I say?"

"I'll visit a lot, since we can afford it now."

"You'd better. I will need as many conjugal visits as I can get."

"Is that all I am to you? A long-distance booty call?"

"Well . . . not *all* you are."

"*Romance!*" she declared. Then she grabbed me and kissed me thoroughly, and told me she would visit as soon as possible. I let her slip out of my arms, got into my car, and drove away, watching her shape in my review mirror diminish into the cold Ohio distance.

I drove all day and into the night. Twenty hours on the road fueled by Red Bull, trail mix, and beef jerky. I tried not to pee until I had to get gas so I could stay in the saddle as long as possible. When I finally arrived in Dunedin, Florida,

I was beyond drained, and stuck to the car seat like a piece of half-melted candy.

I could have taken a first-class flight. All major league camp invitees fly first class on the organization's dime, if they want to. I drove so I could pocket the travel stipend. The organization doesn't care how you get to camp, just that you get there. They are required by the collective bargaining agreement to provide a flight or otherwise reimburse you for your travel up to the cost of a first-class flight. Most players, myself included, say they are going to fly, collect their reimbursement check, and then drive so they can pocket the difference and have their own wheels in camp.

The organization is also required to get each player a high-quality residence and cover its cost. The Blue Jays can provide a room at the Innisbrook country club and resort, which I also opted out of. The country club was a very sweet deal, complete with an all-you-could-whack driving range, gate house, fine dining, luxury apartments, and a sandy beach pool. Last year, Vernon Wells rented out one of the place's multiple banquet halls for the Canada versus United States Olympics hockey match, and Richie Scott and Shaun Marcum chased each other around on roller blades while in full hockey gear. They toppled tables and threw beer bottles at one another, and management didn't say a peep other than, "More refreshment, sir?"

However, taking the default spring-training residence meant forfeiting the housing stipend. A lot of guys, especially journeymen not yet immune to the vertigo-inducing effects of big league paychecks, booked their own discount residences so they could pocket the substantial difference between the bill and the lodging stipend. The cheaper the residency, the more money you made. So of course I booked the cheapest place I could find.

To put the money in perspective, in 2009 I stayed at a friend of a friend's place, in their extra room, paying just over $200 a week. The Jays paid me over a thousand dollars for the same week. I saw no reason to change things up. Unfortunately this twice-removed buddy of mine had just tied the knot and needed my old room for the teenage step-daughter his nuptials earned him. He proposed a new deal: in place of the old room, he offered me his wife's old apartment at the same price of $200 a week. Plus he said they'd leave all their old furniture behind for me. He said it would be like a hotel room, completely move-in ready, and the key would be waiting for me under a rock in the courtyard upon my arrival. It sounded like a great deal: my own place, no roommate, no distractions, and lots of money in my pocket.

Then I opened the door.

Unlike a country club room, the place wasn't cleaned before vacated. The girls just packed up, jumped ship, and left their evacuation mess for me. Lord they were slobs! Spaghetti noodles stuck to the sides of kitchen cabinets. Dust buffalos migrating in herds across the laminate floor. Mystery stains on bedsheets, mold on the bathroom ceiling, and green rings around the toilet bowls. I pulled no less than three hair-brushes, four hair scrunchies, one shoe, one pair of socks, three double-A batteries, a bra, and one—still wrapped, thank God—tampon from beneath the couch cushions.

Before I found the stockpile of feminine products in the couch, it was already unsettlingly sticky. But after I unearthed the tampon, I just pushed the sofa in to a far corner, never to be touched again. Moving the couch across the floor it acted like a dust plow. In its wake appeared more lost treasure: a copy of *Seventeen* magazine, fingernail clippers, a corroded spoon, and a bottle of some mysterious antifungal cream. I stared at it all for a moment—spoon, dust, and mystery cream—then I decided it was best to kick it all back under the couch and not move any more furniture.

I had my choice of two bedrooms, both "fully furnished." The master had a bed, a dresser, and a window. The queen-sized bed was nearly as high off the ground as I was tall. I marveled at this. *Why is this so damn high?* I thought. *I met the woman who used to sleep here. She's like four foot two!*

After summiting the bed, I realized why it was so high: There was a dent in the center of it, like a black hole that sucked your body in from the farthest reaches of the mattress. I wondered if this mattress hole had an exit? Maybe it was like a slide; you went to sleep on top of the bed, but during the night you were sucked down to floor level and crawled out from underneath it.

The guest bedroom had a lot more "character." It was a fourteen-year-old girl's wonderland, with glow-in-the-dark stickers on the wall, collages of boy-band heartthrobs, and various glitter residues stuck to abandoned teenybopper kitsch. The room did have a desk—though it was child-sized—complete with a hot-pink rolling desk chair. Those items, combined with a few lovely unicorn figurines, made me consider making the room my main quarters. Alas, the bed was a twin. Not the end of the world, mind you, but there was also the matter of the closet filled with baby-doll heads. Lifelike, unblinking, baby-doll heads.

Just knowing the heads were there was unnerving. Worse still, there was no door on this closet. Apparently the sliding door tracks had broken off a while ago. The ladies of the house opted to replace the door with hanging beads instead of fixing it. This did little to hide any of the closet's disembodied residents, but it did do a fantastic job of making the space feel like an altar. *God help the boy who breaks this girl's heart,* I thought, as I backed out of the room while making the sign of the cross.

After crawling under the hood of the place, I had half a mind to bail out. I never signed any agreement with my friend; it was a buddy-system contract. I squeezed my phone and considered calling him to say the deal was off. Then, the strangest thought came to mind: Did I, broken and useless, deserve better than this? I shook my head no and thought of the money I'd give up if I went elsewhere. I thought about how, after this year, I might not make anything close to what I was making now. Then what? Trading comfort for cash was an old minor league habit it didn't make sense to kick now. I had to make this place work.

I drove out to Wal-Mart, stocked up on all the necessities—beer, toilet paper, microwaveable popcorn—and a payload of cleaning supplies. I did my best to bomb the place with all manner of sterilizing artillery, mixing off-the-shelf cleansers and disinfectants into a delirium-inducing super formula that could strip paint. Whatever messes I couldn't defeat, or I suspected might be a piñata of vaginal medicines, I quarantined. I thought when the sprays and scrubs hit the place I might hear it groan, like all the filth had evolved into some sentient, apartment-sized organism. Nothing that dramatic, but I did get a look at what the wall color was like before it turned from eggshell white to urinal-cake yellow. I washed my linens, nuked the toilet, and bought new shower shoes—one pair for the locker room, another for home. Finally, I pulled the teenage daughter's abandoned desk and chair into the master bedroom and set the place up like a dorm. I left the unicorn stickers on the desk's top because they matched the chair.

When I'd finished adjusting the room to my liking, I sat down on the tiny rolling desk chair and called Bonnie. I told her about the apartment, how'd I'd managed to disinfect it, and how it wasn't the best scenario but was the most cost-effective. Then I told her how much I missed her, and that I already felt lonely without her.

"Awww," she said, "I miss you too. You won't be lonely after tomorrow. You'll be surrounded by all the guys again."

Any other season, she would have been right. "I don't know. I don't think being lonely has anything to do with the number of people you're around."

Chapter 9

Spring-training testing day came. Viles of blood were drawn, folds of body fat were pinched, and clear plastic cups were peed into. X-rays, checkups, and pants-down, cold-rubber coughing. Long lines of players holding green medical folders, all bored, all tired, all hungry and anxious to get stamped as fit for another season of major league duty.

Introductions were done on day two, in the main classroom of the Blue Jays Spring Training complex. It was a dated facility, but the Jays kept the paint fresh, and there were new photos in the giant picture frames that lined the walls.

Alex welcomed us, manager Cito Gaston gave a speech about competitive expectations for the season, and George gave his famous "Don't shit on the grapes" lecture concerning washing your hands after a bowel movement. Various men in Jay-logoed clothing fell in and out of a line that stretched around the blue-jay-colored classroom when their names were called. Lots of forms were signed, equipment distributed. Mitts were beaten into shape, cleats were laced, and pant bottoms were altered. Old friends caught up, off-season stories were swapped, and laughs were shared. All in all, it was like any of the other spring-training starts I'd been a part of, except for two little details: I did not get my fit-for-duty stamp, and I did not feel like I belonged.

Even after a year with this team, I didn't know many of the guys. Oh, I loved the organization, appreciated the front office now more than ever, and thought the coaching staff was grand. I also had a lot of friends in the minors, or had, rather, as many had moved on during the off-season. Yet, in the face of all this, the big league roster still held a lot of uncharted territory. Uncharted because it was all off limits to me—my punishment for being the team traitor.

I first came to the Jays' organization promising honorable character, despite my literary endeavors. I professed a full understanding of the concept of the team and how it operated. I openly admitted I was a writer, and worked hard to win over the skeptics who said a player who wrote from the inside could never be reliable, trusted, or safe. Then, just when I'd broken through and established myself, when everyone was starting to warm up to me, I fucked up.

A true team is much more than just names on a roster. It is a group of like-minded individuals willing to buy into the same basic values for enjoyment, success, and even protection. It's a trust. I understood that I'd committed a crime against that trust. What I did not understand, since no one was hurt by my actions, was why it was a crime, or how long my punishment would last.

The rules and codes of a locker room are unwritten, but enforced by those players with the most playing time, success, or contract dollars, meaning the codes of the clubhouse are the whims of its most powerful players. These players are not always the most balanced or democratic leaders. They don't always analyze how rules came into being, and they rarely care to hear your side of the story, especially if you're a rookie writing a book and using a voice recorder.

Thankfully there had been a lot of turnover on the major

league side of the roster during the off-season. Along with Roy Halladay, now Kevin Millar, Alex Rios, Scott Rolen, TJ Collins, and Rod Barajas were gone—all pillars of the clubhouse social structure. New leaders would emerge to take their places, and with them would come new followers, cliques, codes, and trust dynamics. In the meantime, I had a blank slate.

If I wanted to break down the walls dividing me from the team, I needed to get in tight with the new clubhouse rulers. Since I no longer had the ability to compete my way into clubhouse power, I had little choice but to ass-kiss my way there.

Every spring training has phases. The first is the Reunion Phase, when everyone is happy to be together again. Next is the Bonding Phase, when the competition starts to thin out, cuts are made, factions form, and social roles are discovered. Finally there's the Identity Phase, wherein rosters are set and players start proving (or failing to prove) their worth to the club.

In the Reunion Phase, players are at their most open-minded. Everyone is typically happy to be together again, playing the game they love. Changes in the social hierarchy have yet to be sorted out. Plus with so many new faces, guys aren't quite comfortable enough to treat one another with the loving vitriol so common to team communication. If you were a player looking for a fresh start with your peers and couldn't play yourself into social absolution, this was the time to do it.

I needed endorsements, preferably from guys with on-field success, service time, and social clout. Guys like Vernon Wells, Adam Lind, Aaron Hill, David Purcey, and Ricky Romero. If they won the part of team alpha males—the part I was hoping to win by excellent performance—while I curried favor with them, I could ride into good graces by association.

Thus, while everyone else made their rounds through the clubhouse, joking and laughing and catching up on off-season exploits, I was executing Operation: One of the Guys. I went from locker to locker, cafeteria table to cafeteria table, spreading my campaign slogan: *Dirk Hayhurst is one of you. He's changed. Forget what you used to know, the new Dirk is here to stay.* I shook hands, asked about family, and shot the bull. When an opportune time presented itself, I'd casually slip in my message, "So yeah, I'm sure you don't really care but I got my book done and I'm not writing anymore, *thank God!* Talk about a load off my shoulders, it'll be nice to actually enjoy a season without taking notes for a change, you know, just be one of the guys again."

Some guys were easier than others. Hill and I actually got along well enough that he volunteered to read a prerelease copy of my book during the off-season. David Purcey and Brad Mills spent a lot of time with me in Triple-A and knew I could be trusted. Lyle Overbay and I made a connection in Baseball Chapel. Shawn Camp and Richie Scott both told me, "Sorry to hear about your injury, bro, but you'll be back out there soon." Adam Lind even made it a point to find me and say, "I heard Bob Costas and Keith Olbermann said your book was amazing."

"Yeah," I said, looking around to make sure the wrong people weren't listening. "They really liked it."

"Keith's a pretty cool guy," Lind said. "I like his show."

"I'll let him know, I'm sure he'll be glad to hear it."

"Do you think you'll write another one if this one is well received?"

I cringed. "Only if I retire!"

"That sucks. What with you being hurt and all, it makes

sense that you'd write more. I mean, what else are you going to do?"

"No writing. Definitely not that. I'm just one of the guys now."

After Lind, I said hello to Jason Frasor and Brandon League and Scott Downs and a few other guys. I kept things light and made sure my message had the same consistent points. To those I didn't know well, I simply smiled or said hello or, at the very least, smacked them on the butt—the ball player's universal greeting. I even bought votes, specifically among those that came up to me and asked me if the doctor gave me anything good for my surgery. When I'd tell them oxycodone, they'd say, "We might have to talk later."

I ran a well-organized campaign, making sure all the parties I wanted endorsements from knew I endorsed them as well. "Sucks I can't be out there to watch you," I'd say with a smile, "because I know it's going to be your year."

Maybe it was because there were a lot of good guys with short memories on the team. Maybe it was because I'd served my time in the shun box. Maybe I was just that good of an ass-kisser. Whatever it was, it seemed that things were going to be alright. I didn't get to everyone, but I got to the players I thought mattered. And if I was consistent and they did what I thought they were capable of, things would be just fine.

After my whistle-stop tour in the cafeteria, I breezed through the hallway that connected the compound's cafeteria to the locker room, where I stopped off at my locker to check my cell for texts from Bonnie. Because my jersey number was a higher number, my locker was among those of the newcomers and first-time auditions, since they always get stuck with nosebleed digits themselves. One player, number 77, was at his locker just across from me. I put my phone away and crossed the aisle with my hand out and said, "Dirk Hayhurst."

"I know," he said, hands remaining at his side. "I heard about you."

My smile faded and my hand dropped.

"You're the guy who brings a microphone out to the bullpen. Yeah, one of my boys who played with you said you like to keep notes on guys and rat 'em out and shit. He said to steer clear of you."

"I've never ratted out anyone," I said.

"That's not what I heard. I heard you got a book coming out this year that's full of the shit we do."

"That's not true. You don't understand. The book is—"

"So that wasn't you talking up the media earlier about a book?" he broke in.

"I talk to the media because they're friends of mine and they help me promote stuff. What's wrong with that? "

"Mmm-hmmm," said 77, not answering.

"Who told you I was a rat?"

"Don't worry about it."

My eyes narrowed and we stood staring at each other. "Yeah, I wrote a book, and last year I had a recorder," I said. "But I never ratted anyone out and I never took a recorder to the bullpen in the big leagues. I've always been open about what I do. Furthermore, you don't even know me."

"I know you broke the rules," he said, producing a can of dip from his back pocket, pulling off the cap and pinching out a wad. "I know my boy don't like you. That's all I need to know." He pressed the dip in his lower lip and massaged it into place with his tongue. "And just because you tell me you ain't doing nothing, doesn't mean you ain't doing nothing."

"Who told you I was a rat?" I asked again.

"I told you, don't worry about it."

"Who?" I asked again, closing the distance between us with a hard step.

He just nodded at me. A smirk broke across his face, tight at the lower lip where his dip sat. Finally, just when I thought he would speak, he turned to his locker, pulled out a pair of sunglasses, slipped them on, and stepped past me, his shoulder clipping me as he went. Not bothering to turn around, he said, "You know who."

Then, before he pushed through the locker-room doors to join the rest of the able bodies for stretch, he looked back and said, "Catch you around, Media."

Chapter 10

I wasn't the only player in camp worried about status. I had a talented rival named Brice Jared. A young and gifted pitcher who'd fallen in love with the concept of himself as a major leaguer; or, more specifically, with the concept of himself as the king among men that playing in the major leagues can transform you into. Brice made it to the Show quickly, experienced instant success, and, with the help of a few established big league influences, left the gravitational pull of humility for things more worthy of a man of his talent. The way things unraveled last season made him hate me. And, if my run-in with number 77 was anything to go on, he still did.

Being injured, there wasn't much I could do to discredit any of the claims Brice was making against me. Spring training for the injured is like detention. While everyone else is out having fun, sharing experiences in the game they love, you're stuck inside doing tedious busywork.

I was sequestered in the Jays' training room, surrounded by blue training tables and stacks of athletic tape. There was an ice machine and a shelf stuffed with towels and heaps of tan elastic bandage rolls. A little gray radio played vacantly in the background. My days consisted of trying to get my hand over my head, where I would trace the letters of the alphabet with a one-pound weight. A *pink* one-pound weight. The exercises were instrumental to my recovery, but they were mindless and boring nonetheless. While the tedium of fielding an endless stream of bunts during pitcher's fielding practice—what all the healthy pitchers were doing—wasn't much better, at least they were outside, on the green grass, under the sun, with a team of guys to horse around with.

I wasn't the only rehabber. There were a handful of others, including Shawn Hill, Richie Scott, Travis Hasher, and the perennially injured Dustin McGowan. But we all had different schedules, predicated upon the different points in our rehabs. Hill and Scott were able to throw. Hasher spent all his time in the weight room with another rehabbing position player we all called Soup. McGowan had his own veteran schedule and kept different hours. There was nowhere near the camaraderie the healthy players had, nor was there any action. Just the radio, and the occasional collapse of ice cycling in the ice machine.

I thought I might develop some deep soul mate connection with the trainers, the kind that makes for great comeback documentary stories about how one man pushes another forward. I didn't. The trainers were primarily hands-off, assigning me my daily routines before scurrying back into their offices to answer phone calls or finish paperwork or other bureaucratic chores. Like any proper civilized health care system, baseball rehab is full of excessive documentation and secretarial duties that keep healers away from patients. I knew the healthy had priority over the broken—that's always been the way of this game—but I was learning that so too did phone calls, emails, and text messages regarding the relatively healthy. Any of the aforementioned could delay therapy at any moment. It wasn't the training staff's fault; they genuinely cared, and worked tirelessly, but the amount of interruptions and sudden demands made for long bouts of lying across training tables counting specks in the facility's drop-ceiling tiles, wondering what was happening on the field without me. But I knew the answer to that: A team was being formed. A team I wasn't a part of.

At first I ventured outside to watch the boys practice after I was done with my exercises. The trainers would pack my shoulder in ice and I'd slip a jacket over the giant lump the ice made and hover in the cuts of narrow mid-morning shadow, watching the healthy go about their days.

Instead of feeling as if the team-shaped hole in my heart was filled, I felt as if I'd turned into some baseball field hunchback who lurked in the dark recesses of the Dunedin spring-training facility. Though I was right next to them, I felt farther away from the action than when I was in the training room.

Nothing stings more than watching others have fun with something you're no longer a part of. Watching the healthy pitchers throw was agony. *Jesus,* I thought, as I watched them wind and deliver, *Romero's change-up is filthy. Purcey's curve is a video-game cheat code . . . When did they all become so gifted?* I couldn't even get my arm above my head, and watching them made me feel it was pointless to even try.

One afternoon, after my pink weight lifting came to a close, I sat slumped and weary on my blue training table with an ice pack lashed to my shoulder by a tan bandage roll. A white plastic digital timer was clipped into the folds of the bandage with an alarm set for twenty minutes, which had long since run out. The water from the pack was expanding across my workout shirt in a damp, gray splotch, and trickling down my arm to my elbow, where it beaded and dripped onto the floor below.

The training-room doors shot open and in flew a flock of Blue Jay pitchers, squawking and chirping as they came.

They were the first of the bullpen throwers and, throwing routines now finished, they'd come in to do their arm maintenance program. Brad Mills, a talented, left-handed pitching prospect and friend, was among them. He requested a pair of ice packs, which a trainer lashed to his arm with a tan elastic bandage, and then he sat down next to me.

"How's it going in here?" he asked.

I blew out a sigh. "Living the dream. How about you?"

"Same old. Work on drills we use once a year, then throw a bullpen."

"Sounds heavenly. How'd your pen go?"

"Good, I guess." He shrugged, but only his unwrapped shoulder moved.

"You guess?"

"They want me to work on a slider, or a cutter, something with that cross-plate action." He shook his head. "Thing is, I don't want to add something that I'm not confident in, then spend all spring training getting beat on a hunch they have. You know how often you hear that, right? Guy comes into camp, coaches all want him to learn something new, player does his best to please them, gets his ass kicked, then spends the whole year in Triple-A because he wasn't true to himself."

"Work on it while they're watching, then do what you want in games," I said.

"What if they ask if I'm throwing it?"

"Say you are. Have your catcher say you threw a couple good strikes with it. Then, so as not to be obvious, have him say"—I raised my left arm and made quotes—"'*it's got the spin, it wants to break,*' or something. You won't be the first guy who bullshitted your way through a new pitch."

Mills nodded, and smiled.

"Did they call you this off-season and tell you what they expected from you?" I asked. Mills was talented, no doubt about it, but the brass was right, he did need a cutter or slider. I wondered what else they thought of him.

"Alex said that I had a future with the club," Mills said. "That older guys were getting more expensive and that I would get my chances. He also said that I'd probably see some action in the same capacity that I did last year but, you know, anything could change in spring training."

I turned and stared at him. He'd just repeated everything Alex had said to me before my injury, almost verbatim.

Mills furrowed his brow. "What's wrong?"

Instead of answering, I opted to slump further down the Blue Jay color-coordinated wall.

I actually believed I was unique to the club and would become one of its future contributors. But there were dozens of guys just like me in this organization, with the only major difference being none of them were stupid enough to run out and get themselves injured. I was an idiot. A stupid, broken idiot.

"You think I should scrap the slider, then?" asked Mills.

"No," I said, "it's not that. You definitely should try the slider. It's just that—"

"Media." The voice rang from my left, opposite Mills. We both turned to regard Brice Jared standing with his hands on his hips, lip curled in a wry smile. When my eyes locked with his, he spoke again. "What's up, Media?"

"Brice," I said flatly. "Something I can do for you?"

"Nah, man," he snorted. "*I'm* great."

I said nothing.

"Saw you making friends with the reporters," continued Brice, loudly to make sure others could hear. "What is it, like three weeks into camp and you're already sucking off the media again?" He was referring to me talking with the gaggle of beat reporters that could always be found in the locker room when the team was there. They were my best chance at getting my book on the public's radar now that I was busted. I had to talk with them, beg them for some plugs.

"I wasn't talking to them about you, Brice, don't worry."

"You're making guys uncomfortable again."

"You're the one that's stirring shit up again. I've met some of your friends."

Brice shook his head. "Me? I didn't do shit. You do it to yourself. I really thought"—he put up two fingers for a trainer inquiring about ice packs—"that after last season you would have learned your lesson."

"I was kinda thinking the same thing about you."

"So that's it, huh?" He seemed offended, as if the conversation had only now become personal. "You gonna spend all of this year pissing this team off, too?"

"Don't go telling people bullshit like you did last year, and I'll bet no one will care."

"Someone's gotta warn them about the shit you're up to."

"And what is that? I didn't do a goddamn—" I stowed my anger when the trainer who'd made Brice's ice bags came to wrap him. I at least had good enough sense not pick a fight in front of the training staff. When the trainer got done strapping the ice on Brice, he gave it a few choice whacks to shape it to Brice's shoulder and elbow, then clipped a timer onto him and walked away.

"Thanks, Frosty," said Brice. Then he looked back to me and said, "Well, I'm sorry about your injury, but karma's a bitch, ain't it?" He shrugged and walked away, leaving me furious, but unable to think of anything fast enough to win the exchange.

"Good to see you guys are still friends," Mills said as Brice walked out.

"Oh, we're *tight*."

"You know, if I were you, I'd keep writing just to piss him off."

"If you were me? Shit, you're afraid of not doing something the coaches want you to do because you don't want to make them think you're un-coachable."

"That's different," Mills said. "We're talking about what a player thinks versus what management thinks."

"You think management isn't weary of me? Please. You have no idea the trouble that fucker got me into last year. I'm a liability now. Thank God Alex likes me or . . . Well, lets just say some of the guys on this team think I'm a time bomb. It's only three weeks into spring training, but if this keeps up I'm not going to have a job when I'm healthy." I stood up and pulled the end of the bandage free and began unraveling it. "Let me ask you something: If you'd come up to the big leagues last year and dominated, do you think they'd be asking you to throw a slider right now?"

"No, probably not," said Mills.

"Of course not. Hell, they'd probably be asking you what your secret was, so they could teach it to minors boys." I let the ice pack fall to the ground. "Success always makes right up here. I can't pitch right now, so I can't afford to piss anyone off. If that asshole keeps playing well and telling guys I'm sneaking around with microphones in my pants and feeding inside scoops to the media, my life will become hell. I'd be better off gone."

"I don't know if it's that serious."

"It's that serious," I said. I threw my soaking wrap and towels into a laundry bin. "In the meantime, I play the social game. I've got to. There will never be a day when I get to round everyone up and have a press conference to address the issue and we all talk about it like civilized men. That's not how baseball works."

"It's a funny game," offered Mills.

"Oh, it's real funny. So why aren't more people laughing?"

Chapter 11

"You should go to the beach, honey," Bonnie said during one of our daily phone conversations. "Get out of that apartment. It will do you good."

"I don't really want to go to the beach," I said.

"Then go to the mall and walk around."

"Guys don't go to the mall and walk around just to go to the mall and walk around, Bonnie. Not unless they're douchebags trying to hit on underage girls, or eighty-year-old men getting their exercise."

"Then go buy yourself a PlayStation and kill something. That always makes you feel better."

"I have one at home. I'd just be wasting money if I bought another. Besides, this place doesn't have a television."

"You're making enough. Buy a television and a PlayStaion."

"Meh . . ."

"You feeling okay? It's not like you to turn down a chance at buying a television and a gaming system. For goodness sakes, you asked for it on your wedding registry and now you're not interested?" She laughed, but when I didn't follow suit, she calmed, cleared her throat, and asked, "Honey, what's wrong?"

I paced around the apartment as I talked, stopping in front of random things, like the crappy art on the wall, or curtains covering the baby-doll heads.

"I don't know," I said. "I feel crappy and I have no reason to. The last couple of days I've been having these weird feelings at the ballpark."

"What do you mean?"

"Like I'm lost."

"Are you depressed?"

"No," I snapped at her, "I'm not depressed. I'm getting paid to heal. I'm accruing big league service time. I'm pocketing the per diem. I'm a damn major leaguer, living the dream. I have no reason to be depressed."

"You can still feel depressed. You don't have to have a reason."

"I'm not depressed," I said again.

"Okay, well, tell me what else you're feeling."

"Well, these last couple days when I've come home from rehab, I get this feeling like I'm trapped in the apartment."

"Oh honey, you need to get out of that place."

"I know, but that's the strange thing, Bonnie. I get all worked up, grab my keys and head for the door and just before I open it, I stop and think about where I would go that would be fun, and nothing comes to mind. Shopping, the beach, even spending money on video games; nothing moves me."

"How long have you felt this way? When you got to spring training? After the surgery? When you got hurt?" There was a great deal of concern in her question barrage. "Honey, how long have you been feeling bad?"

I had shambled back into the bedroom and sat down on the tiny rolling desk chair and was now absently picking at one of the unicorn stickers atop the desk.

"I don't know, maybe since last year? Mostly after that

fight in the locker room. I remember I felt really strange for a while after it happened. I even stopped eating and I didn't know why."

"Wait. Stop. You've been feeling bad since last year?"

I got a piece of the unicorn up, but it tore and left me with half a paper head.

"Not bad, just not good. But, you know, I just chalked it up to writing the book and all the stress of being in the big leagues. It wasn't a big deal."

"You stopped eating. That's a big deal."

"I was still pitching well, and I got the book done."

"That doesn't matter! Why didn't you say something?"

I flicked the half head from my fingers and put my head down on the table top, the phone sandwiched between my head and the desk. "Honey, why are you yelling at me?" I asked. Then, jerking up, "Wait. Have I been, uh, you know, less of a man in the bedroom? Oh God, I heard that can happen. When you're feeling weird it's like your mind has a link to your . . . Oh God. Bonnie, be honest, has my not feeling good somehow impacted my male potency and you just weren't telling me?"

"What? No! No, your potency is perfectly potent. I'm just really concerned. You really should tell someone how you're feeling before you stop eating again, or worse."

"Who do I tell that to, exactly? And what do I say when I do it? Do I walk up to Alex and say, 'Hey Al, I know there are a million guys in the minors who would love to have my job and that I'm making big-time money to be here, money you didn't have to give me, but I'm feeling really sad and I don't know why. It's probably nothing, but my wife told me to talk to you about it. Side note, she's worried about my performance in the bedroom."

"I am not! Will you stop with that? Honey, if you can't talk to Alex, then talk to the other guys on the team about it."

"Oh my god, I absolutely can't do that." I was standing now and waving my arms in the air, like I was trying to prevent a plane from landing.

"Why?"

"You can tell your teammates a lot of things. That you're angry, that you want to get drunk until you can't see straight, that you need them to keep a secret about you cheating on your girlfriend. But you just cannot talk about your emotions. I told you what happened when I did that before I started writing, remember? Baseball players don't do that."

"Why?"

"Because, think of what it sounds like, Bonnie: weakness and whining. A guy is making more money in one night than most of the population is making in two weeks while playing a game for a living and he's sad inside; boo-hoo. And do you think guys on the team are going to feel bad for me? Me, after what I've done? You think coaches are going to tell me, 'It's okay son, you don't have to be mentally tough to do this job'? Hell no!

"Look," I continued, scaling the bed and flopping into the hole in the mattress, "you work with special-needs children for a living. You know people look at mental issues differently. Remember when your client, Ian, had that freak-out, screaming and hitting himself because he was overstimulated and the secretary burst into your office and threatened to call the cops on him if you didn't get him under control because she was afraid?"

"Yes," Bonnie said.

"She didn't understand that child had an issue. I know the team wouldn't understand if I say I'm having an issue. I've seen it happen before and it changes the way people think about you. Furthermore, I don't even know if I'm having an issue! We're just talking about feelings right now, is all. We're just talking about feelings. I'm not talented enough to stay in this game if I'm going to write, be injury-prone, *and* get labeled as a head case."

"But there has to be someone you can talk to about it. You can't be the first person in the big leagues to deal with stuff."

"We have a team psychological doctor, and if worse comes to worst I can talk to him."

"You should talk to him now. Why wait?"

"Because I can handle this. I'm just being a little irrational right now. This is a new routine. I recognize it, and if I can recognize it I can control it. It's fine. I'm fine. We're fine. Okay?"

It took her awhile, but finally she said, "Alright. But what are you going to do to deal with it on your own?"

"I have a technique that's worked for me before. Don't worry, honey. I'm a professional, remember?"

I shook the bottles of oxycodone and sleeping pills like maracas, then sat them on the kitchen counter and opened the refrigerator. A twenty-four pack of Yuengling lager stared back at me. I pulled one of the cold, sweaty green bottles out of the box and popped the cap off. Then I shook out a pair of sleeping pills from its bottle and swallowed them with a swig of Pennsylvania's finest suds.

I'd been feeling things I didn't understand, but I decided that I didn't have to understand them. I just had to turn them off. The sleeping pills made it all go away. Without them I'd get home around noon, fiddle with the Internet, panic about how I was wasting my day, get in the car, go nowhere, get out of the car, go back into the apartment, hate myself, feel strangely emotional, hate myself some more, call Bonnie, tell her everything was fine, then lie in bed for a few hours, wondering why I couldn't sleep. With the pills it was clean, simple, easy. I'd pop a few after my rehab, go to sleep and wake up around six a.m.—after fourteen or so hours of sleep—

rested and ready to face a day of pink weights and social isolation.

By early March, however, I was taking a trio of pills every afternoon, along with several beers. I didn't think anything of it, honestly. Normal tolerance building. It was similar to how I made it through my first year with the Blue Jays. I learned it from watching other guys on the team. I believed that I just needed to ride out whatever it was that was making me feel down . . . and that I shouldn't have felt down in the first place, since I was making such great money and would have my job all year.

Because I didn't have the cross-country-flights-screw-up-my-sleep excuse to get more sleeping pills should my supply run out, I started mixing in the oxycodone (which also made me drowsy), or more alcohol, or both. I never turned to hard liquor because that sounded like something a guy who had a problem would do, and I did not have a problem. I just liked sleeping.

I rationed out the pills to make sure they'd last, stocked up on beer, and made sure not to spend too much time at the park, where I often felt isolated in the training room, inadequate because of my injury, and angry because of Brice. As long as my routine didn't change, I'd make it through spring training by hitting my internal snooze button repeatedly. I projected that I'd run out of pills just after spring training, by which time I'd be throwing again and Brice would be gone. That, I believed, would make all the difference in whatever was bothering me.

Of course, this was all based on the assumption that things wouldn't get worse.

Chapter 12

"I thought you couldn't demote a player if they're injured on the big league roster," I said, standing before George Poulis in his little square office, holding an official Blue Jays memo in my hands. "Am I getting sent to the minors? Is that what this means?"

"No, no, no. That's where we do all the rehab assignments," George said. "It's not a demotion, just standard practice this time of year."

"But why wouldn't we just stay here? I mean, there is going to be like a million bodies over there." And there would be, since minor league camp is about five times the size of big league camp.

"You'll do your rehab when the minor leaguers are out on the field. Don't worry, we have Jep Jasper working over there and he's a really good guy. He'll take great care of you."

But I didn't want to be taken care of by a really good guy. I wanted to stay in big league camp. Over on the minor league side, there were no more five-star breakfasts. No more catered lunches. No more on-demand clubby service. No more extra-wide custom lockers. And no more access to the book-selling, joke-sharing, big league media crew. I already didn't feel very connected to the team, it's true, but getting sent to the minors was like getting unplugged altogether and thrown out of Neverland at the same time.

"I'm sorry," said George, "but you'll adjust. You can come to camp later, sleep in, go out and get breakfast. And of course you're still welcome to come over here after your treatment, you know, and hang out with all your friends."

"Right," I said, defeated. "All my friends. Of course."

"And we still get all your reports, so we know right where you're at."

"Great," I said.

"Great," George said. "You'll start reporting there tomorrow."

Outside George's training room office I wadded up the memo and threw it in the trash. At my locker, my Blue Jay-logoed equipment bag was already open and partially packed. Being on the big league side of the operation meant that the clubhouse staff knew everything you needed before you did. Usually it's a perk. This time it felt like a nail in my coffin.

A question from behind me: "Media, you leaving us?"

It was Brice. I knew the voice, but I did not turn to face it. "All the rehabbers are going over to the minor league side. Happens every year," I said, reaching into my locker's cubby to grab a protein-shaker bottle I'd brought with me.

"Oh, I know, but those guys will probably be coming back," Brice said.

"What's that supposed to mean?"

"Things are changing around here, man. Some good arms in camp, that's all."

"You don't think I can make it back to the bigs?"

"I don't think you can make it back to the bigs here," he said.

"You're an asshole," I said.

"Man, I'm just trying to be real with you. I told you way

back in the day the shit you was doing was going to catch up with you. You didn't listen. Now things are changing around here and I don't think there's gonna be room for guys who don't listen."

"I'll be back, pal. Don't worry about me," I said.

"Media, I don't worry about you. But some of the others guys around here do. That's the problem. People talking about you, bro. People talking and it ain't good."

I wadded up my sweatshirt and slammed it into my travel bag, then turned to face Brice. "And what are those people saying? Huh? Funny how you're always around when people are saying stuff about me."

"I don't go looking for it, man." He held his hands wide.

"Yeah," I said, "but you always seem to find it."

"I guess you're just a popular topic," he said. "Kinda funny how popular you are, being hurt and all. I mean, it's like you wanna be hurt. It's like you don't care about the team no more. You just care about selling books. It looks shady, man."

"And that's what everyone thinks, huh? That I got hurt so I could sell books? Are you a fucking idiot? Do you even understand how—"

"See, there you go again. You're so smart and we're so stupid. You don't listen, man. You don't fucking listen. You can't take criticism, that's your biggest problem, that's why guys don't like you."

"What the fuck are you talking—"

"If I was you," Brice interrupted again, "I'd drag your injury out, man, play that Club Med card and collect everything you can. 'Cause I keep hearing things, you know?" He buzzed his finger around his head as if the voices were coming from secret sources.

"I don't give a shit what you hear."

"We both know that ain't true," he said.

"Why don't you get the fuck out of here and leave me alone?"

"Why? This is my clubhouse. Yours is on the other side of town."

I should have torn into him. Left big league camp with "knuckle contusion" added to my injury report. Instead, I felt like I was about to unravel. My emotions were wrong, busted, scrambled. Rather than focused, directed anger, the kind I had summoned in previous encounters with Brice, the kind that helped me get through tough jams on a baseball field, the kind that made me a ball player, what came coursing through me was raw, unchecked, emotional overflow. I felt my face flush and my eyes start to burn. I was going to cry!

I had to get out of there before it happened. I turned away from Brice, grabbed my bag and zipped it. Brice just stood there, watching me.

"Go fuck yourself," I said, heading for the door.

" 'Bye."

Chapter 13

There were players everywhere. Four levels' worth of minor leaguers, plus two teams' worth of guys who hadn't yet been assigned to a club, all packed into rows of sterile metal lockers. Card games were in session on spare changing stools. Latin players performed high-volume imitations of each other in door jams. Complaints about dirty shoes and wet laundry echoed incessantly. And to top it all off, someone took a shit and didn't wash their hands afterwards.

It didn't matter. In minor league camp there are no grapes.

The lower levels, High-A and down, all dressed in one giant main locker room. Double- and Triple-A had their own private rooms. The big league rehabbers were in the Triple-A locker room. When I came in, I threw my bag into an unclaimed locker, sat down on its changing stool, and stared into the locker's empty space as if it were some infinite vacuum.

I still couldn't understand what had happened to me in front of Brice. I'd had issues with players in the past. It's damn near impossible to play as many years of baseball as I had without running into someone you don't use the same signs as. But this was different. It was like a war, complete with propaganda. I couldn't let him beat me, but there wasn't much I could do from where I was, in the state I was in. I had to get my mental shit together. I had to heal up. I had to make it back to the big leagues, if not for my career, then at least for the chance to shove it in Brice's face.

I met the head minor league trainer and director of rehab, Jep Jasper, in the minor league complex's training room. He was a small, balding man with a perpetual smile and high-pitched, Barney Fife-ian voice. He seemed very happy to meet me. After spending a few moments with him, I realized he would have seemed happy to meet anyone. He was upbeat and well caffeinated. I would talk, and he would complete my sentences, tagging their finish with an automatic, "Oh sure, yeah, I'll bet." It was hard to say if his personality was a byproduct of his environment or just who he was. But on the minor league side of spring training, where bodies and needs outnumbered trainers by about twenty to one, it seemed like a good fit.

I told him about what happened to my arm, and how I was anxious to get it healthy because I hated being hurt and sitting out. As I spoke he nodded along, torquing and twisting my shoulder, periodically spouting an "Oh sure, yeah, I'll bet."

When he finished evaluating me, he gave me an exercise routine and explained, "I have my rehab guys come in a little later in the day, that way I can get all these minor league bodies cleared out of here and focus on y'uns."

"I can do stuff on my own though, right?" I said, looking over the sheet. "In case you get busy?" I gestured around the room, presently crowded with minor leaguers—rationing out pills, getting their ankles taped, dumping powders into their crotches. Jep was in charge of the health of everyone in the place. It was inevitable that he would get busy.

"Oh sure, ya," he said. "And that's smart of you to ask, real smart. Good. Good. Good that you want to work on your own. You're free to be your own boss in here. Don't wait for us to tell you what to do. No sir. You know your routine, you just do it."

"Okay," I said. "Great. So you'll have my routine for me each day?"

"Yessir, you bet. Uh-huh. Right now, ya see, it's all about getting that range of motion back and working through that scar tissue. Then we'll build some strength in there and you'll be throwing 'fore you know it, kid." Big smile. "Shoot, I can already tell you're the type that's going to fly right through this. Why, I'm gonna have to slow you down for your own protection!"

"Well," I blushed, "I am kind of a hard worker. That might be how I got—"

"Yerself injured in the first place? Oh sure, I'll bet."

"So what do I do first?"

His mouth opened, but his BlackBerry rang. He held up a finger, then picked up the phone and slunk back into his office to punch on his computer.

I sat at my training table for a long while, waiting for him to come back. Minor league bodies buzzed in and out of the room, and occasionally one of the other rehab guys came in and nodded at me and went out. When Jep came back out to face me, it was as if his speech reset: "Yessir, first thing we need to do is get that range of motion back, then we'll build some strength, and then you'll be throwing again." Big smile.

I smiled back.

"Uh-huh, yep, let's get you warmed up. Body always works better when it's warmed up. Go ahead and take your shirt off and we'll get some laser on your arm. Get it nice and hot so it moves around easy and then we'll go from there."

The medical laser was an odd, alien-looking tool. It was like an old video game console with a metal cord sticking out of it that attached to a plastic wand with a large, clear plastic mouse ball on the end of it. The laser was generated in the console portion and pumped down the cord and through the mouse ball and into my shoulder. The machine made an incessant *beep beep beep beep* as it ran, and Jep and I both had to wear giant laser-proof glasses while operating it.

"This is real good at heating up the body a little deeper into the tissue," Jep said. During most of this he stared into his BlackBerry and texted with one hand, absently rolling the laser mouse ball all over my arm with the other.

"This doesn't cause cancer, does it?" I asked, mostly joking.

"Uh-huh, sure, yep." He was looking into his BlackBerry, absently. "Here," he said, handing me the laser, "just make sure you keep moving it around real good, I gotta see about this." I took the laser and rolled it around on my shoulder while he went to make a call in his office. I finished lasering my shoulder long before he came back out. When he finally did, I wasn't sure if my arm was still warm from the laser or not.

It went on like this for most of the day, and the day after that, and the day after that. I tried to show up later in the day when there were fewer bodies, but there were never fewer phone calls or BlackBerry messages. I found myself spending more time in the training room doing fewer things, just because I wanted to make sure I was doing everything with the approval of Jep. I learned, however, that I wasn't just *free* to be my own boss; I had to be, if I was going to make it out of the place before whatever the hell was malfunctioning inside me started to break out and suck me into the anxious, lost place that seemed to make the sun grow cold and the air turn sour.

It was a delicate balance of trying to get healthy physically and not unraveling mentally into some anxious, why-am-I-not-healthy mess. It was absolutely paramount that I keep myself occupied. There were several days when Jep was around to push me along, but there were also several days he was gone for long stretches to cover the active players, or other rehabbers, or to schedule appointments. To kill those lulls I spent a lot of hours in the weight room. I couldn't do anything with my upper body, but I was allowed to work my lower body, abs, and go running. It's common to see injured players spend hours in the weight room, overworking the muscles they're cleared to use. Many of the injured rejoin their rosters with massive biceps and pecs, or tree-trunk quads, just because they had nothing better to do. But unsupervised, bored, injured athletes have a way of getting into trouble, and history, as they say, has a way of repeating itself.

One day, while waiting for the rehab crew to come in off the field and put me through some manual resistance drills, I went into the weight room to do abs. Meanwhile, the hulking form of Travis Hasher, silent and stoic, entered the room followed by a trolling Soup. Hasher went to the weight rack and selected a massive set of dumbbells, easily over a hundred pounds each. The tendons in his neck bulged as he carted them to a nearby bench. In one fluid motion, he went supine and positioned the weights above his chest, arms extended with the weights aloft.

I turned my head slightly away from Hasher, as one does when they suspect they may need to shield themselves from flying debris. Hasher let the colossal weights depress like a plunger to a bomb. Then, slowly, steadily, without a complete shoulder explosion, he pumped skyward again. Hasher proceeded to press more than my body weight nearly a dozen times before letting the weights fall and rumble across the floor like faint thunder.

I let out a great sigh and lay back on the floor, ready for sit-ups. Instead of doing them, however, I just lay there with my hands across my chest, connected at each shoulder like a cadaver. I stared at the ceiling thinking of how health seemed nothing more than a gamble, bestowing its blessing on some but not others with no way to tell until you didn't have it anymore, or found out for the first time that maybe you never did.

Working out suddenly lost its allure, and I felt like spending some time in the bathroom holding my head and telling myself I was going to be okay. I rolled to my left and planted my right arm to push off the ground.

That's when I felt something like a tear.

Fresh pain throbbed in the front of my right shoulder. I rolled to my back again, grabbing my right shoulder as I went. Gritting my teeth and trying not to let Hasher or Soup know I was in pain, I pushed myself up with my left hand and lumbered into the training room, still clutching my shoulder.

No one was there.

"Jep?" I called out. "Woody? Vern?"

Nobody home. I swallowed hard. Panic gripped me. Reason collided with emotion and emotion was winning, again. I sat down on a blue training table and tried to control my breathing. Soup watched through the glass panels that divided the training room and the weight room and I tried not to look at him. I held my shoulder like I'd been shot there, and had to keep compression on the wound to staunch the bleeding.

The outside door banged open. In walked Jep and a pair of relief pitchers, Scott and Hill. They'd just finished their rehab throwing. I sprung to my feet, but before I spoke I felt suddenly defensive. A second ago I wanted someone to know I'd hurt myself, but no more. What was I going to tell them, that I'd done something stupid in the training room? Again? Would I cry if I opened my mouth? I didn't want Scott and

Hill to know. I didn't want Jep to know. I didn't want Brice to know. I pulled my good hand away from my shoulder just in time to meet their gaze.

"All done working out and ready for some ice?" asked Jep, setting his sunglasses on his head and flipping his mitt into his office as he walked through the room.

"Uh-huh, sure, yep," I said. Big smile.

Chapter 14

At first the ice helped. But when I got home and my body warmed up my shoulder felt like someone had hit it with a hammer. It hurt worse than it did in the training room, worse than it had ever felt before. It throbbed all the way down to my hand. I couldn't brush my teeth without pain. I couldn't wipe my ass without pain. I couldn't pick up a beer and twist the cap off the pill bottles without pain.

The next day was just as bad. Weaving through the snow-bird-piloted, champagne-colored Lincoln Town Cars on my commute to the training compound was torture. Each twist and turn felt like bone grinding against bone in my right shoulder.

I feared the worst, but I didn't want to tell Jep what I had done. The circumstances regarding any injury would be reported on my permanent medical history. If there was something seriously wrong, I decided that we'd find out together, not because I came running in from the weight room clutching my arm. I already made the mistake once and I was not going to let them write "Stupid" on my injury report.

"I got ambitious, with our rehab exercises," I said as Jep examined me, "just like you thought I would."

"You probably just worked too hard," Jep said. "Just over-worked is all."

"Yeah, probably," I said. "I just can't wait to be healthy."

"You have to be careful of doing too much, even when you feel good. That's how lots of guys have setbacks, they—"

His BlackBerry rang. He dropped my arm and pulled the device from its hip holster. He sighed, lifted the phone to his head with one hand, and showed an index finger to me with the other. Then turned around and walked into his office. He did not come out for nearly an hour. When he finally did, it was to escort Richie Scott and Shawn Hill to the field to supervise their throwing. When he came back from *that*, he stopped at my training table and said, "I've been thinking, we should just take a break. It won't hurt anything at this point to take a break from exercises. I say we just ice you up and calm it down. Yep, get all that irritation out and calm that sucker down."

Jep made an ice pack that looked like an ice-filled burrito, then, with a tan bandage roll tucked under his arm, smoth-ered my shoulder with ice pack. I held the pack steady while he lashed it in place with the bandage roll. He spun it around until it seemed as if it were grafted to my person, then set a timer for twenty minutes, handed it to me and said, "Yeah. We'll just take it easy for today, give it a break, see if it—" His phone rang again. He walked away. Twenty minutes later, I went home and opened my pill bottles.

Three days passed. Virtually nothing changed. I was at the compound for less than an hour each day. We iced my arm. I showered. I left. I worried. I paced. I drank and popped pills.

I wanted to tell Jep what had happened. I wanted to tell him my shoulder felt like shit; that, as a whole, I felt like shit, shoulder to soul. I wanted to tell him that in the last three days, since this setback, I'd slept nearly sixty hours. But when he asked how I felt I always said, "A little better, I think."

"Good. Good. See, just need to get it calmed down in there. I think until you come in here and tell me it's fine, we should just keep doing what we're doing."

But I didn't want to keep doing what we were doing. "Are you sure?" I asked. "Should we maybe do some ultrasound, or laser, or stim?" I named off the other treatments often used to expedite recovery in the training room. Before the setback, we didn't have much of a routine. Some days we'd do laser. Other days we'd do ultrasound. Others we'd do electric stimulation. At first I didn't think anything of how little consistency there was, but eventually I started wondering if it wasn't a result of how much demand there was on the training staff. It seemed when things were slower, I'd get laser, ultrasound, and all the other things that went into the rehab process. Then, on days when more emails and phone calls showed up, I'd be told things like, "I'm not sure if I put too much stock in this laser." Or, "The ultrasound is just a way to warm you up, but you can get warmed up on your own without it." Maybe. Maybe not. We had the machines and I had the time. Why not use them?

"Yeah," Jep said, looking at the clock. "Yeah, we could hook you up with some stim, sure, that'd be good."

His words caught in my ear wrong. "Maybe we should do some ultrasound, too?" I asked.

"We could. That wouldn't hurt you any."

"Do you think going back and forth from hot and cold would help it?"

"Yeah, I think it would. You can ice it as many times as you want, it's only going to help, won't hurt you any."

Jep started the treatment. I was unsure of his answers. If all the tools in front of us were going to help me, why weren't we doing it every day? And if icing multiple times was beneficial, why didn't we do that every day? Why did I spend so much time sitting at my locker, or staring at the ceiling, or back in the apartment passed out when I could have been doing something to heal?

"Let's try this one here," Jep said, pulling out an electric stim machine that looked like it had been used on decades of Blue Jay pitchers. I stared skeptically at the machine, then at Jep, then back to the machine. I had never seen one that old before. It looked like an eight-track player modified for medical purposes.

"Looks like that thing has seen better days," I said.

"Yeah," he chuckled. "It sure does." He unwound the machine's leads anyway, connected them to the sticky pads that would conduct the electricity, then slapped the pads onto my shoulder like some jumper-cable/nicotine-patch hybrid.

He turned the machine on. "You feel anything?"

"Nothing."

"How about now?" He fiddled with the machine's plugs and dials for a bit.

"Nothing."

"Well that's strange . . ." He played with the machine again. "Should be . . ."

I looked away from his tinkering to a new stim machine a fifth the size of the dinosaur I was currently plugged into. It had touch-screen controls, an instruction manual, and came in bright, kid-friendly colors.

"Uh, why don't we use that one?"

"What? Oh, yeah, I guess we could, but I just want to see what this . . ." He went back to the dated machine again. "Sometimes these are more trouble than they're worth, you know?"

"Well, I know that one works," I said, nodding at the new machine.

"Yeah, looks like we'll have to make the switch." But he kept fiddling.

"When's the last time you used that one?"

"I never have," he said.

I wanted to ask him why he felt now was a good time for him to try it on me, but I choked it back. Instead, I watched him unpack the new machine and all its leads and spread them out in front of me. He hesitated, staring curiously at the leads and patches, and in that moment I started to wonder if I was ever going to recover from my surgery.

"You've used this one before, right?"

"Uh-huh, yeah, sure," he said. "Just making sure I have the right wires plugged in. Gotta get them wires right is all."

"I could move over to another bench," I said, noting that there was no one else but us in the room. "We could use one of the other machines you like."

"Oh, huh-uh, no. We'll use this one. This one riiiight here . . . Just got to get the—" His phone rang. He put his finger up and went into his office.

The next day I had to head back over to the major league side of camp for a mandatory security meeting. By this point in camp, some cuts had been made and the team was starting to bond, forming a sense of who was going to stick around and who was heading to Triple-A. In many ways, I was cut, and my presence around the club was like that of an outsider—like someone who gets kicked off a reality television show contest but then gets invited back for a reunion.

I sat in the back of the classroom, silent, listening to the guys joke and mock each other. Most of them had relationships off the field. In fact, they'd held a party in my absence that they referred to as their Boats and Hoes party, wherein players rented a boat, invited a ton of girls, dressed in yuppie

New England boat apparel, and got obscenely drunk. Some of the guys I was rehabbing with were there. I had no idea until now.

The meeting was conducted by ex-law-enforcement officers. Their job was to cover all the pitfalls of the modern athlete's life. They warned us about things like getting your picture taken on cell phones in a bar, drinking and driving, and how, if you own a gun and beat your wife, statistics say she'll use the gun against you—which can be very bad for your career.

One of the guys asked, on behalf of another guy of course, if it was also true for the beating of boyfriends. The answer was still yes. Then a PowerPoint slideshow was done with a half-naked woman mixed in every three slides. Then some advice was given about what to do if a woman was stalking you. Then a volunteer was selected to wear beer goggles and play catch. It was a very comprehensive meeting.

At the end we were asked to sign a sheet saying we'd attended. Then we were given laminated cards with MLB security numbers on them that we could call if we, or anyone we cared about, were in danger as a result of the public nature of our job. I wondered if I should tell them that just about every night I was taking enough pills to wreck a car should I ever decide to leave the apartment and drive. After the beer goggles went on, however, and the jokes about guys beating their gay boyfriends, I decided this wasn't the time or place for that.

I took the card, signed the sheet, and thanked them for the show.

Before I left to head back to the minor league side of things, I made sure to hit up the big league breakfast spread. It was so good to see it again. I loaded up a plate and sat at an unoccupied table. The cafeteria was nearly empty by this point, since most of the guys had already eaten and were getting ready to take the field. I sat alone, eating and reading the latest *USA Today* until a group of relief pitchers came in for a cup of coffee and stopped talking when they saw me. I pretended not to notice, and kept my eyes trained on the paper, though I'd stopped reading, ears open.

One of the pitchers was Brice. The other was number 77. There were two others in the entourage and they all poured themselves one cup each, then took an extra empty cup so they could air-cool the coffee to a drinkable temperature by pouring the contents of the cup back and forth from one to the other. I knew the other two players in the group and yet, it was as if I did not know them. They were fellow relief pitchers with maybe three years of big league time between them. We'd been teammates at one point or another but not for long, and we were never close.

Stoically sifting their coffee, they filtered out of the room save for one player, Jeremy Kitsch, who came over and stood in front of me at my table with his glove sitting atop his head like the butt of an acorn. He poured his coffee back and forth, steam rising from the white Styrofoam after each flushing.

"Hey dude, how are you?" I asked, looking up from my paper as if I'd just noticed him.

"Hey, man," he said evenly.

I watched him pour, waiting for him to speak. There was something he wanted to say, but it seemed like he was weighing the thought, passing it back and forth like he did the coffee.

"Hey, man," Kitsch said again. "You think you could maybe take it easy with the media?"

"What do you mean?" I sat back in my chair.

"Well, you haven't been over here for a while, and the first thing you do when you get here is whore out to the media. It just looks bad, you know?"

When I'd come over to the big league side of camp that day, before the meeting started, I caught up with the media. They were in a scrum, pressed around the lone locker-room television, watching updates and highlights from around the league. I elbowed in, said hello, shot the breeze, asked them if they could plug my book, which would be out soon. If I was to make a run for any bestseller lists, I'd need their help.

"I was just trying to get some book pub, man. It wasn't like I was talking about you guys or anything. It wasn't any big deal."

Kitsch looked down at his coffee. "Nah, man," he said. "It's like, we're here trying to do our jobs and it's like you're here focusing on the media. It's like every time we turn around you're gushing about your book and that you're a writer and it's taking attention away from the team, and that's not right."

"It's not like that," I said.

"Maybe, but that's what it looks like."

"Well, it may look like that, but that's not what is going on here. The media is like free advertising, you know. Besides, I'm hurt, and on the other side of camp. I'm just trying to make the most of my opportunities."

"I understand, man. I think most guys know what you're trying to do, but I also think most guys think you're going about it the wrong way."

"What other way should I be going about it?"

Kitsch shrugged.

"Hey," I said, "Kevin Millar and his Cowboy Up bullshit were paraded around this locker room all last year and no one said anything to him."

"That's different."

"How so?"

"Millar's got his ten years in the Show. He can do what he

wants, man." He made his final pour and placed the full cup into the hollow cavity of the empty one. "Look," he said, "it's just that, you don't have a lot of time and you're hurt. You're in there"—he gestured to the locker room—"whoring out to the media, joking around with them and it's like you're just using this to get a paycheck and sell books while some guys are in there dying to have what you have."

"You think I hurt myself so I could pull a Club Med and sell books?"

"I'm just saying . . ." Kitsch shrugged again.

"No, you're not *just saying*. You're accusing. You keep telling me what this looks like, you say you understand me, but you also want me to stop because it looks wrong. I don't get it."

Kitsch shrugged. "I guess it's not fair, man, but you know how it is. It's baseball. You could be right, but if the whole group thinks you're wrong, then you have to respect the group."

I said nothing. I looked down at my paper, furious at the flawed logic and yet knowing full well in this context it was law. I couldn't believe I was being accused of pulling a Club Med, what with all the pills I was taking just to endure the experience. I wanted to tell him, I wanted him to know exactly what the fuck I was dealing with just to have the opportunity to deal with it. But my face was hot and my heart was pumping. I looked around the room for all the exits, should I need to get up and run, and there, just outside in the hall, I could see Brice and 77 holding their coffee, quiet and watching me out of the corner of their eyes.

"What"—I coughed to make it seem like I was choking—"What do you want me to do?" I asked.

"Be more discreet. Guys think you don't respect the locker room. You're not even supposed to be here today and when

you do show up it's like all you want to do is talk to the media. I mean, think of how it looks to them. Just have some
respect."

"Not supposed to be here?" I shook my head. "If you all
know it's not me trying to disrespect you, why does everyone
feel this way?"

"That's how it is. Guys don't like it, so you have to decide
if you want to respect them or not."

Despite my best efforts, Kitsch must have noticed my
emotional state by this point. His tone changed, but the insult didn't. "Hey man, I know you gotta sell your books, but
take the media outside with you or something. You know,
where no one can see you talking to them. And maybe don't
be talking about your book all the time. Talk about the team
or something. Talk about the game."

"But I've been sent to minor league camp. I don't know
what's going on with the team," I said, my voice uneven.

Kitsch shrugged again. "I'm just trying to help you out is
all."

"Thanks," I said, now hunched over the newspaper.

"Yeah man, anytime."

Chapter 15

Back in the minor league side of camp, after I finished my treatment and took lunch, I sat hunkered down on a toilet in the Triple-A locker room, reading the Money page of *USA Today*. It was becoming harder for me to take a crap. Good for my investment knowledge. Bad for my intestinal tract. The blockage probably had something to do with all the oxycodone and sleeping pills I was taking. I drank a lot of coffee to compensate, but it had its work cut out for it.

Unfortunately, the caffeine didn't do anything to combat the hollow, drifting feeling I had when awake. I felt as though I'd been severed from the team. Worse than that, actually. It was to the point now where some players were trying to be merciful to me, like I'd gone from being one of the guys to a perpetual fuckup. I had no say in the matter, shackled to the training room as I was. I just had to live with whatever moniker was being slapped on me. It shot my self-confidence. I could barely talk to the guys, because I suspected they all thought I was some malicious, selfish bastard, recording their statements and selling them to the media. Even guys who I knew didn't give a shit about me writing or selling books.

I didn't feel like a baseball player anymore. I didn't feel like a human being anymore. I felt like a social disease, and I longed to get away from rehab and back to the apartment so I could go to sleep again.

"Courtesy flush!" bellowed Richie Scott, the click-clack of his cleats on the bathroom tile heralding his arrival. I hadn't even dropped any anchors yet.

"Sorry," I said, reaching around and depressing the toilet plunger regardless.

"That you, Hayhurst?"

"Yeah. Yeah, it's me," I said, getting up from what was becoming a lost cause. I pushed open the door and walked out. Scott was rubbing some sunscreen into his face in the bathroom mirror. He looked determined, alive. I looked like a vampire. For a person who played baseball and lived in Florida, I looked like I'd never seen the sun. My reflection was that of an injured man, not even strong enough to withstand my own gaze. I dropped my head and looked into the sink.

"You alright?" asked Scott.

"I don't know," I said.

"I heard you had a setback," he said, working the sunscreen into the nooks and crannies of his ears. "Everyone has 'em. You'll be okay."

"Oh. Yeah. My arm," I said, giving my shoulder a rolling crank. "Yeah, it's bothering me again. Don't know what I did to it."

"Jep will fix you up."

I looked away. "Yeah."

Scott washed the remaining screen from his hands and dried them on his pants despite both paper and cloth towels being available on the bathroom sink. He grabbed his glove, which sat cupped atop his head. He started to walk past me, then stopped. He must have noticed I was gripping the edge of the counter like I might rip it off. Or maybe vomit my guts out.

"You alright, Hay?" he asked again.

"I don't know," I said.

"You need me to get Jep?"

"No, no. It's nothing like that. It's just—" *Don't say it, don't say it, Dirk. Once you start telling people, it will all become real. DO NOT SAY IT.* "I don't know, sometimes I feel like I'm going to tear myself apart inside." And it was out. I turned to look at Scott, whose eyes went left, then right, then back to me. "I mean, I have these moments of panic, like I could fly apart, you know? But then, after a little, it all calms down and I just feel empty. Like life is just something you do until you die." I laughed as I finished. Indeed, the words sounded crazy to me. Then, for some reason, I stretched out my hands and looked at them the way people do when they're high and find opposable thumbs infinitely fascinating, rich with philosophical consequence. After a few seconds, I dropped them uselessly at my side and looked at Scott with my eyebrows furrowed. "Do you know what I mean?"

Scott looked at his feet. He rolled a cleat over and inspected it. Then he smacked his mitt with his bare hand and said, "Injury is some hard shit, bro."

"Yeah. I know, but . . ." But I didn't know.

"Injury is hard. Jep will fix you up."

"Right. Sorry. I guess I'm just feeling down about the injury."

"For sure, man. It's cool," he said, while backing away, slowly.

I moved closer, though. "You think this is all normal? You think what I'm feeling is normal?"

"Injury is some hard shit, bro," he repeated.

I stopped pursuing him, and began nodding as if he'd dispensed timeless wisdom. He kept moving, however, disguising his retreat with, "I got to get out there and get my throwing in, you know, before Jep gets another phone call. I swear I'm going to take that BlackBerry and smash it. But, uh, you should talk to Jep, he'll fix you up."

"It hurts," I said to Jep the next day. "I don't know why, I haven't done anything to it these last couple of days besides ice and rest."

"Well, we'll just keep icing it and see how it feels."

"Should we hit it with the stim machine again?" I asked.

"Yeah, we could. It wouldn't hurt ya none."

It wouldn't hurt me none. I was getting tired of that answer. It wouldn't hurt me none, but what was going to help me? I was getting tired of suggesting treatment options. The logic behind why we did one form of treatment one day, but not the other, didn't add up to me. I was no doctor, but could only assume that the lack of consistency wasn't good. But this wasn't a hospital, it was a baseball training room. Before I arrived here, I had my choice of surgeons and my choice of rehab options. I was advised that one was as good as the other, and, having never been injured before, I had no frame of reference from which to argue. I guess I assumed with the organization paying me so much money to get better, they would provide the absolute best. And yet, here I was, doing things that *wouldn't hurt me none.*

As I pondered the quality of my care, Jep made up an ice pack and set it down next to me before getting out the old stim machine. The same stim machine he couldn't figure out a few days ago.

"You sure you want to use that one?" I asked as he plugged me in.

"Yeah, we'll see if we can't get it to work on you."

"Why would we try that one if we couldn't get it to work last time?"

I watched him fiddle with the leads and patches and dials.

"Feel anything?" he asked.

"Nothing."

"Well if that don't beat all."

"You know," I said, "I've been wondering about the lack of routine we have."

"I don't like to get into a stuck routine in case something changed or you come in here not feeling right," he said, adjusting the dials again.

"Okay, maybe routine is a bad word. How about our lack of structure?"

"Anything now?" he asked.

"Nothing has changed from last time we tried this."

Jep changed the wires and looked at the back of the stim machine.

"Maybe," I said, "we should try getting into a routine with what we know works?"

Jep said nothing.

"You sure this thing is the best choice?"

Jep said nothing.

"Why don't we use the other machine instead?"

Jep said nothing.

"Why don't we just—"

"*Why! Why! Why!*" Jep snapped. He threw down the leads and slapped his hands at his sides. "Always, *Why?* Always questioning what I'm doing." A vein bulged in his neck, and his voice deepened. "*Goll-eee,* don't you think I know how to do my job? Can't you just relax and trust what I'm doing here?"

Jep stared hard at me, his little frame shaking and his hands balled into white-knuckled fists. His eyes twitched while he waited for me to answer.

I did not look away from him only because I was too stunned. He was such a gentle-natured guy. I often felt he wasn't really paying attention to me, the way he buzzed around the room, juggling a million things, supplying answers to most of my questions before I finished asking them. But now that I had his full attention, I was a little scared of it. Maybe all the distractions were the best way to keep this side of him from coming out and killing all of us?

"I'm sorry," I said slowly, like I was talking to a man with a gun. "I didn't mean to upset you. It's just that I'm new to being injured, and I want to make sure I'm doing everything I can to give myself a chance to get better. I don't always understand why we do the things we do and I want to understand.

"Please, Jep, help me understand."

He seemed to relax. The mental gun he had pointed my way slowly dipped to the floor. The vein in his neck receded. He took a deep breath and did a bobbing figure eight with his head. The country-boy smile returned to his face. "Golly," he said, "Golly me, I'm sorry. You're right. I get it. You're just trying to get better. You're right, partner. I shouldn't have come off like that."

"It's okay, man," I said, calmly. "Injury is some hard shit."

"Yeah, it sure can be. Well, let's just focus on getting you better."

"Right," I said, nodding and looking to the new stim machine sitting just beyond hand's reach.

"Right," said Jep, as he picked up the old machine and adjusted the switches again. "Anything now?" he asked.

"Nothing."

Chapter 16

After rehab, I came home to the apartment. As I walked through the door, I felt like an inmate returning to my cell. I sat down at my computer desk, but did not touch any keys or navigate through any icons. Minutes later, I held the fridge door open and searched for meaning among its contents. I didn't find any. I paced the apartment, stopping at random spots, purposeless, like some clockwork man who had become unwound.

I picked up my car keys and wandered to the door. I stopped just before it, and gently let my head fall to its lacquered wooden surface. Then, after listening to nothing for an indefinite amount of time, I lifted my head and let it fall again, and again, and again, each time more deliberate than the last, until I could feel my teeth rattle and saw white flashes inside my eyes. When I could feel the skin on my head become taut from swelling, I spun around and rested my back on the door. I slid to the floor, where I sat with my head drooping between my knees as if someone had socked me in the gut. Then, for reasons I couldn't explain, I started to cry. I didn't know why. I didn't feel sad. I didn't feel anything.

*   *   *

I went to bed around one in the afternoon, after a meal of beer and pills. I took them in the largest quantities yet, and when I woke up at around ten that night, I took more and went back to bed. I did the same thing for the next few days. I'd float into rehab like a ghost, do whatever Jep did or didn't tell me to do, nibble whatever was left in the minor league cafeteria, and float back to my bed.

Sometimes I would feel that lost, despairing feeling at the compound. Sometimes I would freeze and stare off into space. Sometimes I would entertain morbid questions in silence, weighing the value of life and death, only to panic and run to the bathroom and hide in a toilet stall until it blew over.

I didn't answer Bonnie's calls. I slept through them, actually. She left concerned voice messages, to which I replied with brief and vague text messages. I loved her, and thinking of how much I loved her made me feel ashamed of myself and the way I was feeling. When we did talk, I was distracted and unarticulated, telling her all was well, things were good, and that I was just tired. Always tired.

Five days before my birthday and ten days before the launch of my book, I became so miserable and sensitive that anything said to me out of key ran the risk of breaking me. I was an exposed nerve. I wore a smile as a mask but had lost virtually all my confidence in communicating with anyone. I had been on the mound before when I'd lost the command of my pitches, the ability to throw strikes disappearing, leaving me stranded and sinking. This was similar, except instead of the ability to pitch, I feared I was losing the ability to simply function. I was paranoid, thinking that maybe some giant conspiracy had been hatched to punish me for breaking the baseball codes. It was preposterous, I knew, but I thought about it anyway. Constantly. And the more I thought about it, the more I was convinced I was going crazy.

Finally, the weight became too great to bear.

Via text message, I was informed by Mike Shaw, the team's travel coordinator, that my major league per diem and housing stipend were available for pickup in the office at the minor league complex. I was instructed to get my money from the intern who worked at the middle desk in the main office.

I put on a happy face and walked to the main office. The intern I was supposed to talk to was eating lunch with one of the minor league coaches.

"Hey," I said, over-projecting to compensate for my utter lack of self-confidence. "Mike Shaw told me you had something for me?"

The intern put his plastic silverware down and picked up his napkin to wipe salad dressing from his face. Irritated, he wiped his face with enough pressure to scrape paint from siding, then slapped the napkin on the table and turned to face me.

I knew this intern. He was with the club last year in the same capacity, in charge of the minor league meal-money dispersals, and always bitter about it. In his defense, it's not a uniform operation. Players don't form a single-file line at the same time every two weeks and ask for their money, one after another, hands out like vagrants at a soup kitchen. They show up whenever their schedule allows, or just whenever it happens to cross their minds. Often, it doesn't cross their minds until the last minute, and then they run into the main office and beg for their money well after official collection hours are over. I could see how this would get irritating, but that's what this intern signed up for: a steady diet of random players at random times with random needs, all of them thinking their need was most important.

The minor league coach stopped and looked at me in mid-chew, then looked at the seething intern.

"Do you have my per diem?" I asked.

"You're just going to come in here and interrupt me while I'm eating lunch and demand your meal money?"

I was surprised by his tone, which led me to believe there was some misunderstanding. I knew he hated dealing with the minor league guys who probably ran him ragged. So, attempting to clarify that I was not his enemy, said, "Whoa bro, I'm a big leaguer."

It came out all wrong. I meant that I was on a different schedule than the minor league guys, but what it sounded like was, "I've had big league time and that means I get to do what I want, bitch."

"Seriously? Are you serious with that?" he asked.

"Well," I started to stutter, "I'm just saying, I'm not—"

"No, I know what you're saying and it's bullshit. I'm in here eating with one of my friends and you come in here like I should stop everything to get what you want?"

"I was told to come talk to you," I restated

"And what, your eyes don't work? You couldn't look at the scene here and think it might not be a good time?"

I looked at the minor league coach. He swallowed looking back at me.

"I think you're overreacting," I said. "I was told to come in here and ask for my meal money and that you would know about it."

"I don't have any money for you." He picked up his fork again.

"You could have just said that."

"And you could have just used your brain." He shook his

head at the minor league coach. "Damn," continued the intern, "and they said you were smart 'cause you're a writer."

That's when things went to hell. I stood there, locked on to him, my head sinking slowly until my chin nearly touched my collarbone, eyebrows overlapping, eyes twitching. My teeth were gritted so tight I my jaw hurt. I could have punched a hole into his chest and ripped his heart out.

I was on the verge of becoming the Incredible Hulk. All my emotions were at the boiling point. And then, instead of the monster, it was the mess. Everything backfired. My eyes welled up. The pit of my stomach tumbled into free fall. I could feel the gazes of all the other people in the main office watching me, shaking their heads in disgust, thinking, *Who does he think he is? Serves him right, that arrogant big league jackoff.*

This intern was a disgusting, pasty little fuck with long chest hairs sprouting from a white undershirt he layered under a cheap cotton polo tucked into pleated khaki pants. His shoes were dress but his socks were white. His wristwatch was made of plastic and rubber. He had acne despite being well into his twenties, and had to shave his eyebrows to keep them from connecting.

And he'd broken me.

"I said I don't have anything for you," he repeated, without even looking at me.

I nodded and turned to leave. My nose was running before I made it to the hallway. By the time I made it back to my locker, my face was flushed red with tear streaks under my eyes. I was so full of anger, and yet all that was coming out was water. I sat with my head dipping forward into the locker while the rest of my body dangled out on my stool. I was hyperventilating, practically gasping for air. It was as if I'd just been pulled from a game in which I got my ass thoroughly kicked. No, it was worse than that. I'd never cried after a bad outing, nor had I sat with my bottom lip quivering, or snot running down my face. I bawled like a spanked child.

Dear God, what the hell was wrong with me?

Chapter 17

"Hey," I said softly as I stood just inside the door to Jep's office. He had his head buried in email, and it seemed as if every thirty seconds or so there was a new alert sound on one of his various communication devices.

"Hey partner, what's up?" he said, smiling up at me.

My face was drained, still damp. I came in and sat in one of the chairs in front of his desk and, trying not to fall to more hyperventilating, said, "I don't feel right."

He waved a hand at me and let his seat recline. "I know," he said, "but sometimes arms, 'specially the shoulders, get aggravated. You got scar tissue in there, and inflammation and, well, it's still healing. It's only been about three months. Heck, not even!"

"That's not it," I said.

"Your elbow?" He sat up straight. "Sometimes guys who have their shoulder go wrong start to feel something in their elbow on account of the compensation."

"No, not that." How was I supposed to explain what I was feeling to someone else, when I couldn't even explain it to myself?

"I think I'm depressed."

"Oh, well, sure, uh-huh." Jep tossed his hands up and

smiled. "It's normal to feel a little down during rehab. Injury is a real grind, partner."

"No," I said, now looking down at my feet. "I've felt a little down before, and I know what the grind feels like. This is different. I think there is something wrong with me."

"Talk to your wife. Call up some family. They'll fix you up."

"Jep, I just had an argument with an intern and had to go into the lockers so no one would see me crying. I'm a goddamn major league baseball player that just got talked down to by a chubby witless intern and I was so rattled I was dripping snot in my damn locker." I drew a deep, quivering breath, then went on.

"I go home and I feel like I'm trapped. I don't want to talk to anyone, and I desperately want to talk to someone. I don't want to be at home, and I don't want to leave. My emotions are all over the map. I'm afraid of talking to guys on my own team. I—" I grabbed my head and squeezed it. I could feel tears coming at me again. "I feel like I'm going crazy, Jep. I don't want to be alive anymore."

I was hyperventilating again.

"Golly," said Jep after a moment.

I swallowed, pressed the back of my wrist across my leaking face, collected myself, and asked, "Do you have Dr. Ray's number?"

Jep snapped free of the curious stare he'd fixed on me. "Yeah, sure, you bet," he said, reaching for his phone. "Got it right here."

He read me the number and I typed it into my phone.

"Thanks," I said and stood up. "I'm going to give him a call right now."

"Yeah, uh-huh, that'll be good. Talk to Ray, he'll fix you up."

I left the office. Jep got up and followed me to the door,

where he stopped and held the jamb, his concerned gaze following me all the way to the locker-room exit.

I went outside to a blue metal picnic table near the locker-room doors. Sitting on the table top with my feet on the bench, I pulled up Dr. Ray's number, but before I dialed it, I stopped to consider what would happen if I did.

Dr. Ray Karesky was the Blue Jays' team psychologist. He also worked in the same capacity with the Padres, which is how I first met him. At the time I was pitching for the Lake Elsinore Storm, the Padres' High-A affiliate in Lake Elsinore, California. Ray occasionally came to town to check up on the team. Sometimes he'd make us watch steroid videos, or talk about what would happen if we got busted with an illegal substance. Sometimes he would conduct general lectures about basic psychological approaches to the game, like dealing with failure or coping with stress. Every time he visited, he made himself available to anyone who might want to talk to him about personal issues. Not unlike a reporter, he'd meander around the clubhouse, butting into conversations when the opportunity presented itself.

Most of the players avoided him, especially in public. They called him a brain fuck, a blanket for the mentally weak, or a wet nurse for guys who couldn't handle the stress of baseball life. They'd beat their chests and say, "If you can't handle the grind of the game, you don't belong in it."

There were also some players, mostly the paranoid and superstitious, who thought Ray was there to sniff out those not mentally strong enough to make it to the big leagues. It was believed that once he figured out who wasn't tough enough—and he could do it using his special shrink magic through simple conversation—he'd take that information and report back to the brass. A week later, out of the blue, you'd get released. Players kept exchanges with Ray brief; that way, the doc wasn't afforded a chance to pick them apart.

Over several seasons in the minors, I realized how silly our assumptions about Ray were. He wasn't part of some covert operation to rid the game of the weak, but was genuinely committed to helping players deal with the unique hardships of trying to play professional baseball for a living. Every year the sport brings in untested, immature, and naïve minds. It dangles superstardom in front of them, exposes them to a world where booze, affairs, and drugs are coping mechanisms, and expects them to withstand daily public scrutiny. Ray and other team doctors like him were a way for organizations to protect their investments from breaking.

It stands to reason that sports psychology should work like any physical maintenance/injury prevention program an organization institutes. However, unlike all the other medical fields in the game, sports psychology has a polarizing effect. It's associated with weakness, and sometimes thought of as a dark art. Players and coaches still looked at it like a crutch. Some even feared the doctor would crawl in your head and make you not like baseball, or competition, or girls, or America. Physically speaking, players only need to see a measurable gain in their performance to rationalize the augmentation of their body. But mentally speaking, asking a player to change the way he looks at the game, the way he thinks, or what a competitor looks like, is, in many ways, like asking them to renounce their faith.

I sat at the blue picnic table looking at all the manicured practice fields I'd never been farther away from. I could call Dr. Ray, let the organization know I was breaking under the weight of my present circumstance. But once I dialed, I would invoke everything that came with it. I would broadcast that I was mentally weak. I would be labeled a head case. I would feel like a failure.

I held the phone for a long time, weighing my options. I told myself calling wouldn't help. I told myself I was strong and I'd just had one bad moment, an anomaly intensified by a run-in with a stupid intern. I was a goddamn big leaguer and I needed to act like one. Suck it up, be strong, and get through the rest of this day. Just make it back to the apartment, take a few sleeping pills, and forget about the whole thing.

"Sleeping pills . . ." I mumbled. They weren't performance-enhancing drugs. They were just performance *sustaining*. And this had been a very bad performance.

My head fell.

I dialed Ray's number.

Chapter 18

Ray didn't pick up while I was at the complex. When I told this to Jep, he told me, in a deliberate, *it's going to be okay, partner* kind of voice, that Ray would call back. I resented him talking to me that way. Just because I said I was falling apart didn't mean I wanted to be treated like I was falling apart. Funny how you tell people you're feeling abnormal in hopes that they'll treat you like you're normal.

Ray returned my call when I was back at the apartment. I sat outside my door, on a set of stairs that overlooked the apartment complex. I couldn't go in. I was afraid I'd feel trapped once the door slammed shut behind me, and lose it shortly after. I was afraid I'd eat the whole bottle of pills and maybe something else this time . . .

Instead I sat watching two portly elderly couples play shuffleboard just beyond the parking lot while another equally large couple watched them play, sunbathing across chaise lounges like two wrinkly sea lions.

"Hello, Dirk," came the cheery voice of Dr. Ray Karesky when I answered. "How are you feeling?"

"I'm okay," I said.

"You're okay?" He adjusted his phone, which made a

piercing scratch against whiskers. "It sounded from the message like you weren't so okay."

"Well, I'm not okay. But, you know, I'm okay."

"Okay?"

"Let me start again. I'm stable right now, but I think I'm going crazy."

"What are you feeling?" asked Ray.

"Anxiety, fear, depression—even though I'm not sure what that is entirely. I'm mad at an intern . . . I'm confused. Really confused. I have these attacks."

"Attacks?"

"Violent mood swings. Emotional freak-outs." I explained the whole process, from the inability to leave my house to self-loathing, crying in place of anger, physical pain stemming from mental impetus, and mental pain from physical impetus. All of it. "I can't go into my apartment, Ray. I'm sitting outside right now. If I go in, I'm afraid it will all happen again." I paused and thought about all I'd said. "Am I going crazy?"

"More crazy than the usual ball player?" He attempted to lighten the mood.

"I'm serious."

"Have you stripped naked and run through the streets covered in your own feces yet?"

"Uh . . . not yet." I wondered if that was coming next.

"Then you're fine. Now tell me what you do after you feel loathsome."

"I try and go to sleep."

"You can go to sleep feeling that way?"

"Well, I take sleeping pills."

"Okay," he said, not skipping a beat, but his voice shifting to a more therapeutic candor. "Anything else?"

"I also take some painkillers."

"What kind?"

"Oxycodone."

"Mmm-hmm." He seemed to make a note of it on his end. "From your surgery, I'm sure . . . You take them all together?"

"Yeah. With beer."

"Do you know the doses? How much do you drink?"

I told him.

"You do this to make you sleep?"

"Well . . ." I thought about it. "Not because I want to sleep, but because I want to stop feeling what I'm feeling. I don't go to the park drunk and medicated or anything. I mean, you know me, Ray, I'm no addict . . . But, I suppose that's what all addicts say, right? That they're not addicts? Well, I'm not. I mean, you've known me for a long time and"—I thought about what I was saying and how when you want people to think you're not crazy, you sound crazy—"ah Jesus, forget it."

"Relax. I don't think you're an addict, and I don't think you're crazy. I just want to get my head around this so I can help you. It's obvious you're going through a rough time right now. One question: Is there something in particular that makes you feel all this? A trigger?"

"Baseball," I said.

There was a stretch of silence while Ray waited for me to elaborate. When I didn't, Ray piped in with, "Well, there's a lot to baseball. Any particular part that is bothering you?"

"It's hard to pin it all down. I'm just a mess. I can't . . . I'm not . . . I just . . ." I started to fracture again, cracks forming in the dam of my soul. I wanted to continue, but the words were hard to form and I felt embarrassed and disgusted that I felt embarrassed and disgusted.

"I don't feel like I have control of myself right now," I said, my voice unsteady. "It's a long story and I want to talk about it, because I think context is important, but I . . . God, this is so embarrassing. It's . . ." I snorted back the snot that was now running from my nose.

"It's okay," said Ray. "We can talk about this when you're in a better place."

"How do I get to that better place?" Deep, gasping inhale.

"I know you say you're having trouble going out, but I think you should get out of your apartment for a while, go do something different besides the broken routine you have. Do you have some friends on the team you can maybe get some dinner with?"

"Not really," I said. "That's part of the issue. Guys who write books while playing aren't known for their robust selection of friends," I said.

"I imagine not. Well, is there anything else you can think of?"

I looked across at the six-pack of elderly playing shuffleboard. One of the couples had won and was doing some sort of geriatric victory dance while the pair on the chaise lounge smacked their flippers together in congratulations.

"I suppose I could go play shuffleboard with the neighbors," I said.

Ray coughed. "That, uh, that sounds great," he said. "Do that."

"Okay," I said.

"Dirk, before you go, do I have your permission to share this conversation with Alex Anthopoulos?"

"What?" I said, alarmed. "I thought I was telling you all this in confidence." I thought back to the days when former teammates suspected him of searching for the weak minds on the team, and helping management weed them out. "I don't want Alex to know I've been eating sleeping pills and painkillers to get through my days. Fuck no, you don't have my permission!"

"I won't tell him the details," said Ray. "I can be as discreet as you'd like, but, after your conversation with Jep, I think it's better for me to let them know you are okay, and that you are getting some help, than leave them with the last impression you gave them."

"But, but . . . I just said I'd go play shuffleboard with the neighbors."

"I don't think shuffleboard is going to fix this."

"I don't want to lose my job, Ray!"

I hadn't meant to shout, and I felt embarrassed again at my lack of control and started to apologize, then I started to sob, but Ray paid no notice, calmly saying, "Dirk, you're not the first person to go through this. I know it feels that way, but you're not. A lot of players face stuff like this. More than you'd believe."

I let the phone line sit quiet for a while I collected myself. Going public with a physical injury was one thing. Going public with a mental one was something entirely different. I was scared of what it would mean for my future, but more scared of waking up and not feeling like I had anything worth living for. "I don't want the organization to think I'm weak, even if I am. Okay?"

"I won't tell anyone you're weak. Trust me. Can you trust me?"

"I trust you."

"Alright. You go play some shuffleboard. I'm going to make a few phone calls."

"We'd like to send you home," George said via phone call a couple of hours later.

"What?" I was stunned, and pulled my phone away from my face and checked to see if it was lying to me. "But . . . no, I don't want to go home." Especially now that I'd discovered how good I was at shuffleboard.

"We really think this would be the best thing for you."

"George," I said, almost pleading, "one of the issues I'm having is being away from the guys I know, and feeling like I'm out of the group and broken. So you're going to make that even harder on me by sending me all the way back home? I don't understand what I did."

"We don't want to compound your physical issues with any mental ones." He sounded like he cared about me, but all I heard was, "You're crazy, and crazies don't belong 'round these parts."

"Other guys have gone through post-injury depression before," George continued, "and we've sent them back home so they could have some support groups around them. Guys are less likely to get into bad habits that way, and in my experience those can take more time to fix than the physical stuff. Really, it's just that we want to do what's best for you."

That's not what it felt like. I'd told Ray I didn't want to look like I was weak, but the more time I spent in this conversation with George, the more I felt like damaged goods. The goal of confessing all my inner issues was to get help, not to be banished. This didn't feel like help; it felt like exile. It felt like the Prophecy of Brice coming true. I knew I never should have said anything.

"So, what now? I just pack up and head back to Ohio?"

"Yes. We'll get your rehab set up with the Cleveland Clinic, and you can be under the supervision of the surgeon. I heard you had a setback, so we'll get you reevaluated with your surgeon as well. It will be great. You'll be in a much better place, and under the care of your physicians. You won't be the first person to do this."

"How come I've never heard of anyone else doing it?"

"I don't know."

"I don't know, either."

"Hey," George said, trying to shift gears, "I understand it's strange, but when you're feeling like you are, it's good to have loved ones around you. A safe place. Why don't you take some time to talk with your family about it and see what they think. We can't make you, but think it over and let me know. We just want to do what's best for you. Call me when you've made a decision."

We said our good-byes, and I immediately called Dr. Ray.

"Well, what do you think?" Ray asked, assuming I already knew about the plan to exile me back to my home state, as far away from the healthy as possible.

"I think you ratted me out. I think they think I'm unbalanced, or worse, because you told them I wasn't strong enough to stick it out down here. I asked you not to make it sound like I was too weak to do this and now I look like a fucking mess!"

"Dirk, I didn't tell them anything, except that you were dealing with some post-injury depression. I didn't tell them about your medication or drinking or any of that. I just told them you were struggling. I had to tell them something."

"I don't want to go home," I said. "I'm strong enough to handle this. For God's sake, you know how much shit I went through just to get to the majors! Do you know how much crap I've taken writing a book while playing? Do you know what a mess my family life was before this? I can handle being injured without being sent home . . . I can. I can fucking handle it!" But the way I shook with frustration and fatigue said otherwise. In fact, as I fell into the disgustingly sticky sofa, breathing like a man in the grip of a heart attack, it was pretty obvious I couldn't handle it at all.

Ray listened until my breathing steadied out. Then, in a measured voice, he said, "There is no weak or strong here, Dirk. There are only those who get help and those who don't.

Don't think about this in terms of your career. Think about this in terms of your quality of life. You play baseball to improve your quality of life. Look at your quality of life. Do you want it to improve?"

"Here we go with the questions again."

"There are going to be a lot of hard questions from here on. The first one you need to answer is this: Do you want your quality of life to improve, or do you want to keep feeling the way you are?"

I packed up everything the next morning. I told my buddy who rented me the apartment that I had to rehab somewhere else, but I didn't say why. I paid him the remainder of our rental agreement, then drove home the same way I came to Florida: nonstop.

At three a.m. the next morning, I pulled into my driveway. I entered the house and quietly pushed through the bedroom door. Bonnie turned the light on by her bed, the glow illuminating her face. I stood where I was, hovering between the light and the dark. She got up and came to me. Hugging me tightly, she said, "Everything is going to be alright."

If that had even a remote chance of being true, there was something I had to do first. I broke free of her embrace, went to my luggage, pulled out my toiletry bag, and took out the bottles of pills. I went into the bathroom, lifted the toilet-bowl lid and dumped the contents of the bottles into the water and flushed. The pills swirled like snow in a snow globe, then disappeared.

I threw the empty pill bottles into the aluminum trash can at the corner of the room. Then I went to the bathroom sink, to the counter, to the mirror and stared at myself and what I'd become, Bonnie hovering behind me. Our eyes caught in the reflection. She wore a look of pity. I felt like an animal that, in its own ignorance, had wounded itself mortally and then slunk off to some dark place to die.

Then I went into the bedroom and took the framed jersey down.

"We're going to get you better," said Bonnie, wrapping her arms around me once more.

"How?" I asked. "How do you fix what you don't know is wrong?"

Chapter 19

I didn't sleep well that night. I woke several times, staring at the ceiling or at Bonnie swaddled in her blankets. I felt too disgusted to sleep, and with no pills to help me break the infinite loop in my head, I lay beneath it all.

I was out of bed early, my body still in tune with spring-training time. Bonnie found me at the kitchen table, chasing coffee around my cup with a spoon. She kissed my cheek and got her breakfast. She said she didn't want to leave, but she had to work. We needed her job now since mine was probably on its last legs thanks mostly to me being home. I told her it wasn't a problem, that I'd see her that evening. Before she left, she made sure I knew that if I was really feeling terrible, *drastically* terrible, I could call her or her parents or my parents, or just about anyone because they would be there for me.

I nodded and went back to my coffee cup.

Everyone would soon know why I'd come home and I hated that. Not only had I been knocked off the playing field, but I was also injured in the game of life. Not long ago it was only a surgery, just a bump in the road of my pitching career. Now, with the admission of depression, I was a big red flashing question mark. Was I feeling okay? Would I do anything drastic if left alone? Was I stable? Was I normal? It might have been difficult keeping all my emotions under control when it was just me and the pills and the beer, but at least there was no public shame.

To give Bonnie confidence that she could leave me alone, I told her she had nothing to worry about, that I was never suicidal. Even though I felt hollow and that life didn't excite me, I'd never thought of killing myself, I just didn't feel like being alive. I thought the distinction was fairly clear, but after I heard the words come out of my own mouth and saw how they twisted Bonnie's face in concern, I realized words were a poor medium through which to convey such emotions. They were all I had.

George set up my rehab at the Cleveland Clinic. I went three times a week to their rehab center, about a half hour from my house. It was a fantastic facility, modern, clean, equipped with all manner of gadgets and—the best part—people who actually knew how to work them. Unfortunately, the clinic was also for-profit, which meant when my time with a therapist was up, it was up. No more multiple icings or long sessions with a stim machine. I had to do my work and go so the next patient could get in and receive the time he'd paid for.

Meanwhile, Ray set me up with a psychologist who specialized in sports counseling. I was not a fan of the idea, especially since the guy had never been inside a locker room, never played the game, and could never understand how my life inside of both were going to hell besides what he learned in school. But it was out of my hands. It's what the organization wanted me to do and so I did it.

This expert sports psychologist asked me to talk about my family life and my childhood. He asked me about my marriage and my sex life. I asked him what any of that had to do with the fact that I had a hard time dealing with being a baseball player. He told me that's what he was trying to get me to answer.

"Me? That's why I'm paying you, man," I said.

He smiled dismissively and scribbled some notes on his yellow legal pad while I glared at him. "I don't think I know you well enough yet to make any calls on why you feel anything," he said, calmly.

"But we've been at this for six sessions now. Can't you take a guess?"

"Why don't you take a guess and tell me why you feel that guess is valid?"

I rolled my eyes.

"Fine," I said, settling back into the plush leather couch. I slapped my hands on my knees and let it rip. "It's like this: This whole industry is morally bankrupt. It's full of fakes and bastards and arrogant SOBs who can get away with murder as long as they play great. And then, on the flip side, there's a pocket of decent guys who deserve respect, but don't get it if they don't play well. Everyday dumbasses get on the Internet and debate your worth like you're a fucking commodity. But instead of trying to say we're not a commodity, we just want to be the most valuable commodity possible. Everyone wants to be the hyped, processed, nostalgia-injected product instead of being an actual fucking person. Peasants and lords. Gods and worshipers. Separation and isolation. Both sides say they hate it and yet both sides wouldn't have it any other way. If you tell the players' side of the story with any kind of honesty, they get pissed unless it's the type of honesty that makes them look good. If you tell the fan they don't know what they're talking about, they call you an arrogant asshole. It's all a giant act, everyone being what everyone else wants. How can we perpetuate that kind of stupid, limited thinking? It boggles the mind, I tell you.

It's voyeurs and egos and idiots and massive paychecks that somehow make sense of mountains of bullshit. Huge mountains of dehumanizing bullshit. It's just"—I shook my fists as I searched for the word—"it's just . . . fuck, man, it's just *fuck*."

The shrink made several notes on his legal pad, and when he finished he pressed his glasses back up his nose, crossed his legs, and calmly asked, "Do you think your choice to remain a virgin until marriage makes you feel less fulfilled as a player?"

"I'm not going back to that guy," I told Ray. I called him immediately after I left the sports shrink's office, tearing down the potholed Cleveland area highways as fast as my little black CRV could take me.

"Wow. I don't blame you," Ray said after I explained everything. "It's important to establish a good connection with your therapist, or it can do more harm than good. I can see if there is someone else in your area."

"I can't talk to a guy who studies sports from the outside about what it's like to be in a sport on the inside, unless he's been in there himself. Talking to shrinks is strange enough as it is. Hold on. Cop." I set my phone down and took my foot off the accelerator as I rolled by a police cruiser lurking in the median of the highway. Once it was out of sight, "Okay, where were we?"

"Why is talking to shrinks strange? You're talking to one now."

"I don't think of you as a shrink. I think of you as that guy who is in our locker room, ready to help us if our heads explode."

"I should consider listing that on my résumé," Ray said.

"Why can't I just talk with you about all this stuff?"

"You can, if you'd like. We can check in with each other a

couple times a week, and chat. I still think it would be good for you to have someone local, in case I can't set aside time with you. I do have the rest of your organization to 'keep from letting their heads explode,' remember?"

"Then tell me what's wrong with me and we'll fix it now." I kept stealing looks into the review mirror to make sure the cop wasn't following me. He wasn't, but I kept looking anyway. I always felt like I was doing something wrong lately.

"I'm not sure what's wrong with you, Dirk," said Ray.

"Guess."

"Well, uh, based on what you've told me and my observations of you over the years, I think you're dealing with some mania issues and some depression issues."

"Oh Jesus. *Manic-depressive,* that's just what I need the organization thinking about me."

"And a tendency to jump to conclusions," Ray said, with a soft chuckle. "I didn't say you were manic-depressive. And even if you were, that's not a bad thing. It's just the name of an issue. People assign scary definitions to things without even knowing what they are."

I smacked the top of my steering wheel. "Exactly! That's why I didn't want to say anything. It's probably why I got sent home."

"You were sent home because the Jays want you to get better, and be in a situation where you can better deal with this."

"Well, I'm home. Now how do we get this fixed?"

"I know you're getting tired of all the probing questions, but I have to ask you a few more. The first time we talked, when you were in Florida, you said you'd wanted to tell me everything so I could get all the context, but you weren't feeling well enough to hash everything out. You seem like you're in a better place now."

"Yeah," I said. I changed lanes. "I am."

"Well, you can tell me as much or as little as you like, but

I think it would be good to work through whatever issues you think are contributing to your present situation."

"I can try. But I'm probably going to run out of highway before I finish it."

"Then slow down," said Ray, "no one is chasing you."

Chapter 20

June 2, 2009—the previous season

We flew back to Vegas on a Southwest-evening knuckleball. Hot desert air ran into cool mountain breezes, slapping our jet all over the sky. Nothing rough enough to stop the boys from seducing free booze from the stewardesses, but too much to let you fall asleep without cracking your head against the cabin wall. Sacramento to Vegas was a short trip, and if the boys were to get drunk before landing, they couldn't let a little thing like turbulence slow them down. Ask any player who's ever played in the City of Sin and he'll tell you the best way to endure the onslaught of buzzing casino ads and blitzing light at the Vegas airport is to have a good buzz of your own.

Vegas. Probably the best and worst place imaginable to put a minor league baseball team. The brass bit their nails every time they sent a prospect there. On-demand gambling, drugs, prostitution, cathouses, drunk driving, stolen goods, real fights, bar fights, bum fights . . . If you were a young man with an itch to get crazy—as almost all minor leaguers are—you were a kid in a candy store. In Vegas you could get high, naked, rich, broke, drunk, beat up, and arrested. All in the same night. Case in point, one of our best relievers tied on a white tiger-print headband, got smashed at an eighties tribute concert, and spent the night passed out in a shrub outside the Luxor. He woke up when the sprinklers went off—and that was just his Monday night out.

Ironically, for all the ways a player could destroy himself in Vegas, it's one of the best cities for training future big leaguers. It's uncanny how many similarities the legendary Vegas charm has with the motivation behind making it to the top of professional baseball. Both offer life above the rules, constant action, and adulation if you're a winner. Both have an aura about them that compels you to live for the moment. And both can have you playing under the influence of some will-sustaining drug long past quitting time. At least in the big leagues, the locker rooms aren't packed with elderly in Hawaiian-print shirts, or foreigners handing out coupons for call girls . . . Well, not *all* of the locker rooms.

This big league training mechanism has nothing to do with Cashman Field, home of the Las Vegas 51s. That place is a hotbox with a concrete infield, gusting winds, and towering wooden fences for hitters to play racquetball against. No, the real training happens off the field, starting about a month or so into the season, when the charm fades. The boys start to realize they're *living* in Vegas, not one-night-standing it. The reality of trying to do your job in a place where fantasy is the hottest-selling item isn't all it's cracked up to be. Locker-room conversations shift from the standard masculine exploits of how much was drunk, won, lost, and screwed, to how much everyone hates going out because "the damn tourists don't know how to act here!" In short, most guys get a taste of the wild side and realize that while it's fun to escape to every now and then, there's no way they could live in it forever, nor would they want to.

Most guys. Not all. There are always a few who don't want the party to stop.

The plane's in-flight intercom crackled as Brice Jared, a freshly minted big leaguer who started the year with the Jays but was recently busted back to the minors, made an announcement. I recognized the frequency of his voice, even through my noise-canceling headphones, and pulled them off to see what the fuss was about.

I wasn't particularly fond of Brice. I didn't mind him so much in spring training, before he was a big leaguer. Back then he was just a touch cocky, typical for a high draft pick like himself, but he wasn't overbearing. After he made the big club, however, that changed.

Brice the Big Leaguer was a whole new animal. He'd been to the Show and came back wearing it like a billboard. His wardrobe changed, starting with his suits. In every major league locker room there are catalogues from custom tailoring companies who want to slap their wares on big names. For the low, low price of around ten grand, anyone can wear a big league suit. Brice got six. Everyone else on the flight was wearing a blazer and slacks, thrown together to satisfy the travel dress code. Not Brice. He looked like he'd just stepped off the fashion runway.

He also got himself a new car, new watch, new shoes, and new sunglasses—which he wore even now, on an evening flight. Big League Brice blew money on ridiculous stuff because he could. Because "that's what big leaguers do." And that was the real problem.

When Brice came back from the Show, he could no longer have a roommate during hotel stays on road trips, because, "in the big leagues, you have your own room, and I can't go back." Brice couldn't eat the spread in the minor league clubhouse anymore because "in the big leagues, they have real food and personal chefs, not this PB&J bullshit." He'd also grown a little more liberal with his mouth, chirping at umpires when they didn't give him the calls he wanted. He bitched about the travel, the clubbies, and the stadium lighting, making sure that we, his minor league teammates, knew "things are different in the big leagues."

It was irritating. Especially since most of the guys on this Triple-A Vegas roster had big league time; in some cases, several years' worth. We all knew players who had more money, experience, and time in the majors than Brice, but didn't "do what big leaguers do." And if those players, who had years of service and high-dollar contracts under their belts, wanted to splash the social pot with their wallets and titles, at least they had the service time to back it up. Brice had two months of service and was spending more bonus money than actual big league earnings. Despite his new look, swagger, and affinity for complaining, he was just another Triple-A player now, albeit with a bad case of Big League Withdrawal.

After the intercom crackled, Brice's voice came over the speakers. "Hell-ooooo everyone," he began. "Thanks for flying Southwest, the official airline of your Las Vegas 51s." It came out in a drunken-but-trying-oh-so-hard-not-to-show-it slur. He might have gotten away with it if he hadn't started laughing hysterically at himself. Two flight attendants stood by his side with nervous looks on their faces. Brice had most likely paid them for a chance to use the cabin announcement intercom. Before acting on any notions of backing out of their arrangement, Brice slurred on. "Hey," he resumed, breathing heavily into the mic, "we got a new guy on our team . . . Ffff-irst timer here in Triple-A, and we have a special way of intro-ducting"—he made quotes for that word—"them. Rookie's gotta sing karaoke, y'all!"

"Uncle," said my seatmate, fellow reliever, and friend Bryan Bullington, or "Bully." Like me, he had slid off his headphones and was watching this spectacle unfold. We took a quick survey of the plane to see where the coaches were sitting, and if they were going to do anything. They were low in their seats, trying not to let anyone know they were affiliated with the performance.

"Aaaaand this is really going to happen," Bully said, letting his head fall into the seatback.

"This guy is a ten-year big leaguer in his own mind, Dude," I said, nudging Bully. "You've got more time than him, and you were a first rounder. Why don't you tell him to rein it in a little?"

Bully shook his head. "Other guys have said something already. It doesn't help. Just makes him bitter. He's got it bad, maybe the worst I've ever seen. Someone up there probably encouraged this out of him. And now he's our problem."

Like Bully, I let my head fall into the seatback. I didn't have as much time in the big leagues as Brice or Bully did, but I'd seen transformations like Brice's before. Some guys go to the Show and they come back different. They succumb to the myth that they are as big as the league they're in purely because they are there. Worse, some of them stay up there. A cycle starts. Young players who don't know how to act show up in the bigs, look to an older player to show them how to behave, and wind up following the lead of some established, veteran jackass. A high-dollar prospect already into digging himself is the perfect candidate to continue the tradition of unchecked jackassery. When the two meet, it's like the uniting of a Sith Lord and a devoted apprentice. The majors have plenty of oversized egos, but you don't learn the kind of swagger Brice was throwing around unless you have a master to help you hone it.

At Brice's command, one of the younger pitchers who'd just joined the club appeared from behind the galley curtain. He was a country boy: shy, quiet, and not ready for flight-attendant work. Ironically, he was probably a bigger prospect than Brice. The difference was that Brice had been to the Show and Shy Country hadn't, and service time means everything in baseball.

A group of relief pitchers close to the action—those who'd been testing their alcohol tolerance at high altitude—snickered at our country rookie like a pack of goons about to run someone's underwear up a flagpole. Bully and I, though annoyed by Brice, chuckled as well. Even the coaches, who probably needed a drink more than anyone else on the jet, were laughing. It was the minors, a place of irony and over-the-line gags. To take any of it seriously would be the real sin. If it made Brice feel better to think he was living the Big League Life on a cattle-car flight where drinks came in plastic cups courtesy of a lispy attendant who sang the preflight safety instructions to the tune of a Broadway hit, so be it.

"Tell the audience what you're gonna be singing for us tonight." Brice pushed Shy Country out into the aisle.

Country gingerly placed his hands on the microphone and told the audience, " 'Friends in Low Places,' by Mr. Garth Brooks." The goons in front applauded heartily while the coach passengers offered a meager, out-of-sync clapping of hands.

What followed was a real mess. A jet plane's intercom is not built with a CD player, an MP3 hookup jack, or the ability to stream music from iTunes. In all our other rookie hazings, which we did in the outfield with a boom box and a microphone, rookies at least had musical accompaniment. Poor Shy Country had nothing. He had to stick in an earbud from his iPod and sing *a capella*. He sounded like a baying dog in need of euthanizing.

"Jesus, where's an air marshal when you need one?" I said. "If this isn't an act of terrorism, I don't know what is."

"No kidding," Bully said. "I've heard this song sung a million times by a million different drunk guys and this is the worst rendition yet."

The music trolled on long enough for Shy Country to hit the chorus. When he did, a few of the white-haired passengers—soon to be clogging buffet lines and slot machines—sang along. Then, one of the attendants, probably feeling he'd kept up his end of the bargain, cut the music off and ushered everyone back to their seats. At this, the first universal round of applause was issued.

Following the performance, the voice of the plane's captain came on and instructed everyone to take their seats for landing. Everyone did. Except, of course, for Brice. One of the flight attendants had to walk him back to his seat, and when the pair passed by Bully and me, Brice said, "In the big leagues, you fly private jets and can stand up when the plane takes off or lands. It don't matter."

"That's nice, sir," said the attendant, "but this isn't the big leagues. This is Southwest Airlines."

Chapter 21

"Did you patch things up with Basso yet?" Bully asked as we shuffled through McCarran Airport. We did our best to talk over the insistent whirling of McCarran's casino-sponsored advertising campaign. It was like the spirit of Vegas was there to greet you as soon as you exited the plane, ready to shove every Cirque du Soleil, magic, and musical act it had down your throat.

I looked over my shoulder. Mike Basso, our manager, was only a few feet behind us. "Not yet," I said. "I'll give him a day and then broach it. It's been a long one."

I had pissed off our manager. That day in our game, he'd called me in for a relief appearance. I pitched well enough to warrant another inning of work. At least, I thought so. Basso had different ideas and told me thanks for the effort, but that I was done. I objected, told him I wanted another inning. Told him I was hot, and needed to capitalize. He said he appreciated my spirit, but the answer was still no. I objected again, at which point he silenced the dugout by screaming, "I said no, now shut the fuck up and sit the fuck down." It wasn't one of my finer moments.

"I really could have used that outing, though," I said to

Bully. "I got off to such a rough start this season, I need all the hot outings I can get."

"I don't think they'll look at your starting numbers now," Bully said. "They know from spring training that you can do relief. Starting was an experiment, and it didn't work. I wouldn't worry about it."

"Yeah, I hear ya. But there is always next season. These stats might not mean much to the Blue Jays, but they will mean something to the next team if I'm a free agent after a year kicking around this place."

Bully, I, and the rest of the team arrived at the baggage claim like a flock of birds. We landed on our carousel in one big cluster then dispersed around it, ready to peck out our luggage.

While we waited, the team broke up into its little cliques. Cell phones were flipped open, text messages checked, wives and girlfriends called back. The coaches stood off to the back of the operation. They were a seasoned bunch and gave the players their space. This was Triple-A Vegas, after all: The less you knew as a coach, the easier it was to plead ignorance when someone got into trouble.

Our team's clubby met us at the carousel with a trolley he'd use to haul all our bags. When I saw him, I slipped out of the pack and moved close. Reaching into my shoulder bag, I produced a multitrack recorder. I fiddled with the settings so they wouldn't pick up the general chaos of the baggage claim, but more localized sounds. Then I waited.

Soon the bags were spitting out onto the carousel. I hit the Record button and held out the recorder to catch the rumble of the gears turning as the luggage conveyer kicked into motion. The yowls of guys who'd placed bets on which bag would surface first and last. The friction zip of nylon bag against nylon bag. Clunking hard-shell cases tumbling down the chute ramp like polycarbonate boulders. And then, the distinct rattle of a bat bag stuffed with tempered lumber clattering to a hard stop. It was the symphony of minor league travel, set against the doodles and dings of McCarran's slot machines. I let the recorder feast on it all.

It was one of my best captures yet. It would make a fine addition to the steady chirping of kids begging for baseballs in the bullpen. The classic belch of hecklers with failed humor. The artillery-themed report of a long batting practice. I tried to catch other things, but not everything I thought would turn out well did. I was still a novice at capturing sounds, but practice makes perfect.

It was part of my little plan to do something no one ever had. That is, after all, one of the reasons we play: to stand out. But I thought I could stand out not only because of how I played the game, but what I did while I played it. At the end of the season my first book would be done. Other players had written books from inside the game, but no one had ever done a podcast or an Internet radio show from inside it. Thanks to social media, Internet tools, and a little artistic vision, I could do something no player ever had. The landscape of the game was changing thanks to the power of the Internet and I wanted to be at the front of it.

"Digs, what the fuck are you doing, man?"

It was Brice, calling me by the nickname I had before I became Media. I'd been asked about the recorder before, even yelled at because of it. But I knew my motives and I didn't feel I needed to explain them to anyone. Not in the minors, anyway.

"Recording," I said, looking down at the little recorder, its mesh microphone aimed at the whirling luggage rack with all its rotating instruments.

"What the fuck are you recording?"

"I *was* recording the sounds of minor league travel, but now I'm recording you swearing at me." I turned to face him, microphone up. "Anything else you'd like to say?"

"That's bullshit, bro. I'm going to take that thing from you and . . . and . . . smash it into pieces so you can't record shit no more." He was still a little drunk.

"Relax. It's off. You've got nothing to worry about," I said, exaggeratedly pressing the Off button. We looked at one another, one of us drunk on airline liquor mini-bottles, the other on idealistic vision. McCarran, meanwhile, buzzed and hummed around us, filling the void with its unceasing agenda of excess.

"I should take that thing and fucking smash it. Do you a favor."

"I heard you the first time. This is just a hobby. You don't need to worry."

"It's a real stupid hobby, bro. Know where you're at," he said, as if reciting some higher truth. He gestured to our surroundings, implying that we were in the land of professional baseball, and in Pro Baseball Land, things like recorders don't fly. When I looked around, however, I saw nothing but irony. We were in Vegas, the city where anything goes. Where relievers slept in shrubs, and more than one guy on the team had been robbed by a prostitute. Our mascot was a carpeted version of Jar Jar Binks, and rookies sang Garth Brooks on economy flights.

"*Know where I'm at?*" I repeated back at him. "Really, dude? You're saying that to me after telling a flight attendant it's okay for you to stand up for landing because you got two months in the Show? Know where *you're* at is more like it."

"You got a lot to learn, bro," he snorted, and crossed his arms. He wore a leather Gucci bag slung around his shoulder. It looked like a woman's handbag but he insisted it was a status symbol, only for men.

"Have I?" I laughed, "And you're going to teach me huh? You're, what, six years younger than me?"

"Don't hate just 'cause you're older and got less time up than me."

"Oh my God . . ." I looked away. I had to, just to confirm I wasn't in some bizzaro reality. But I was. I had been for seven years now. "Time in the Show doesn't justify everything."

"A'ight then, lemme ask you this," he said, nodding toward my recorder. "You think you gonna get away with that shit up in the bigs?"

"We're not in the bigs. Are we, Brice?" I took the recorder and slipped it into a beat-up nylon sling bag I carried. It held my journals, pens, and headphones.

"Yeah, but you think the shit you're doing here isn't going to follow you up there? 'Cause it is."

"I'm not going to record in the bigs."

"Then why you doing it here? Why you stirring shit up here?"

"I'm not stirring shit up. I'm recording sounds. I take notes on life in baseball. I've been open about that since I showed up in the organization. I've told you what I'm doing and you don't listen. You invented this plot you think I'm up to, just like you've invented your new big league persona. You got more time than me. Congratulations. You want the best seat on the bus, fine. You want the better locker, okay. You want to tell me how to live my life, you can fuck off."

"Don't be a punk bitch, I'm trying to help you," Brice said.

"I think you got enough of your own problems to worry about," I said.

One of Brice's friends came over and tugged at him to walk away, but Brice shrugged off the hand of the would-be

intercessor and glared at me. "A'ight," he said, "but just remember though, ain't nobody bigger than the game. Nobody. You keep trying to be and see what happens." He threw
his hands out wide and backed away from me.

"Is that a threat?" A few of the guys had stopped talking
to watch us now.

"Nope. It's a promise, baby." Brice spun around and strode
back to his side of the baggage claim, back to his friends.

I watched him go, burning holes in the back of his big
league suit. I was angry, but I'd said what I needed to say. I
went to the far side of the baggage carousel. Away from Brice.

My suitcase was just sliding down. It was crushed on one
side and had a tear in it. I wrested it from the herd of bags
and inspected the damage.

"They'll give you a new one in the bigs," said the voice of
Basso.

I popped up and looked at him. "Yeah," I said, confused.
"Sure. Say, listen, about today—"

"Congratulations," he interrupted, extending his hand.
"You're going up. That's why I couldn't run you back out
there today. You were in line for the promotion and I just
got the confirmation message in my voice mail when we got
off the plane. Screaming at you was the only way I could shut
you up and keep the news secret. Woody"—the Las Vegas
team trainer—"has your flight info. I think you leave early
tomorrow, so you'd better grab your shit and get moving."

"You're serious?"

"Yeah, I'm serious. Unless you don't want to go?"

"No, no. I'll take it. Thanks, Skipper." I took his hand and
shook it.

"Don't come back," he said with a smile.

"I'll try not to."

I whirled away, grabbed my itinerary from Woody, hugged
my pitching coach, and collected all the congratulatory sen-

timent my friends on the team had for me. Brice even blew me a kiss. That colossal prick. Then I grabbed a cab and made fast for my Vegas apartment. In less than twelve hours, I'd be on a flight north to become a Toronto Blue Jay.

Chapter 22

I was put up in the Rogers Centre Marriott. The lady at the front desk upgraded me to a room with a view of the field. You might say I sweet-talked her, but if I was charming it was unintentional. A lot of Blue Jays passed through the place, keeping low profiles as they came and went. There is a saying in the big leagues: "Act like you've been here before." It refers to the cool, natural demeanor with which a player is supposed to carry himself when promoted to the status of elite citizen. Unfortunately, acting cool often gets skipped and players move directly to acting cold. They're terse and demanding with the service workers, and their behavior leaves a bad taste in people's mouths.

I was anything but cool, which worked in my favor. Giddy, and dying to tell someone I'd made it back to the big leagues, I drowned the lady at the front desk in a vomitous word stream regarding my promotion, practically telling her my life story, oblivious to the line of guests forming behind me. In return, she told me she'd met several Blue Jays, including—probably prompted by my own offering of too much information—her personal list of which Jays she liked most and which she liked least, based on interactions with them and their "bitch" wives. I listened to all of it, which made her extremely happy. I told her I was writing a book, which prompted her to tell me she had stories that could make me millions. Then she said, "But I can tell you're one of the good ones. You know what, I think I can change your room to one that faces the field. Make the day really special for you."

The room was special indeed, and it was a hell of a game to come into town on. From my window above right field, I had the pleasure of watching Roy Halladay mow through the Angels' starting line on his way to a complete-game shutout win. As soon as I entered the suite, I dropped my bags, went straight to the window overlooking the field, and stayed there until Halladay and his blue birds shared victory high fives. It would have been a memorable game for the pitching performance alone, but considering that watching it in person could only have been possible for me due to a major league call up, the experience graduated to magical.

Whoever I was replacing on the roster would not be told of his bad luck until after the game. Until then the roster was full, so I was forbidden to join the team until the sterile math of player shuffling was resolved. Not going to the field seemed moot since I was technically in the stadium, close enough to yell at Alex Rios in right field.

But the details were irrelevant. I was here now, and that's all that mattered. I was a big leaguer again, and as I stared out my window at the millionaires playing under the bright lights, the expectations that came with this level settled upon me once more. As exciting as my new status was, it was also unnerving. My last and only experience with the big leagues was a bloody encounter, one that sent me home with busted confidence, a bruised ego, and a numerical black eye. I lasted just over a month in my debut with the Padres, and I made it that long only because it was September and the team had nowhere to demote me.

The off-season had given me a long time to think about what had gone wrong. I realized that regardless of how many people claimed otherwise, big league baseball was not the same game I had played back in the minors. Yes, the bases were the same distance apart, the mound the same elevation. But you can use the same deck of cards whether gambling for quarters or quarter millions—it's not the cards, it's the circumstances. Even the most talented players can fold when they're under big league pressure.

This time, I was going to fix that. I proved I could handle it in big league spring training. I had enough talent to hold my own. I just needed to win the battle inside my head long enough to show it. At this level, with so many physical talents all capable of doing the same things, the mental side was the separator. Everyone could control their bodies like precision instruments, but it was now about who could handle the mind.

Strategies for getting one's mind right are different for every player. Some choose religion, and some choose family. Some choose eastern meditation, chants, and yoga. Some find answers in a bottle, or a needle, or a prescription. Some, like Brice, stop making decisions for themselves and default to the big league ego. And some, like me, try to convince themselves that the big leagues aren't that big of a deal just so they can get some sleep. Which, on this particular night, I couldn't get.

"Screw this place," I said after restlessness and nerves took me out of my big league bed and brought me back to the window's view of the field. "It's stupid. It's just a field, like any of the others."

I didn't mean it, though. I wanted to mean it. I wanted to not care what happened from here on out because, more than anything, I didn't want to be standing there in the middle of the night overthinking it. I didn't want my thoughts holding me captive well into the morning, like they had almost every single night in my last go-around in the bigs.

I turned away from the window, sat down at my room's desk, and pulled out a sheet of hotel stationery. I was going to write all the emotions out, put them into perspective.

But there was really only one thing to write.

I took a complimentary pen from the drawer and started writing *I can do this* over and over again. I filled a page with three tight columns of the phrase before stopping. I looked the page over, reading the phrase back to myself. Then I crumpled up the page and threw it in the trash. On a clean page, I wrote *You belong* in the center of the paper, in one single line.

Then I stared at the phrase, wondering if I had written fact or fiction.

Before my first outing as a Blue Jay, Cito Gaston pulled me aside and said, "All you have to do to be successful here is throw strikes, just like you did in spring training."

I nodded and said he was right, prompting Cito to pat me on the head like a good dog. When I came in to pitch, I struck out the first two batters I faced and put a zero on the scoreboard. However, I did give up a hit to Vladimir Guerrero, which, after I exited the field, prompted Cito to pull me aside and say, "You never throw strikes to that guy! Not ever!" I nodded, said he was right, and he patted me on the head again.

In my second outing, I faced the Rangers in Texas. I retired the side one-two-three, including a broken bat and a strikeout. I felt very good about myself because this was my longest streak in the bigs without giving up a run—two whole innings! But it was success in the bigs, and you don't question such things; you enjoy them when they come because they may not come again. To celebrate, I stole a few bottles of El Presidente from the locker room and got buzzed in the complimentary bathrobe provided by the five-star hotel we were staying at. An hour later, when the cheap beer wore off and I didn't know what else to do, I called room service and ordered a bran muffin. I was a rock star.

My third outing came back at home, against the Marlins. I put up another solid outing, no runs in an inning and a third. After I left the game, Roy Halladay and I bumped into each other in the training room when I came in to get ice. He told me I did a good job. It was the most I'd heard him talk since joining the club.

I stayed at the Rogers Centre hotel again through the home stand, even though my seven nights of meal money and free big league housing had run out. I could have moved out of the hotel, but I didn't know how long I'd be around, so it wasn't wise to get locked into an apartment contract. Besides, I had made friends with the hotel's staff and liked how easy it was to live in the same place where I worked. I took the service elevator in the hotel's restaurant down to the field level and entered via the back door. I made friends with the ushers and the security people and the field crew, and would come down early to chat with them about their jobs. They all told me they were excited to hear I was coming, because they'd read some articles I'd written on the Internet and thought it would be really cool for me to write about what it was like to be a Jay. I told them I'd need a few more innings before I could write about it, and they said if I kept pitching the way I was, I'd play forever.

My fourth outing was against the Marlins in the same series. Brian Tallet started the game. He gave up ten hits and eight runs, which got me into the game in the fourth inning. I pitched two clean innings except for hitting Hanley Ramirez with a pitch. It was an accident, but he took it personally.

After the game he called my hitting him bullshit, and said we, the Jays, were trying to scare him because he was such a good hitter. At first I felt bad that I hit him. I had no incentive to do it, because every outing was an audition to keep a spot in the big leagues. But after I heard the rest of the guys in the locker room saying what an egotistical douche Ramirez was for making a big fuss, I embraced it. It was part of my job as a rookie to be all things to everyone, so I said, "Hell no, I don't feel bad about it! Serves him right!" Everyone appreciated this. Nothing brings a team together like a common enemy.

My next outing was in the City of Brotherly Love, against the Phillies. I gave up my first run, a home run to a guy who had hit three of them off me in the minors: John Mayberry Jr. I covered my face after he launched it and started rounding the bases—not to curse, but to laugh. Away from the field, I was finishing up a chapter that included a character hitting an important home run off me in a minor league game. That character was John Mayberry Jr. It seemed almost divine that he would do it again here. I retired the next hitter, and it was another big league inning completed.

On the bus ride home from the park that night, I was called up front to tell jokes. Rookies must obey, and so I gave my best effort from all the good material I'd written down over the years. The guys laughed. On my way back to my seat, I got smacked on the ass, and nothing says good job like a firm, open-palmed smack on the ass.

The guys liked me. I liked me. I didn't feel guilty or unwelcome or unworthy or upset about giving up the home run. I was doing my job and earning my keep. I was really, truly living the dream. Wherever I went, I felt like I belonged. And after the bus pulled into the hotel, I was invited to the bar with the fellas and we got beers and wings and made jokes and laughed at each other and talked about money and toys and wives and life was good, better than it had ever been for me in baseball before. Later that night in my room, when I wrote I belonged, I felt that I'd written a fact. A beautiful, fulfilling fact.

Chapter 23

The weather changed. Rain came into Philly and drenched the park before the next day's game. I believe the excessive rainfall played a key role in the toilet backing up. The fact that I might have eaten too many chicken wings the night before? That might also have played a role, although which played the bigger part in the incident was hard to tell. Regardless, one thing was abundantly clear: the toilet in the visitors' bullpen was clogged, and the water level inside the bowl was rising with me on top.

Actually, it had already risen, quietly, inconspicuously, all the way up to the brim, so that a turd was able to kiss the back of my thigh. Luckily, I was just finishing up when my bathroom experience became aggressive, and so I was able to leap from the bowl, thus saving my uniform from the ensuing overflow as it poured onto the floor of the visitors' bullpen bathroom.

Pants down and fresh sewage drying on my ass, I watched chunky brown liquid gush over the rim of the toilet bowl like some porcelain volcano. Panic gripped me. The ramifications of what would happen to me if this event made it outside the bathroom doors washed over me like a tidal wave of poo. Surely this would turn into an utter social catastrophe, a rookie blunder for the record books.

I played it out in my head. Camp, Frasor, Downs, and League would probably laugh about it. Of course they'd make their best jokes, then report to the rest of the team so they could make *their* jokes, but then the incident would fade. Skip Sunday, aka Rabbit, would have a fit. He and his collection of psychological tics would go into full system meltdown. Rabbit, a man who ate the same pregame meals, listened to the same pregame songs, and drank the same flavor and size pregame Red Bull. Rabbit, who could not walk over certain things or talk about certain things or even be *near* certain things before a possible game appearance. Rabbit, who equated success to taking the same pregame shit during the same inning of each game, was just crazy enough to think I'd do this to him on purpose. He'd go into one of his spastic freak-outs about ritualism and results, luck and karma, and how none of it was crazy if it kept him in the bigs.

His tantrum would fire up his surrogate mother, TJ Collins, lord and master of the bullpen, and then I'd be in the doghouse. Between Rabbit and TJ, they'd make me carry every last ounce of this putrid mess out in a paper Gatorade cup. Once TJ spoke, Downs would follow suit on the ruling. League would plead the fifth right behind Frasor, and Camp, depending on how much caffeine he'd had, would either make fun of me, or Rabbit, or both. Probably both.

It was imperative this event not leave the room, which, considering the sloping of the floor toward the door, seemed guaranteed. Luckily, the bathroom doubled as a storage shed for the grounds crew, which meant there were tools at my disposal that most normal bathrooms would not have. Most notably, a push broom, some Turface, a shovel, and a hose connected to a spigot in the wall. There was also a drainage grate in the middle of the floor.

I calculated that I could use the hose to spray the sewage down the grate, busting up any stubborn logs with the power of the water pressure. Any standing water that remained could be absorbed with the Turface, which I could then broom into a pile and shovel into a trashcan. I could spray off the toilet and wipe it dry with toilet paper. By then, I hoped, whatever was still standing in the bowl would have sunk to a level of disgusting more tolerable for the average baseball player.

First, I sprayed my legs off with the frigid (yet strangely exhilarating) hose water. Then, pants up, I began the process of shepherding toilet runoff down the drainage grate. Three minutes in, I knew I had a problem. The drainage grate started regurgitating, just as the toilet had. In an effort to stem the flow, I grabbed the shovel and tried to stab the handle down into the drain hole, hoping to break up any clogs. This method failed to unclog anything. It did, however, do a remarkable job of speckling my uniform, hands, wrists, and even my cheeks with dirty brown water.

My only recourse would be to soak up everything on the floor with Turface. I decided to spray off the toilet, use Turface to absorb the water, then sweep it up and cut my losses. But the puddle had grown sentient. It was expanding with a mind for chaos, oozing toward the crack below the door, intent on escape.

I assailed the puddle with Turface, working to beat it back one handful at a time. When I ran out of Turface, I grabbed the shovel—still slimed and fetid from its failed audition as a plunger—and spooned the water into the trashcan. But I couldn't spoon fast enough.

In a reckless attempt to overpower this mess, I leapt onto the puddle and slashed at it wildly, hoping to spread it out and weaken it. The gamble paid off. With the filthy water slung on the walls, equipment, pants, and shoes, the beast finally retreated into its hole. I brushed up what I could of its carcass, washed what parts of myself I could fit into the sink, and braced myself before turning the door handle to exit.

"Guys," I said, stepping from the bathroom while smoothing out an impossibly disgusting jersey, "I think there might be something wrong with the toilet."

"What did you do, dude?"

It was Rabbit, as expected. Even under normal circumstances, he'd get nervous if someone went to the bathroom before him, fearing they might still be in there when his internal clock of superstition struck potty break. He sprung to his feet to investigate.

"I didn't do anything, I just tried to flush the toilet and . . ." I gestured as if pushing down a plunger to blow up life as we knew it.

Rabbit rushed into the bathroom. It looked like someone had tried to put out a fire. And then, of course, there was the smell . . .

Rabbit's body language did all the talking. His gaunt frame of skin and bone contorted in anguish. League slid up behind Rabbit and peeked in, then started laughing hysterically. This induced Frasor into looking, then Camp, then Downs, and finally TJ.

Rabbit spun on me, veins in his eyes bulging to the surface. His hands rose up, briefly stopping level with my neck before continuing up to his shaved, malnourished head, which he grabbed trying to hold his freak-out at bay. After me, Rabbit was the next youngest player on the staff. He was the former rookie in the pen and that made him dangerous, because players fresh out of rookie-dom are always looking to show current rookies how grown-up they are. I had just given him his big chance.

Laughter hit Rabbit from all sides.

Frasor was first, talking down to him sarcastically the way one might speak to a dog who couldn't find his favorite toy. "*Oh no,* Rabbit, what are you going to do? You won't be able to pitch today? *Oh no!*"

Camp was next. "Uhhhggh. I'd better start warming up now," he said, slipping off his jacket. "You owe me, Rabbit, always bailing your skinny ass out."

"Downs," League said between giggly fits, "get Cito on the phone and tell him Rabbit can't pitch because he can't take his mid-game shit." Then, back to Rabbit, "Don't worry, Rab, you know how Cito *loves* the bullpen. He'll understand."

"Fuck, dude!" erupted Rabbit. He spun back to me once again. "You gotta fix this, Hayhurst. I gotta take a shit!"

"I did fix it. It overflowed in there and I was on the toilet when it happened. It got all over me. I had to spray my bare ass off with that frigid hose. Do you know how cold that water was?"

"Will it flush now?" asked Rabbit.

"I wouldn't try it if I were you," I said.

"Dude! Fuck! Ugh! Man! Dude! C'mon!"—contortions between each word—"You'd better make it flush."

"Come on, Rabbit, I got bit in the leg by a turd and you act like you're the one that has to suffer."

"You're a rook, dude! Find a way to fucking fix it. You got"—he looked at the scoreboard clock—"an inning to fix this. Tell em, Teej."

TJ, bullpen master, surveyed us all. He had the most service time of the pitching staff. He was loud, abrasive, and cocksure, old-school, hard-nosed, and a smashmouth. The kind of guy you wanted to have on your side in a fight, but not the kind of guy you wanted to screw up in front of, or piss off. He was quick-witted, too, which, coupled with his imposing size, personality, and volume, made him not to be trifled with.

"Hell, Cock"—a pet name he had for Rabbit—"you knew this was going to happen eventually. But who would have thought Hayhurst would be the fucking guy to do this to you?"

"Yeah, but . . . but . . ." Rabbit was not pleased with this response. But TJ's word was law in the social hierarchy, and so he'd have to swallow it.

"Go down there and ask the Phillies if you can use their shitter," Camp suggested.

"I can't . . . I'm not . . . C'mon, dude!"

"Relax, Rabbit," Frasor said. "Have Hayhurst go fetch the grounds crew guys and get someone up here to fix it."

"Yeah!" Rabbit snapped the idea up instantly as if it was his own. "Go get the grounds crew up here to fix this shit, Hayhurst." Rabbit shook his head at me. "Fucking Hayhurst."

"Don't take that from *Rabbit*," Camp said. "Make him go down and use the Phillies' pen."

"No way! He's the rookie, he's gotta fix this!" Rabbit glared at me, waiting for me to obey, while others watched with smirks, hoping that I wouldn't.

I glanced around the group, reading faces and expectations. There was hidden meaning in each choice, even with something as ridiculous as a clogged toilet. As crazy as Rabbit was about routine and superstitions, the whole big league operation was like this, placing a ludicrous amount of weight on things that produced on-field results whether there was any direct correlation to those results or not. The ends always justify the means in the bigs, which has a way of elevating routine preparation to divine ritual. So much is at stake on every play and every pitch that every toilet flush takes on meaning as well. And guys will do just about anything to keep themselves in line for success, to the point where they don't really understand why they do what they're doing anymore. The routine absorbs them like Turface on a brown puddle, and soon you can't tell which is the player and which is the crap he's sucked up.

"I'll get a grounds-crew guy," I said. "I don't want to screw up anybody's routines." Rabbit nodded his head that I'd done right. Frasor spun sideways as if I missed a key foul shot. Camp just snorted.

"You're lucky, Rabbit," said Frasor. "I'd make you use the Phillies' pen."

"You would, Fraze. That's the kind of guy you are."

"You're too nice, Hayhurst. You're too nice. But you'll learn."

Chapter 24

The next day I was in the training room lying on a table and getting my arm rubbed when Downs came strolling in. He needed some Gold Bond Medicated Powder—the official powder of big league ass cracks—to get his day started right. However, when he saw me, he stopped dumping powder down his shorts, looked me over, then barked out the decree, "Rookies: Get the fuck out of the training room!" He pluralized it, so it would sound more like the recitation of a rule than a personal command. But since I was the only rookie in the training room, this was my personal cue to exit.

The rule concerning rookies in the big league training room is simple: don't be in there. Unless you've exploded on the field in plain view of everyone, or have some well-documented illness, younger guys are assumed healthy until proven otherwise. Therefore your presence in the training room only serves to waste time that a trainer could use to grease up older, crankier talent. This is yet another of the unwritten but universally understood rules of the major leagues. In fact, in some organizations, the trainers quietly enforce this rule by refusing to treat rookies under the pretense of always being busy with "unforeseen" demands. In other organizations, like the Jays, the older guys police the rule by shouting orders while jiggling their nuts in so much crotch powder they could have them deep-fried.

I didn't question it. Obediently I rolled off the training table and scampered for the door, a smile on my face as I left. As bizarre as it may seem, Downs's yelling was a good thing. If a veteran likes you, he'll look out for your best interests, even if he's insolent about it. If he doesn't like you, he'll let you stumble onto every social land mine there is. And believe me, there are a lot of them. A major league locker room can be like a goddamn demilitarized zone. This is why you should always be wary of guys who don't talk to you in a clubhouse. It's a surefire way to tell you're in trouble.

I made it a point to cultivate communication channels with everyone. I didn't want any secrets or false conclusions to be drawn from what I was doing by writing on the side. I knew it was senseless to hide this from the team. They'd find out eventually, so I decided it was best they heard it from me. I first let everyone know during the Reunion Phase of spring training, and since I stuck around till the end of camp, everyone had gotten comfortable enough with me to know I wasn't out to get them.

Well, almost everyone.

"Stay out of the training room, rook," Rabbit said as I walked into the Phillies' visitors' kitchen. It was like a miniature café, right inside the locker room, with round tables and chairs spaced around them like petals on a flower. Polished metal tins with cold cuts and condiments and multiple types of bread. A rack covered with potato chip bags of all flavors. And a fully functioning staff with—just like Brice was so fond of saying—a personal chef that would get you just about anything you wanted. I was going to request a famous-around-the-league Philly cheesesteak. It looked like that would come with a side of ass-ache, however, courtesy of Chef Rabbit.

"Sorry, coach," I said, walking past him to place my order.

"You should be. That's fucking rule number one."

Rabbit was sitting at a table eating a peanut-butter-and-jelly sandwich with the crusts cut off. This one came with smooth peanut butter; chunky would come in another hour. He ate two a day, every day, one chunky, one smooth, always at the same times. They represented the yin and yang of peanut-butter-based superstitions.

"What are you going to do when I come in here early and remove all the peanut butter from the place? How will you function?" I asked, coming to a stop in front of the café's chef.

"I pack my own, just in case," he said, eyeing me as if I meant to invade.

"Wow," I said. "You're ridiculous."

"Whatever, Hayhurst. I'm not the one that draws moose-o-raffes on shit."

"Garfooses," I corrected, referring to the fire-breathing, half-giraffe, half-moose cartoon signature I drew for fans.

"Even worse." He took another bite. He ate only the jagged edge of the sandwich, consuming it like it was a peanut butter puzzle.

"Fans like it," I said. "When's the last time you talked to fans, Rabbit?"

"I don't talk to fans during a game. I'm all business," he said, prideful.

I smiled at him. Rabbit was definitely one of the most interesting players I'd ever known. I placed my order for a cheesesteak and the chef whirled away to make it as if it was life or death.

"Don't you ever worry that your whole day is going to become a set of superstitions?" I said to him, walking to the chip rack and making my selection. "That you'll just be in a prison of your own making? That you'll wind up in a mental hospital for having a meltdown when you go to a stadium that has no toilets in the bullpen?"

Rabbit snorted. "Stupid rookie. All the big league bullpens have toilets. And it's not superstition," he continued, "it's routine. It's how I do work."

"No, it's definitely superstition," I said as a cheesesteak appeared in front of me. I took it and thanked the chef, then sat down at a table across from Rabbit. "Routine is something that if you stopped doing it, would prevent you from doing your best. Superstition is something that you *think* if you stopped doing it, would prevent you from doing your best."

"Whatever, Hayhurst, you don't know."

"What don't I know?" I took a bite—fantastic.

"Anything. I get the job done up here doing things my way, so what does it matter how I do it?"

"It just seems like your life would be a lot easier if you didn't put so much weight into things that had no real bearing on your actual results."

Then, because I worried this was getting too personal, I generalized a bit. "It just seems to me that a lot of things we do up here we put on ourselves, ya know. I mean, we have all these extra, unspoken rules . . . and . . ." My words ran out of steam as I looked at Rabbit's stone face. "I dunno, never mind."

"Why don't you write about it?" Rabbit said.

"Ha, yeah, right." I took another bite of my sandwich.

"Yeah," Rabbit said. "Is it superstition, or routine, to bring a recorder into the locker room?" He stood abruptly and threw his trash away, despite a clubby saying he'd take it. "What the fuck's up with that, Hayhurst?"

I choked on my cheesesteak. "Where did you hear that?" But I knew where he heard it.

"My boy Brice told me," Rabbit said. "Is that shit true?"

"Uh." I pushed the cheesesteak away. "Yes, it is, but it's not what you think.

"Doesn't matter what I think. It matters what Teej thinks."

Chapter 25

"We're going to get that fucker," said our MLB security rep, smacking fist to palm as he addressed us in the Blue Jays' major league locker room. "Don't you worry."

We sat in front of our custom major league lockers, in our executive-class leather rolling chairs, reclining in our underwear listening while he spoke. We'd made it back from the Phillies and were in the home clubhouse again. It was like a swanky hotel lobby with comfortable leather couches, subdued lighting, ambient—though raucous—mood music, and attendants. It was hardly the place for a police task force meeting.

The security rep telling us not to worry was an interesting choice of words since Halladay, the person this emergency security meeting was held for the sake of, couldn't have looked any less worried about what some Internet troll said about him. In fact, if anything, it seemed like a giant waste of his time—time that, knowing Doc, he would otherwise be using to prepare for his job.

Rumor control was part of the business, however, and there was an issue that had to be addressed. A lot of juicy speculation was swirling about Doc getting traded. His contract was expiring at the end of the season, and his next deal would surely be an expensive one. The Jays might trade him to a team in the hunt before the trade deadline to get some talent. Since Roy's departure would be epic news, a sneaky Internet troll was taking advantage of it by faking a Twitter account in Roy's name. Just a few hours ago, this imposter confirmed a trade to the White Sox. The dominos started falling: networks asking questions, fans assuming the worst. Even some of the players didn't know what was going on.

While the Jays' public relations crew took care of the media side of things, our MLB security correspondent was stirring up a contagion of paranoia about the powers of social media. "I want you guys to know that we're already working with investigators, and we're waiting to hear back from MLB's security offices to see how hard we can prosecute this guy. He's not going to get away with this.

"But," he smiled, suddenly amiable, "just so I know. None of you guys are doing it, are you? As a practical joke or something?"

He took a sweeping review of us. Some of the guys packed their mitts. Others text messaged obliviously. Of course no one raised their hand. But, when eyes started to dart around the room to see if someone actually might fess up and risk getting torn in two by Halladay, a few sets of eyes lingered expectantly on me, including Rabbit's.

I sighed. The recorder issue was spreading.

"I didn't think so," our security guy said, rocking back on his heels with his hands in his pockets. "Alright." He hitched up his waistline. "If anyone else has any similar issues, let me know. And if you are on the Twitter, be careful. You've all seen players who've gotten on these websites and gotten themselves in trouble saying stupid stuff. It can really hurt your career. If you haven't yet, think about going on there to make sure your name isn't being used, or saving it for yourself. This way, even if you don't use it, no one else can be you."

We all nodded along and the security rep adjourned the meeting, walking over the giant Blue Jay logo in the center of the clubhouse carpet as he left the room. The blaring pre-game tunes and flat-screen television panels flicked back to life upon his departure.

Most of the team returned to business as usual. But some of the guys asked how something like this was possible. *Who were these deviants who dared imitate us, and how could people believe these poor facsimiles?*

I had a Twitter account. I was the first guy on the team to have one in the history of the franchise. I listened to it all feeling rather like Hunter S. Thompson when he attended the Drug Convention in Las Vegas with a head full of mescaline. Hearing the group talk about what they didn't understand was both funny and sad, but opening my mouth to clarify would only get me in trouble. I nearly laughed when they talked about prosecuting this guy for pretending to be someone he wasn't on the Internet. For God's sake, that was the number one pastime of the web.

Some of the more paranoid players took no comfort in the promise of justice. They were worried they were going to get impersonated, and what might that impersonator say? MLB's security agent did his best to reassure them, but there was really no way he could—the Internet was bigger than all of us. I knew that. I knew that with the modern stuff now directly available to the player, he could become his own brand. But all these guys were so gripped with fear, the best they could hope for was that the imposter was more articulate and thoughtful than the genuine article.

When the meeting broke, I yawned and spun my chair

around to face my locker. I had my laptop open in one of the wooden cubbies. I used to have it out in the wide open when I was first called up, but recently I'd been getting the feeling it was bothering guys. Now I had even more reason to feel that way, what with a Twitter app running in the background.

Footsteps behind me. Someone grabbed my chair and shook it. I slammed my laptop closed and jettisoned it into my locker. The hands on my chair whirled me around, bringing me face to face with Richie Scott.

"What were you doing?" he demanded. "Impersonating Halladay on Twitter again?"

I relaxed. I even managed to laugh a little as I rubbed my eyes. Scott was a friend. "Ya got me," I said. "If I can't be Doc in real life, at least I can pretend I'm him on the Internet."

"Jesus," Scott said, sitting down in the neighboring locker's empty seat. He took a hard look at me. My face was pale and my eyes bloodshot. "Did you sleep at all last night? If the travel is screwing you up, talk to George. A lot of guys get on sleeping pills up here to help them. Seriously, you should think about it. Just tell George the travel is getting to you."

"I don't know about sleeping pills, man. I don't like the sound of that."

"Stop it. Lots of guys take them. This is the big leagues, remember? You've gotta get your sleep in. You know, just in case you pitch this month."

"Hey, if Cito doesn't want to pitch me, he doesn't have to," I said. "I'll gladly sit on great numbers and collect big league checks for the rest of the season. I've got a good thing going. As for World of Warcraft, shoot, sometimes I wish that's what I was doing . . ."

"Oh, here we go," he said, rolling his eyes. *"Gotta stay up late to write my booook,"* he mocked. He kicked his feet up and reclined his chair and said, "I suppose your life story would be pretty difficult to write, what with your closet homosexuality and all. How are you going to talk about that, exactly? I suggest you just come right out and tell the world you love balls. In fact, I think you should title it that: *I love balls*. You know, like a play on words."

"Clever," I said. "And FYI, you might want to retire after the chapter detailing your penis size goes public."

"I heard you've been bringing recorders into the bullpen, but a camera into the shower? So that's why you're always bending over in there—anal-vision!"

"Wait. Stop," I said, waving off our customary sarcasm. "Who told you about the recorder in the bullpen?"

"Who do you think?"

"What did he say?" I scooted to the edge of my seat.

"That you've been hiding a microphone and recording their private talks."

"I never . . . That's not . . . aww, fuck," I said, reeling back.

"What did you do, Garfoose?"

I cautiously surveyed my surroundings—card games, trash talk, bat tapping, crotch powdering—then spoke. "I got a recorder for cataloguing sounds in the minors. Seriously, I know when you think of recorders you think media, voice capture, et cetera, but I wanted it for collecting sounds. You know, isolating the minor leagues' unique tonal qualities?"

"Jesus," Scott scoffed, "you are such a fucking nerd."

"Yes! That's it exactly: I am a nerd! Not a spy, or a snake, or a traitor. I'm just a nerd! Thank you." I slapped him on the knee, though his face did not change at all.

"So you did it?" he asked.

"Yes," I whispered. "But, you know, for nerd purposes."

"And, uh, you didn't once think to yourself, '*This might be a bad idea*'?"

"Oh, sure," I said, "but I thought they'd understand when I explained it to them. I wasn't trying to hurt anybody."

"And how's that working out for you?"

"Well, *obviously* I made a mistake. But you can take voice notes on your iPhone right now. You can take video or snap pictures or post stuff on the web through just about any cell phone. I mean, if anything, a recorder is the least undercover recording device a player could have. And that recorder is long gone. I left it in Triple-A. If guys up here are getting upset, they're getting upset about old news."

"Can you blame them?" Richie asked. "They all know you're a writer, so they're worried. Next thing they know you'll be talking about them on Twitter."

I dropped my head.

"Oh, come on. Tell me you aren't."

"No, I'm not. But I do have a Twitter account."

"Does anyone know?"

"I don't think so."

"I'd keep it that way. At least until all this blows over."

I gritted my teeth and shook my head. "Why?"

"Why what?"

"Why"—I scooted in closer—"do I have to keep my head down about it all? I mean, I haven't done anything to anyone."

"Because that's the way it is up here, man. Fans have perceptions of us, we have perceptions of each other, and there are expectations built on those perceptions. It's the game within the game." He shrugged and scooted his chair back from mine to get some breathing room again. "You're a rookie with no power. It doesn't matter what you're doing. It only matters what other people think you're doing."

"Goddammit," I moaned. I spun my chair in a full circle and said, "It's shit like that!" I was forced to point at Richie because I couldn't point at his words. "That's why I"—I hushed myself again—"*write*. Because I'm tired of just being pressed into some stupid social mold. It's like, we all got into this because we want to be great individuals. But, the higher you get, the less of an individual you become. *Uhhhggh . . .* We're all better off just trying to be what everyone else wants."

"Hey, when you're a superstar, you can do whatever you want." Richie nodded at Kevin Millar, who was throwing a football across the locker room, dangerously close to million-dollar athlete heads, shouting, "Cowboy Up!"

"That's not the point," I said, watching the ball zip by.

"Maybe, but it's reality. Look, *I* get what you're saying. I hate being pushed around by dipshits who have less life experience than me, or when fans tell me I have no concept of what I went through to get here. But you've got more to gain by keeping your head down and your mouth shut, and, uh, your pen cap on. Just keep hiding in the bullpen with your 1.00 ERA and you might find yourself pushing rookies around in a couple of years, signing books instead of baseball cards . . . if you don't get killed for this recorder thing first."

I spun around in my chair again. "Fine," I continued. "Since you're so full of wisdom, how do you think I should handle this mess?"

"Grab guys one-on-one and explain it. Avoid the groups. You know how these guys get when they're in a group and trying to look cool."

Adam Lind walked into the room. He was my locker neighbor and wanted his seat back. He looked at Scott and said, "S'cuse me, Richie."

"My bad, Lindy." Scott popped out of his seat and righted it for Lind. A football drilled Scott in the chest. A chorus of "pass interference" and "fumble" assailed him. Scott scrambled after the ball and fired it back to the other end of the locker room.

"Sorry to interrupt your girl talk," joked Lind, plopping down.

"Nah, you weren't interrupting anyth—" I stopped myself. "Actually, do you have a minute? I'd like to talk to you about a rumor that's been floating around."

Chapter 26

I started with the position players. They were the easiest to chat with, since they were farthest removed from the issue. I worked them over, youngest to oldest, refining my telling each encounter. By the time I was sitting in front of Vernon Wells—the team's captain—I was able to make the whole thing sound like the massive misunderstanding I believed it was.

The majority of the position players blew the whole thing off. They didn't think showcasing a recorder at the ballpark was smart, but they didn't draw the issue out. They took my forthright confession as a form of penance and moved on with their days. Probably because they had more important things to do, like work on their swings or scout opposing pitchers. Actually, most of our conversations started with me offering to reload the batting tee they were practicing hitting off.

It was probably just the nature of the position. The hitters were generally far less pretentious than the pitchers, and that was a precedent set from oldest to youngest. Kevin Millar, one of the position-player vets, wasn't much help on the field for the Jays, but he did make the locker room a lot more entertaining by incessantly shouting whatever stream of madness popped into his frosted-tipped head. Vet Scott Rolen would start pretend swearing matches with bench coach Brian Butterfield. Marco Scutaro danced around the Spanish-speaking side of the clubhouse like a carnival act. Even youngsters like Travis Snider stoked the fun with various jokes and exploits.

The veteran pitchers were much less lax. The incomparable Roy Halladay would march from Point A to B, the living, breathing face of seriousness, work eternally on his mind. It was rare to hear him speak, rarer still to hear him laugh. His intentions were pure, and he was a kind and genuine man, but his solemn personality coupled with his work intensity made many of the younger pitchers afraid to get in his way, lest he vaporize us with lightning from his eyes.

TJ Collins was the more vocal pitching vet. Loud by nature, you could hear him anywhere in the locker room. He had the most service time of any of the pitchers on the team, and expected the locker room to run in a certain order. As I said, older guys make the rules, and while those rules are unwritten, they were not unheard, not when a mouth as loud as TJ's makes them up. All the pitchers wanted to be on his good side since he was not afraid to shred you, in front of the whole team, with a combination of loud insults, jokes, and threats. He was smart, knew the lay of the land and how big leaguers were supposed to act. And he was very black and white about breaking the law. There were a lot of veterans you did not want to piss off, but him most of all. Once you burned a bridge with TJ, it was never getting rebuilt.

Complicating matters was the fact that TJ was having a terrible season. He'd just signed a huge contract and he was wetting the bed. In fact, he was the worst pitcher on the team by far. He tried to play the injury card, but when he got healthy enough to compete again, he went right back to getting his ass kicked. Fans booed him off the field. News outlets ate him alive. And, as they tend to do, the media were all over him with speculations on what had caused him to fall apart. Rumors that he'd stopped using steroids or HGH were starting to fly, which suggested that all his earlier success was a result of drug use. In a way, the media was stripping him of everything he'd ever accomplished. In his mind, anyway. He wasn't taking it very well. But then again, what player would? I might have felt sorry for the guy if I wasn't so afraid of him.

When I started talking to the pitchers, I went to the guys I knew were on the more balanced end of the spectrum. Those who would look at the issue more like a person, and less like a big league baseball player. I confided in Camp and Frasor, League, Downs, and, of course, Scott. I didn't bother with a lot of the rookies since they would go along with whatever the older guys decided anyway. As for Rabbit, I already knew how he felt, so why bother? I was flat-out afraid to talk to TJ, but it was either him or Halladay. As scary as TJ was, Halladay was so powerful that pissing him off would probably result in a permanent exile from Canada, plus there were all those social-media issues he was already dealing with. No, it had to be TJ. I knew it was risky, but if I could explain it to him in the calm, cool, rational way I did with all the others, life would go on just fine.

"Well, I . . . I just . . . I. . . . The thing is"—the sight of TJ cracking his dense battery of jagged knuckles made me nervous to the point of babbling—"I thought it would be a cool idea if, well, I mean, I would *never* do it up here—"

"It was a terrible idea, Hayhurst. Fucking terrible!" TJ roared. He seemed to get larger when he was angry, and he was already much larger than everyone else.

"Yes, yes. Oh yes. It *was* a terrible idea," I sniveled. There was no use arguing. Even if I had some great truth on my side, propelled by infallible logic, I was a rookie, and rookies are always full of "terrible fucking ideas."

I stood in front of TJ, in front of his locker. The conversation started with him sitting down and me addressing him as if he were on a throne. But TJ was on his feet the instant I mentioned the word "recorder."

TJ could destroy me, physically and socially, and there was nothing I could do to stop him besides beg, and beg I did, backing away and wringing my hands, pleading no harm intended.

For better or for worse, I'd hoped to at least keep the conversation private. But now, with TJ's booming voice spilling through the locker room, the issue was no longer personal. Everybody could hear him bellowing at me, and many of the position players were gawking at us. My fellow pitchers, however, looked away. They knew better than to let their eyes linger on TJ for too long, lest their curiosity divert any of his frustration to them.

"Do you still have it?" TJ asked, sniffing me over.

"No," I said, backing away farther, "I got rid of it. It was just an idea. A bad one," I placated. "I decided it wasn't worth it. I never thought it would cause so much trouble."

"Yeah, you didn't fucking think. That's for sure." TJ looked sideways, shaking his head in disgust.

"It was a minors-only thing. Besides, it's old news. It happened over a month ago, down in Triple-A. Some guys just now heard about it up here and got anxious. I'm trying to handle it. I figured I'd come to you privately and clear it up." I took a step forward, my hands out wide.

"What a fucking stupid idea!" TJ erupted again. "What kind of rat fucking bastard brings a recorder into the locker room? I mean, of all the stupid shit I've ever heard of. You've got to be one of the stupidest motherfuckers I've ever met."

I don't know why I felt the need to object. I knew I shouldn't, and yet, out of my mouth it came: "But Accardo has his camera here every day. And we can all take video on our cell phones."

TJ's face twisted with what looked to be nausea. "Are you serious with that shit?"

"I'm just . . . I'm just saying."

"Stop talking."

I obeyed, and looked at my feet.

"Are you mic'd up right now? Under your shirt?" he asked.

"No. I was never 'mic'd up.' It was like an iPod with a microphone attached to it. I just carried it with me, you know, like a member of the media." I winced as soon as I heard myself say it: *media*. I could not have picked a stupider choice of words.

"Is that what you are? A member of the fucking media?"

I threw my hands up and backpedaled. "No, no. Look, everyone could see it. I used it to record sounds of the game, like the crack of a bat, balls being caught, and fans heckling us. I never went for players talking. I wanted to do a podcast to promote my writing online—"

TJ flinched when I started talking about Internet tools, and I stopped before I could dig myself any deeper. I was saying all the wrong things. Honest, but wrong. TJ was Old Guard. He came up in an era when players didn't have all this tweeting, Facebook-ing, blogging bullshit. No one outside of the game needed to know anything other than what they saw on the field. There was no use in explaining to him that the game was changing, that sports and technology were converging, that some teams were already encouraging their players to interact in social media. That times were changing and we had to change, too—if we didn't, we'd all live in fear of someone snapping a picture of our penis and tweeting it.

"You writing about anyone here?" TJ gestured to the

room. Some of the players looked at us and waited for an answer. Some looked away.

"No. I don't write about people who don't want to be written about."

"You say that shit now, but *then* you start bringing your recorder into the locker room, or out to the pen, or wherever the fuck else." He threw his hands out wide as if lassoing the whole stadium into his argument, as though I might have microphones planted anywhere and everywhere.

My shoulders slumped. "You've got to understand—"

"No, you gotta fucking understand!" His volume peaked, silencing me. Everyone watched us now, pitcher and position player. We stared at each other across the chasm between our ideals, and then, for the first time in our conversation, his voice grew soft. Low and controlled, it had a more unsettling effect on me that his customary volume. He got close, leaning in so he was sure that I would hear him privately. "If you write about me, I swear to God, I'll kill you. I got the money, and connections." He let the statement hang like a guillotine before asking, softly, "Are we clear?"

"Yeah," I said. "Yeah, we're clear."

"Then get the fuck out of here."

The event spread among the pitchers like wildfire, and though no one confronted me about it, they didn't have to. Their silence spoke volumes.

A day later, during batting practice on the Rogers Centre turf, the team divided up into its normal cliques: relief pitchers with other relief pitchers, fielders with fielders, starters with starters . . . and I stood alone, somewhere in between.

The roof of the dome was half open, and the sun shone through, stretching an obtuse rectangle of light across the diamond, inching toward me. Bruce Walton, aka Papi, the bullpen pitching coach, came over and stood by my side.

Papi was like the bullpen's den leader, or babysitter, or spiritual adviser, or some combination thereof.

"So, what's this I hear about you carrying a microphone out to the bullpen?"

I took a deep sigh.

"It's true then, huh?"

"I had a recorder," I said, sorry to be discussing it once again. "I used it in the minors to record things. Sounds I thought would be cool to catalogue." I explained the rest, and how I had done my best to tell everyone what I'd been doing, and why it shouldn't scare anyone. "It was never my intent to record players, or sell their conversations to Oprah, or ESPN, or the Nazis, or whatever people are thinking."

"Did you bring it to the pen up here?" Papi didn't look at me while he spoke, he just watched batting practice.

"No," I said.

"You understand that guys hear that you're doing stuff like that and it makes them nervous?"

"I've noticed. I've apologized to everyone about it, even though most of them never had anything to do with it."

"I think they just want to make sure you keep your priorities straight."

Keep my priorities straight? He meant to pitch well, get results, and not hurt the team. If that was the case, then I had been keeping my priorities straight. But this writing and recording stuff wasn't about priorities; it was about me wanting—needing—to do something unique, just for me, that wasn't based on baseball competition. Would Papi understand that if I explained it to him?

"I don't want to make the guys uncomfortable. I want to be a good teammate. It's just, I want to . . ." I let the words go, and packed my mitt in their place. Papi wasn't even looking at me as I spoke. My explanation held no power here, and was better kept in my head.

"We're an elite club up here," Papi said, eyes still ahead. "The average person walking around on the street would love to hear about even the most casual stuff we talk about. But that's not their business."

I nodded.

"We're a family," he continued. "We take care of each other, look out for each other. This is a sacred place and when you do things that don't acknowledge that, it causes problems."

I nodded again. Papi paused, watching freshly struck balls scoot across the turf, in and out of the rectangle of light. There was something else he wanted to say, I could tell; he just didn't know how to ask it. Then, after stepping on a ball to stop its roll, he picked it up, looked it over in his hand, and asked, "You're not putting any of *this* in your book, are you?"

"No," I said, trying to not sound annoyed. "My book is about stuff that happened years ago, and it's about more than baseball."

"Are you going to write another one?"

"I don't know," I said.

"So you could still write about what happens here?"

"Well, this is part of my life, and I write about my life, so I guess I could."

"Then you see why guys get nervous. They don't know what you're doing."

What I'm doing? I thought. This team had guys who cheated on their wives, were functioning alcoholics, and were hooked on painkillers. Potheads, steroid users, and porn addicts. Anger issues, abuse, and gambling problems. Baseball was full of it. Lives, marriages, families, and bank accounts—all set to self-destruct if the good play stopped and they were worried about what *I* was doing? I was just trying to express a part of myself, my view, my world.

"I guess they don't know what I'm doing," I said, finally.

"Well," Papi sighed, bowling his caught batting practice ball toward the center-field ball bucket, "just remember, this is a family, and you don't hurt your brothers."

I nodded again, before looking around the field and measuring the distance all my teammates were keeping from me. "Right," I said. "You don't hurt your brothers."

Chapter 27

"And that's how we got here, Ray. George helped me get the sleeping pills shortly after the fall-out with TJ and the chat from my bullpen coach. I told George it was for the travel, but it wasn't. Everyone in the organization knew about the recorder incident, they had to. It made me so anxious and stressed thinking about what they were thinking about that I just couldn't sleep. The pills helped turn the emotions off until I made it to the off-season. I thought things would reset then, and be better in the spring. I thought I'd be fine. Then I got hurt . . . And now . . ." I took a deep breath and exhaled, marking the conclusion of my tale. "I'm here, sitting at home on my ass, branded a rat bastard head case—that's why this isn't just an injury."

I'd long since made it home from the shrink's office and was now sitting at my kitchen table, lying across the top of it on my left arm and facing my phone, now on speakerphone. I was alone in my little gray house with all the lights off and the curtains drawn. Bonnie had placed a cluster of votive candles on the table as a centerpiece. I'd absently lined them up in a tight row as I spoke to Ray.

"Rabbit and a few others quickly started calling me Media

soon after the fight," I said, moving a votive out of the line and back to the table center. "Some of the other guys did the same." I moved a few more votives.

"TJ was actually released later in the season, while I stayed on the roster. I thought it would make the atmosphere better, but it didn't. It was a shock to a lot of guys, considering the money he was making. A few guys thought I had something to do with it, like I recorded something that ended TJ's career." I moved all of the votives back to the center save one, which I played with the wick of.

"For a while, it seemed like every empty room, every end of the bench, every silent conversation found me. I had trouble finding a catch partner. I found myself hoping another Triple-A guy would get called up so I would have someone to talk with who wasn't infected by the whole issue. Everything I did was scrutinized, every personal thing was subjected to someone's opinion. I got sent down, then recalled in September, along with Brice and a few of his cronies. By that time I had more service time than him, but it seemed nullified by what I'd done.

"My pitching spoke for itself. It was the one thing I did right. Ray, I'm convinced that had I not pitched so well, I would have been truly blacklisted. I think that's why things are so bad this season: I no longer have redeeming qualities. First I ruined my reputation, and then I did something classically stupid to get myself injured. And now the guys that don't outright hate me probably think I'm nuts."

I put the single votive I was picking the wick of down, outside the centerpiece. Then I stood up and walked to the window and pulled back the curtain and peeked out. I held the phone just out away from my face. I could have switched Ray off speakerphone, but hearing his voice in the room made it feel as if he was there.

"Wow, you've had a rough go of it," Ray said gently. "I can understand why you'd be having some strong emotions lately. I think anyone in your situation would."

I smiled. It was nice to get it all out of my system and to talk to someone sympathetic. That's what I really needed right now: someone who got me, and could tell me how it wasn't my fault and how unjust the whole thing was and what a bunch of bastards baseball players were.

"I have to ask you, though," Ray continued, "have you ever stopped to consider how incredibly selfish you are?"

My head jerked up. "What?"

"Selfish," he repeated, flatly. "How remarkably *selfish* you are."

"Explain yourself, doctor," I said, fumbling to switch the phone off speaker and back to the handset.

"Well," he laughed, "you keep using this language, 'everyone.' 'Everyone hates me. Everyone likes me. They all think I'm nuts.' It's a pretty selfish way to think, wouldn't you say? Believing that at any given time every person you come into contact with hates or likes you, or even cares about you at all?"

"But—it's—well . . . What's your point?" I said, kicking the chair I previously sat in at my kitchen table out of the way in favor of sitting atop the table itself.

"Would you agree that most baseball players think of themselves at least as selfishly as you do? That they are concerned with their careers first and foremost, and that they don't really care much about what other people do around them?"

"I don't think I'm as selfish as some of them can be, Ray."

"You willfully wrote a book, fully knowing it would piss people off—you're a little selfish. Okay, maybe *self-centered*. How's that?"

"Is this a joke?" I said, shifting the phone from ear to ear. "You're a therapist?"

"Okay, would you at least agree that other players, in their own way, are just as self-centered and self-seeking? *Self-seeking*," he repeated, "yes, how about that one?"

"Uh, yeah, I guess I'd agree, but—"

"Then, what makes you think now is any different? What makes you think they're all thinking about you as intensely as you think they are?"

"I don't follow," I said.

"Let me rephrase: What makes you think that all of the people you are playing with, motivated by their own self-seeking needs, suddenly give a flying fuck about what you do, when chances are they've never stopped thinking about what they think they need long enough to notice?"

I gritted my teeth. "Because, *doctor*. It's like I said: I'm breaking the code. You've heard of the baseball code? A universally understood baseball law? Plus, the older guys and some of the coaches, they have issues with me. They told me!"

"And they are everyone?" Ray's voice was so very calm and controlled.

"Well, not everyone, but they're enough." My voice was intense and indignant.

"What if you had as much service time as, say, Halladay, and you were the head of the locker room. Would you care about what everyone thought?"

"Of course not."

"Then why do you care about what they think now?"

"Because I'm not the head of the locker room!" I shouted, as if it were obvious. "I'm a rookie, and I want to be accepted into the group. I don't want people to think I'm out to get them, or that I'm a bad person."

"Are you a bad person?"

"No."

"So why does it matter what they think?"

"Ugh." I slammed my palm on the table then got up and paced around the kitchen shaking my fist at the sky. "Doesn't anyone understand this? Ray, there are *codes* and *rules* players go by—"

"Oh, I understand." Ray cut it, still pleasant and jovial. He almost seemed to enjoy my frustration. "I know all about expectations and codes and unwritten rules. Most players spend their entire careers subscribing to one form of them or another. Most people, for that matter. You think baseball players are unique in code making?"

"In baseball code making, yes."

"Please." Ray swatted my assumption aside. "You're not as special as you think. People everywhere, in every walk of life, make codes. People everywhere worry about how the group will see them if they break those codes. Codes they never even had a hand in making but take on as all-encompassing. We all do. And we all project the assumed consequences of breaking those codes onto ourselves or others, to the point that we act on them irrationally—even to the point of hurting or killing ourselves."

I stopped and stood as if fastened to the table. I'd been thinking about that last subject a lot lately.

"Dirk, fear of how others perceive or will perceive us is one of the most common things I help guys deal with. In your case, it's your perception of your teammates' perception of you. For many other players, it's the media, or the fans' perceptions. Players are afraid of what is said about them, from people who don't know them—not a damn thing about them other than what has been reported. Lots of players want to be liked by everyone, teammate or coach or parent or some person they've never met. They want to be winners. Seen as winners. And it bothers them very similarly to how you're feeling now when they think they're not."

"But what fans think has no basis on a player, not like what a fellow player and peer thinks."

"Why?" Ray asked.

"Because a player is a peer, so his opinion means more."

"Why?"

"Because we're a team."

"So, because you're on a team with another guy who is thinking irrationally about his relationship to the outside world, and as a product of those irrationalities, makes you think irrationally about yourself, it's okay? Dirk, it's *not* okay. It's not okay to let others define your perception of yourself in unhealthy ways. I don't give a shit if it's Brice or TJ or Babe fucking Ruth."

I pulled out the seat from the kitchen table and sat down slowly. I felt like, finally, someone was helping me explain something I felt but couldn't articulate.

"But if I don't listen to those people, those icons," I said, "they'll think I'm arrogant, and then—"

"Let them," Ray interrupted. His voice was surprisingly firm. "It's okay to be arrogant when the other option is letting everyone outside you control how you think about yourself. As long as you are prepared to deal with what might come from it."

"I guess I wasn't prepared," I said, picking the last votive candle again, spinning it between my thumb and forefinger. I pressed the wick down so hard that brittle from the wax and soot, it snapped off and rendered the candle useless.

"Do you think . . ." I cleared my throat and started again. "Do you think I'll ever recover? Not my arm, but, you know . . . my head? Do you think I can be fixed?"

Ray's voice was genuine. "Confessing all this is hard. Working through it is harder. I was serious when I said you're dealing with a lot, but I was also serious when I said you've been incredibly self-centered in the most negative way possible, focusing a ton of perceived hate onto yourself. I'm not going to fix you, Dirk, because you're not broken. I'm just going to help you learn about who you are, underneath the seams."

Chapter 28

In the coming days, Ray and I chatted on regular intervals, and he was right: it was hard learning about me. Telling Ray about how I'd felt like crying or hurting myself or not wanting to be alive was humiliating. I felt weak, irrational, pathetic, and damaged. But more than anything I felt guilty. I was dealing with issues someone in my walk of life should never be dealing with. The money was still coming in and my book was coming out. To me, it was a crime for me to be feeling bad. And yet I couldn't turn it off. The only thing I seemed to be able to feel was bad, regardless of how many reasons I had to feel good.

Wednesday afternoon, a week after our first chat, I was back home pulling laundry from the washing machine when my cell vibrated in my back pocket. It was my editor in New York. She was calling to tell me *The Bullpen Gospels* was a *New York Times* bestseller.

It was a huge accomplishment, and she was ecstatic. I, on the other hand: not so much. I told her I was thrilled because that's what you're supposed to say when people tell you big news designed to thrill, but I wasn't. I wasn't stunned, or shocked, or incapable of grasping what it meant. If anything, I was sad. I knew it was a grand thing to write a bestseller, but because I wasn't myself I was incapable of enjoying the fruits of my labors.

I thanked my editor for her news and assured her I'd go out and celebrate in high style. However, after she hung up, I pulled the blinds around the house shut and sat in silence at the kitchen table, drumming my fingers across its dark wooden surface.

It's strange to think about what an excited person will do in order to act like you're excited. It's also strange when great news is how you discover how few people you have in your life. I decided that I should call someone, but in thinking of who, I realized Bonnie was working at the hospital and couldn't answer, my parents were at work or asleep, and I hadn't talked to anyone on the team in weeks.

I picked up my cell and called Ray. He was the only person I could think of who would understand what I was feeling. Also, I knew he'd call me back if I left a message saying I was suicidal. I guess that's the one perk of being mentally unstable: people tend to prioritize your calls.

Ray answered. "Dirk, how are you?"

"I should be better, I guess."

"You guess? What's making you guess?"

"I wrote a *New York Times* bestseller."

A long series of coughs came through the line. I was about to ask Ray if he was okay when his voice exploded. "You guess! You *guess*! What are you, stupid? That's fantastic! Congratulations! Lord Almighty, I've been writing a screenplay for the better part of a decade. I still haven't finished it and will probably never get it produced, and you rattled off a bestseller on your first try and *you guess* you're good? I should recommend you for a lobotomy because you *are* crazy!"

I smirked. "I *guess* it is pretty cool."

"It's very cool! How are you going to celebrate?"

"Well . . ." I looked around the room, then at the loaded

clothes baskets I stacked next to the steps leading down toward the basement. "I'm about to do some laundry."

I'm fairly sure the smacking sound I heard through the line was Ray hitting himself in the forehead. "Remember when I told you that running through the streets naked and covered in your own feces is crazy?" Ray asked. "Well, I'm not telling you to cover yourself in feces, but my professional opinion is that you should celebrate closer to that level than the one you're presently operating at."

"Public nudity?" I asked.

"Pretty damn close," he said.

I thought of myself running down the streets of my historic little town naked and screaming that I'd written a best-seller while gawking mothers fainted. Then another vision came to mind and my smile faded. "Ray, do you think the guys on the team are going to be pissed that the book did this well?"

"I'm not sure. Why does that matter?"

"I know you'll say it shouldn't, that I shouldn't let what others think or could think bother me, but this does. Why? Why can't I just turn it off?"

"This isn't how I expected you to respond to a prescription for public nudity."

"Ray, seriously, I don't know how I'm going to make it back into baseball now that this book has come out. I agree with all you had to say about not letting perceptions control me, and yet I can't stop. It's pathetic. Coaches have told me for years that I think too much. I know it's a flaw, but I can't seem to fix it. I've always wondered if I was really cut out for the big leagues, if I belonged or not. Now, after talking with you, I'm pretty sure I don't."

"Oh, bullshit," Ray said.

"Excuse me?"

"This, among many other things, is one of the problems I

have with many coaches today. This hopelessly esoteric communication style, as if nothing outside the world of baseball exists. Coaches forget they were players once, and management invests virtually nothing in teaching coaches how to teach. You'd think that with all the money the MLB has they'd . . ."

While Ray ranted I stood up from the kitchen table and started to pace. I could hear the laughter of a neighbor kid from outside my living room window. I wandered over and cracked blinds just wide enough to see a boy and his father practicing hitting in their gravel driveway. The father was tossing tennis balls to the boy, who, all of four years old, swung an oversized toy bat in futility trying to hit them.

"It's not a flaw to think, Dirk. It's not a flaw to be observant. It's not even a flaw to be concerned with what people think of you," continued Ray. "It's called being human. And you'll be happy to know you're not the only baseball player dealing with being human."

"Maybe," I said absently.

"You don't play baseball and struggle to get to the top because you *don't* want anyone to notice you're up there. The public validation that you're the best is just as much a part of chasing the dream as the money, or the competition. That's why elite groups withhold it from one another, use it to set up social codes, and take it away as punishment. Sometimes players will do it themselves. They'll win, and it won't be good enough because they didn't do it the right way."

I just stood there, watching the boy and his dad outside my window, hoping the little guy would get a hit. When he finally connected—his dad's toss finding his bat more than anything—the ball dribbled down the gravel driveway and into the blacktopped street. The boy ran, but didn't know where to go. He ended up hiding behind a tree in my yard. He must have believed he wasn't supposed to be there because his smile faded and he looked to my house to see if he was being watched. His eyes met mine from behind the blinds and he ran back to his yard, scared. I felt bad for stealing his moment and I shut the blinds.

"When does it all stop being just for fun?" I asked.

"When we realize other people have opinions about what we were doing, and those opinions become more important than our own."

"How do I turn this all off?"

"You don't."

I sighed and sat down in a chair in the living room.

"The only people who truly don't care what others think are ideological zealots and sociopaths. It's not about turning off something that makes you you. It's about understanding it, and learning that other people don't hold the right to control how you feel about what you've done."

"And how do I master this trick?"

"Start owning who you are: an observant person, very aware and sensitive to your surroundings. I grant you it's hard to be that way and endure pro sports, but it's not wrong. It's who you are, and it's okay. In fact, I doubt if you could have written a bestseller if you weren't these things."

"I . . . I'd never thought of it that way," I said.

There was a long stretch of silence, and then the sound of an oversized plastic bat hitting a tennis ball followed by the purest laughter.

"Are you alright?" Ray asked.

"Yeah, I think I am."

Chapter 29

As the weeks passed, I hit the bestseller list four more times. Every time the rankings were published, the publishers called to congratulate me. My mom cried, my wife bragged, and my agent sent me a fruit basket. My phone rang nonstop with radio shows looking for interviews, and my email inbox always had a message from someone who wanted me to know they enjoyed the book.

A couple of the messages even told me that I'd changed the lives of the reader; that their experiences, in or outside of the game, were similar to mine—an underachiever who had trouble reconciling grand dreams with harsh realities and the damage the collision was doing to their self-image. Some said it helped them fill the vacuum of their lives after baseball. Others said it helped patch up relationships with their dads. I just wanted the book to sell well and avoid getting into too much trouble for writing it. I had no idea I might positively impact someone's life.

Ray and I talked every week. I no longer doubted what he told me or why it mattered so much. We worked hard to check my unhealthy and irrational thinking. Ray called it "reality testing." I'd tell him some inner fear or irrational thought process, and he'd help me pull it apart to see if it was helpful or hurtful. Over time, I got better at slowing things down and taking control of the space between my ears.

There was one peculiar side effect, however. The better I felt, the more I wanted to return to competition. As the depression lifted, the more I felt the desire to compete. I was a baseball player, and I wanted to get back to the game, and back to proving I had something to offer it.

But it didn't much matter what I wanted. My arm dictated what I was allowed to do, and things weren't going so well on the rehab table. After a little over a month at home, I'd progressed to light catch, which I played with my Cleveland Clinic therapist, Mark Autumn. He said he'd played baseball at some point in his life, but it must have been a brief experience since he threw the ball like a shot-putter. The Clinic's sports-rehab facility had an indoor batting cage for limited throwing, but if you needed to stretch your arm out any farther, the only option was the parking lot. Even then, to throw the ball far enough to meet the required distances set out by the Blue Jays rehab guidelines, Mark had to ask doctors to move their cars. When Mark shot-putted the ball at me, he'd often miss wide, with the ball bounding across the pavement, under or off a Mercedes or BMW. I'd race after the misfires, occasionally crawling under cars to retrieve them.

I probably would have made fun of Mark if my own throwing wasn't just as bad. I never actually got to the end of the program: something like 120 feet. I couldn't. It hurt too much to throw long distances. It wasn't like the first time, when the hot bolt of pain ripped into my arm, and it wasn't like when I had my setback and my arm felt like I'd been hit with a hammer. Instead it was a dull, deep, throbbing ache that slowly grew in intensity until my arm felt as heavy as an anvil and half as nimble.

It went like that for several weeks, nothing improving.

Mark scratched his head over it and made a lot of phone calls. He said it was probably a bad thing, but he didn't know for sure since he'd never thrown with a professional athlete before. He didn't know if I should push through it or seek help. I didn't know either. My surgeon prescribed more anti-inflammatories and we kept throwing.

Meanwhile, another negative physical development took place, possibly a side effect of trying to throw through the pain. Shortly after starting the throwing routine, a pinch developed in my back. I felt it when I pulled my scapula together, or stretched my arm, or turned my neck a certain way. It just showed up one day after throwing and never seemed to go away.

That was just the beginning. The pinch heralded a whole pack of symptoms. First, the pinch spawned a choking sensation. It would start in my belly and head north to my neck, then to my lower jaw. Pain would blossom around my spine and scapula. Then, as if some invisible constricting snake was looping itself around my throat, I felt like I was going to suffocate.

It was hard to pinpoint where it came from. I contorted in odd stretches, tried to get a finger, wall corner, door handle, or wooden spoon into a part of my back tissue that could produce relief. I lay on a baseball and slid my back across it for an inverted massage. I took yoga classes and worked on backstretches. I even slept on the floor and hung upside down like Batman. Nothing changed. The pain was part of me, and once it started, it would not stop until it had run its course.

I called George. He set me up with just about every exam imaginable: CT scan, MRI, X-ray, everything. The Jays even flew me down to Birmingham to see Dr. James Andrews, the most renowned orthopedic surgeon on the planet.

Nothing.

After a month of dealing with the back issue and hitting a wall in my throwing, I consulted yet another local doctor who saw that I was on a cocktail of pain killers and anti-inflammatories—Indocin, Celebrex, naproxen, cortisone, and the Hybresis patches—and declared, "Good God, with all this in your system, I wouldn't be surprised if you have a hole in your stomach!" He decided I should have an endoscopy ASAP.

When I called George to tell him I might have a hole in my stomach, I was pretty upset. It was supposed to be a simple surgery with a simple rehab. Why was all this happening to me?

"Why didn't anyone tell me a hole in my stomach was a possibility when they started pumping me full of all this shit?" I asked.

"It's very rare that anyone has ever had a problem like that," George said. "In all my time, I can think of maybe one guy who had any stomach issues. At most, the docs would prescribe some kind of antacid as a countermeasure."

"Well, why didn't they this time?" I asked. "Shit, George, if I go in there and they find I have a hole in my stomach and I'm looking at more surgery, or lifelong pain . . . I mean, it's like, *who do I sue*? Ya know?"

George fell silent.

George was a good man. Caring to a fault, even when it wasn't his job to be. When he hushed, I knew I'd crossed the line. It was a legitimate question, but if there was one thing that spooked an organization more than injuries or mental issues, it was the potential of legal action. I'd become the boogeyman, and I knew he would have to report what I'd just threatened—or at least the fact that I was mentally unstable to the point of making legal threats—back to the organization.

To add insult to injury, the tests came back negative. No

damage to my stomach, but, thanks to one frustrated slip of the tongue, there was damage to my relationship with the organization. I tried not to feel bad about it all, that my health was worth protecting, but I knew that the worst possible thing to have on my injury paper trail was a note that read, "Will sue if mishandled."

It was decided I had severe acid reflux, or GERD, even though no proof was found. I was immediately put on the correlating medication.

Even at the maximum doses, nothing changed.

I knew there was something wrong, but after all the tests revealed negative results, what I thought stopped mattering. I would tell the doctors and therapists I was having an issue, they would look at all the tests that came up negative for said issue, then see I was dealing with depression and make the connection: "It's all in your head."

In fact, when I told George I was still in pain after the endoscopy came back negative, he said, since I had a lot going on atop the injury, that it was probably related to depression and anxiety issues, that I just needed to calm down and talk to Dr. Ray about it.

"It's not depression or anxiety, George. It's real pain. I know what real pain is."

"I got it, too, when I was in college before big exams, Dirk." He spoke very deliberately to me, like I was on some roof edge. "You just need to relax. It'll pass."

"It's not going to pass. I keep taking pills but they don't do anything."

"It takes a while for them to really start taking effect."

"How long?"

"It's different for everyone. But I think, in the meantime, you should just relax because I'm sure getting worked up isn't helping. You should discuss this with Ray, he'll get you right."

Reluctantly, I consented.

Considering all the tests the team had done, complaining further would just worsen our relationship. Every additional complication was just another reason why I should be released. My playing career was dying on a rehab table and I knew it. If I was going to have any chance of playing in the big leagues again, with the Jays or any other team, I had to get healthy. Fast.

Chapter 30

Early estimates had me recovering and close to game-ready by the middle of the season. A month before that date, I couldn't throw across a parking lot without four kinds of inflammation medication, maximum-strength GERD pills, and a conversation with a psychologist. I needed to get back on track. I needed to get back with the club, with the healthy. The Cleveland Clinic and its forty-five-minute, three-times-a-week rehab schedule was no longer sufficient. I needed more attention.

I told the Jays that if I didn't get back to the complex where I could do rehab every day of the week for as long as I needed, I was only hurting myself and wasting their money. I also told them that my spinal-pinch-acid-reflux-psychosis was under control. This was technically true if by "under control" you meant I pretended it didn't exist, just like everyone else seemed to want me to do. I wasn't feeling perfect, not by a long shot, but I knew the chance of "perfect" ever happening again was scant. I also knew that if I was going to have any medical insurance as provided by a professional baseball job, I needed to show the world I was healthy heading into the next off-season.

The Jays dragged their feet. Not surprising—they *were*

dealing with a crazy person after all. I had to lean on Autumn and Dr. Ray to get approval to return to the Jays' rehab complex. But, after a couple of weeks, the Jays finally acted—just not in the way I was hoping.

"I don't understand," I said to Jep, standing in his training room, BlackBerry buzzing and email alerts sounding. I was flown down for an evaluation, but nothing else. "Why wouldn't you have just sent me there from my home if this was your plan?"

"Oh sure, yeah, that makes sense, partner," said Jep, shifting in his rolling desk chair. "I think they just wanted to get you back down here to get you checked up. But I think sending you to Birmingham will be the best move for you from here on out."

"But, but, the rationale for why I was sent home was because I couldn't handle being trapped in an apartment by myself, isolated from my family. Now you're going to send me off to Birmingham, to a hotel room, isolated from family and team?"

"I know it, partner." Jep picked up his accursed BlackBerry and regarded it for a second. "But if you go and you don't like it, or you feel like it's not a good fit, we can always bring you back here."

I let my hands flap out and them smack hard against my sides before collapsing into one of the office's guest chairs. I didn't believe his *bring me back* line. I only managed to get back to Florida from home this time because the docs and trainers in charge of my recovery lobbied hard for me. Factor in the oops about the lawsuit and the bestseller about life inside a professional baseball team, and, well, keeping me away from the action suddenly made a lot of sense.

In Birmingham I'd be up against Dr. James Andrews, master of the Andrews Sports Medicine & Orthopaedic Center, or what we players called "the Andrews clinic." Andrews was a god among surgeons, the unofficial team doctor to all professional sports. He used his legendary healing powers to resurrect billions of dollars' worth of athletes, everyone from Drew Brees to Albert Pujols to John Cena. Andrews was like the head of the locker room, only replace locker room with orthopedic surgical world. He was not the kind of doctor a guy like me could lean on simply because I was a pro athlete. He'd patched up the biggest names in the business; who the fuck was Dirk Hayhurst to him?

As a matter of fact, when I went to visit him for my consultation back when I started having all the GERD issues, he slapped me around like he owned me. Literally. He waltzed into the room and gave me three stinging raps to the cheek. He didn't bitch-slap me, but it was something you would do to a horse or a dog or, at best, a stupid football player. And then, when I lay down on the examination table, Andrews clunked me in the top of the head with his giant Tampa Bay Rays championship ring. Right on the crown. I felt the blow all the way into my teeth. He did it just as casually as you please, knowing full well if I wanted him to work on me, I'd take it.

If I went to Birmingham I had to get well, because it would take more than Dr. Ray and some nagging phone calls to trump the all-powerful James Andrews.

I shifted in my seat and winced at Jep, considering my possibilities.

Jep cocked an eyebrow in return. His BlackBerry buzzed.

I'd pushed the organization pretty hard. If the Andrews clinic really was the best place to rehab on earth, going there was the best choice I could make. For the Jays and for myself. If Andrews endorsed me as healthy, then I was healthy. If not, my career really was over.

"Alright," I consented. "If you think it's best for me, I'll give it a shot."

"Yeah, alright. That's good. Dr. Andrews is real good. He'll fix you up."

The night before I left for Birmingham, while getting ready for bed, I called Dr. Ray from my room in the Innisbrook resort. I was concerned about being stuck in a hotel room in a city I knew nothing about.

"I don't want to start feeling trapped and depressed again," I said.

"We could consider some form of mood-regulating drug to help you cope," Ray suggested.

"No," I said, "no more coping through pills."

"There is nothing wrong with taking responsible medications, Dirk. If they help make your life better, maybe they're what you need. Remember, you can't make yourself less aware, but you can get help dealing with what you are aware of."

"I don't want to do any more pills," I said again.

"But—"

"My mom, dad, even my brother are on those kinds of pills. I'm not doing them."

I had packed everything in my room and was wheeling my suitcase over to the door to make for an easy exit when I realized I'd packed my toothbrush and contact case and had yet to brush or take my contacts out. I sighed and pulled the suitcase back into the bedroom to open it up again.

"Your family might be an indicator you should consider," Ray said. He was probably right. I was definitely predisposed. My dad was bipolar. My mom had anxiety. My brother had both. The pills helped them.

"I don't want to do them," I said, more sternly, pulling out my toothbrush and resealing the bag. "I don't think they're evil. I understand they could help me. I just don't want to do them. I don't want anything else messing with my mind. I don't care if I have bad days. I don't want to do pills. I'd rather change my environment than do them."

"Even if it meant quitting baseball?" asked Ray.

"I . . . I just don't like the idea of doing something for a living that requires me to take mind-altering drugs to make it possible. Doesn't that seem wrong?"

"Maybe," Ray said. "But you wouldn't be the only player who does it."

"Other players brush their teeth, just like I do," I said, putting my toothbrush down in the bathroom only to realize I left the paste in my suitcase, "but it's not about what other players do. Brushing your teeth doesn't make you look crazy. Popping brain pills does."

"We talked about perceptions, and how you can control those," Ray said.

"I know. But sometimes the perceptions of others really can hurt you. People associate a lot of negatives with mood-regulating pills and mental issues. People have started treating me different since I've started dealing with all this. I know it's changed the way the trainers see me, and I'm fairly confident it's going to affect my employment."

"It might," Ray said. "You can't control that, though, so do what's best for you."

"What's best for me"—I wrenched the toothpaste out of my suitcase—"is not letting people think I'm crazy so I can keep my job."

"So what if they think you are crazy?" Ray asked.

"What? Because I'm not," I said dully, slapping the tube on the bathroom countertop. I looked at myself in the mirror. My contacts where still in my face, while the case, solution, and glasses were still in my bag. My head fell. Back to the suitcase.

"You and I know you're not, what does it matter if they think you are?" asked Ray.

"Because sanity tends to look good on a job application, Ray."

"What I'm saying here is, what is crazy? I've spent a lot of time helping players, and a lot of them fit the diagnosis of things like hypomania, narcissism, bipolar, attention deficit disorder, unhealthy fixations, behavioral imbalances, and addiction issues. I'd say about twenty percent of the guys in any given locker room are dealing with some kind of psychological issue. Those are just the ones that you can openly tell, who aren't privately doing something like what you were doing, self-treating with alcohol or pills. If an expert came in and did a full study, I wouldn't be surprised if it was double."

"And I'm part of that percentage of damaged goods, huh?" I threw my entire toiletry bag into the sink and, the phone on speaker, plucked my contacts from my eyes and cased them.

"What I'm saying is," continued Ray, "those numbers comprise a normal locker-room environment. You've told me how most of the time it feels like no one is accountable to anything other than success or failure on the field of play, and you're right. The stuff you see a lot of players do daily would be seen as abnormal or self-destructive behavior in any other profession. In this one, however, it helps them succeed.

"You're not crazy," Ray continued. "You may be different from the group, but you're not crazy. And your choice to get help is not crazy. You can either make your environment adapt to you, or you can adapt to it."

"Pills would help with that?" I was brushing my teeth but pulled the brush from my mouth, white foamy paste around lips, to ask.

"Maybe. There is only one way to find out."

I thought of all the pills while I finished brushing. I though of how my life might look if I had to take pills for the rest of it just to feel good about myself. How all this seemed to be the result of a busted arm. I spit out the paste.

"No," I said. "No pills. I don't have anything against them. They could work, but they're not for me. Either I can learn to cope with the stressors of this game, or I can't. I'm not going to numb myself just to keep doing it." Glasses on, mouth rinsed, I clicked the bathroom lights off and headed to the bedroom.

"You're not going to lose control of yourself if you take them, Dirk."

"It doesn't matter. You told me to take possession of who I am. Well, this is who I am. My reactions to my environment make me who I am. I'm not going to filter them any more with drugs."

"Fair enough," Dr. Ray said.

"So what else can I do?" I asked, slipping into bed.

"Own this choice. If people think you're crazy, be crazy. Be you and don't worry about what they might think or say until they actually say it to you. You can't spend all your time in other people's heads; you have enough shit to worry about inside your own. Hell, we all do. Even I need a psychologist sometimes—dealing with guys like you is enough to make anyone go nuts!"

"You want me to go to Birmingham and practice being crazy?" I asked.

"No, I want you to go to Birmingham and be yourself, worry free."

"I'm not really sure I know what that looks like."

"Well," Ray said, "I'd say it's about time you found out."

Chapter 31

I landed in Birmingham midday. The landscape wasn't like the flat, jungle-scrub of Tampa, Florida, nor the rolling, tree-speckled hills of northern Ohio. It was a combination of the two, with a little more Spanish moss, and Turkish-sauna-style humidity that sat on you like a bully on a first grader. The Jays got me a rental car, and the first thing I did after loading it with all my gear was crank the AC.

I drove to a Hilton hotel in the northern part of the city, my new residence. The hotel was eight stories tall and hollow in the center, with all the room doors facing one another. Some of the doors had windows next to them, even though they were inside, and the elevators were glass. The lobby was home to a check-in desk, a bar, a koi pond with a waterfall, a garden, a pool, and a Ruth's Chris Steak House. It was all smashed together, like the first floor of a cheap mall. Attempting sophistication, the hotel erected bridges to connect all its different portions together, winding them through the koi pond and garden, but all this really did was keep you from taking a straight path to the exit.

The hotel pool was behind the check-in desk, and walled off by glass from the garden/restaurant/bar/pond/lobby. Inside, a herd of massive women floated listlessly across the surface of the water like drifting hippos, while their children repeatedly cannon-balled, trying to splash as much water out of the pool as possible. Every so often a child would plunge too close to one of the great hippos and the beast would come up for air and croak and moo before drifting once more.

Above it all was a roof of glass panels. The light of the sun waxed and waned as clouds passed between it and the hotel. Somehow, a couple of birds had gotten inside and fluttered around in a spastic search for escape. I wondered: How could anyone come and eat at the top-dollar steak house, half of which was exposed to the chaos of the lobby where fish and birds and hippos and gawking guests were a part of every meal?

When I checked in, I gave the lady at the desk my hotel-rewards card and asked for an upgrade to a quiet room. I told her I was a famous bestselling author and a major league baseball player and that I needed quiet for both my physical and mental health. She put me on the seventh floor in a cor-ner suite with a large living space and a separate bedroom. I thanked her, gave her a signed copy of my book, and told her I'd put her in the next one.

When the door slammed shut in my room, I could still hear people eating at the restaurant below, the clanking of forks, the shuffling of dishes, running water, and the slam of every door as it struck shut. I took off the couch cushions and piled them near the base of the door to muffle the sound. Then I stood there, wondering if I was right to shut out the outside world and its noise. Wasn't this the first step to re-peating what I'd done to myself in Florida?

An hour or so later I changed into a set of workout clothes and drove to the Andrews Clinic to meet with Kevin Wilk, the man who would be taking over my rehab. Jep raved about him. Said he was the best in the business. But after getting passed from George to Jep to Autumn, back to Jep, and now here, I was jaded about rehab in general. My expectations were low.

I arrived at the clinic check-in, a glass room populated by big leafy plants, smiling receptionists, and magazine-ogling patients. I made the acquaintance of a southern-drawled receptionist, signed my name on a check-in list, and waited.

Minutes later, a young man, younger than myself, came out from the rehab clinic and met me. He sported the standard rehabber apparel: a company-logoed polo tucked into khaki pants. "You must be Dirk," he said, reaching out his hand.

We shook. "That's me," I said.

"I'm Luke. Come on in, let's get you set up."

He led me into the clinic. It was much bigger than the others I'd been in. It didn't have as many high-tech toys as the Cleveland Clinic, but it did have an abundance of staff. The ratio of beds to specialists was nearly one to one.

The clinic was a long, rectangular room with about ten tables on its long sides and two or three on its southernmost end. There were windows on the west side, a weight room toward the north side, and in the middle were various machines for strength building. There was also a track, if you could call it that. It ran between the tables and the weight machines, and it would take a person about fifty laps on it to do a mile, but it was a controlled distance for those who needed to work on mobility again.

The real spectacle was the walls. They were covered with framed jerseys and posters depicting famous baseball, basketball, football, golf, and wrestling stars—a who's who of athletic greatness. Some had designer encasing with placards, others were framed posters with messages scrawled over them in black Magic Marker. But no matter who the athlete or how his image was framed, all were addressed to the man I was there to see: Kevin Wilk. Whoever this guy was, he'd worked on close to a billion dollars' worth of athletic talent.

"Kevin will be right out to see you," Luke said, and then, like some medical butler, retreated, presumably to perform some unknown training-room task. I was left to sit on a training table, my feet dangling off the end, scissoring in boredom.

After a couple of minutes I lay down and stared at the wall above and behind me. A poster of a professional wrestler, Triple H—code for Hunter Hurst Helmsley, which in turn was code for the wrestler's real name—hung there. He'd been oiled down to make his muscles gleam, and he wore a menacing scowl, tall boots, and a pair of nut-hugging leather undies. And, of course, there was the inscription saying he owed his good health to Kevin Wilk. I started to wonder if Wilk was some kind of divine healer. Would he materialize before me in a blast of smoke, or on a beam of light with doves fluttering in his wake?

"There he is," declared a new voice. "There's the author I've heard so much about." A shorter man, about half the size of Triple H, was walking toward me. He wore a long-sleeved, button-down dress shirt with a tie stuffed into one of the gaps between the buttons, along with dress slacks, polished leather shoes, and a clinic nametag. His stride was so easy and confident, he must have been either the man all the posters were bearing witness to, or the prom king.

About fifteen feet from me, he stopped, threw up both hands and shouted, "I'm open, Luke, I'm open!" Luke, who was filling out some chart or graph, dispassionately picked up a basketball near his feet and passed it to the man with the tie who, as if about to score the final shot in the game that decided the championship of the universe, dribbled, juked, and did a fadeaway jumper, launching the ball at a small, square, wooden box that housed several other sports balls. The basketball hit the corner of the box and shot away across the floor into an unoccupied training table. Game over.

The man with the tie feigned devastation, then spun on Luke and said, "Bad pass. You make a better pass and we win, Lukey." Luke rolled his eyes but the man with the tie was already moving again. He stopped in front of my table, smiled at me and said, "Hello. Kevin Wilk. Nice to meet you."

"Dirk Hayhurst," I said. "I'm sick of being hurt."

"Well, it's your own fault," he said with a sigh. "You should have come to me first. You've seen the rest, now it's time to see the best. Right, Luke?"

"Of course," Luke said.

"Shut up, Luke," Kevin said, not taking his eyes off me. "Luke's kinda sensitive," Kevin said in a softer voice, but still loud enough for Luke to hear. "I'm trying to toughen him up a little. He needs it if he's going to work around athletes. Besides, he's dating this Roller Derby girl and I think she beats him."

"We're not dating," Luke said, shaking his head.

Kevin nodded and mouthed the word "love" at me.

"I care about the health of my employees, Dirk. I'm a healer," Kevin continued, taking a seat on a rolling stool and flipping through a manila folder with what appeared to be my medical history in it. "Since I can't tell him who to date, I have to toughen him up to make sure he survives. It's hard to find good help these days."

"We're not dating, Kevin," Luke said, again. "We just share an apartment."

"She brought him a homemade lunch to the clinic. That's love."

"Whatever. You can think whatever you want," Luke said.

"Shut up, Luke. Respect your superiors."

Luke shook his head again.

"So." Kevin closed the folder and looked at me. "Jep couldn't fix you, the Clinic couldn't fix you, George couldn't fix you—now they send you to me." He cracked his knuckles. "Who did your surgery?" Kevin was on his feet now. He was both intense and yet spastic. In complete possession of himself, and yet doing his best to make it seem like he was flying out of control.

"Dr. Schikendantz," I said. "From the Cle—"

"Yes, yes. Chicken Dents, I know who he is. You've had some shots, some pills, a little depression . . . But you also had an evaluation with Dr. Andrews. How'd that go?"

"That guy . . ." I gave a frustrated exhale.

I caught myself and thought about my answer, about what I wanted to say versus the politically correct response. I made a promise to myself that I would let my real feelings play, and stop trying to say what I thought everyone wanted to hear.

I began again. "That guy had me lay down on the table with my shirt off, got me talking, and then, out of nowhere, he cracks me in the top of my skull with that honking championship ring of his. I felt it in my teeth, man. Then, after asking me how I felt, in mid-answer, he slaps me in the face." Both Luke and Kevin had stopped what they were doing to hear this story, as did a few of the other trainers in the room. "I mean, he didn't give me his pimp hand, but he stung me, man. I'm sure he had good stuff to say about my health during the meeting, and I know he's the orthopedic surgery genius, but who the hell slaps a damn patient in the face? I've been through all kinds of shit this year and then this dude cuts me off by smacking me? I tell you what, man, I'm sure you run a great operation here, but if that guy hits me again, I'm going to hit him back. That's how the fucking examination went."

Luke and Kevin were staring at me. I wondered if I just

pulled another "lawsuit potential" moment, as I had with George a couple of weeks ago. But so what, it felt good to tell the truth. I needed to get it out there. For all I knew, this Kevin character could think he was King Shit, too, and make me bow down to his rule with a strong backhand.

Kevin turned to Luke with a thumb pointing back at me and said, "I like this guy!" Looking back at me, he went on, "I can't promise Andrews won't slap you again. But if you ever need surgery, I don't recommend hitting him back. You can hit Luke instead. Like I said, he needs it."

Luke sighed.

"Alright," I said, rolling with Kevin's sarcasm. I shot Luke a hungry look. "At least I get to hit *someone* around here. The Cleveland Clinic didn't like when I did that."

Kevin flipped my medical folder at Luke. "Alright, punchy, assume the position." Kevin gestured that I should lay back and let him evaluate my right arm's range of motion, as so many doctors and therapists had done before him.

I went supine on the training-room table. Luke appeared next to Kevin holding a plastic dial with two clocklike hands on it. My arm was laid on the table in such a way that if I were standing up I might swear an oath. Then I scooted far enough to the side of the table that Kevin could bend my arm backward like he was loading a catapult. Luke placed the dial on my elbow and Kevin bent my arm backward and forward. Luke used the dial to measure the degrees my arm went either way; combined, they totaled my external and internal rotation, aka my range of motion. Pitchers have much more of this than normal human beings, probably because of how our bones twist during our years of throwing. Luke and Kevin measured both my right and left arm—to get a comparison—and Luke marked all the information down on my folder, while Kevin acted like he was playing a television game show. "Come on, baby, come on, baby," Kevin would say as he tried to get my arm as far as it would go. The numbers were low, and Kevin scoffed.

Next he put my arm through all the other tests I'd become accustomed to: getting it over my head, out to the side like an airplane, and then across my body as if I might use my right arm to scratch the back of my left shoulder.

"Ouch," I said. "I'm not good with that one."

"Oh, stop being such a baby," Kevin said, pushing my arm even farther.

"I'm not, man. It hurts."

"No, it doesn't," Kevin said, still stretching.

"Yes, it does."

Kevin dropped my arm and looked at Luke. He started to hyperventilate like a child about to cry. *"It hurts, stop it. It hurts. Dr. Andrews bitch-slapped me. Waaa."*

I tried to sit up so I could fight back but Kevin put a hand on my chest and pressed me back down. "Relax," he said, and took my arm again. This time he grappled with it as though he might incapacitate me in some wrestling match—probably a move he learned from Triple H. Then he pulled it away from the socket, turned my thumb down, and moved my arm toward the area of my body I'd complained about earlier. This time there was no pain.

"Wow," I said.

"Wow, says the author," Kevin said, dropping my arm again so he could raise his own like he'd scored a touchdown. "Someone should write a book about me. Actually, I've already written a few of my own, mostly about how to fix you knuckleheads. But someone should write one about me: Kevin Wilk, the Wow Maker."

Luke choked back something under his breath.

"Shut up, Luke," Kevin said.

I sat up and looked at the pair of them. "Look, I'm going to shoot you straight. If I don't get better here, this could be it for me. I'm fairly sure I've become a liability to the Jays now, and because of this authoring stuff, I've made a few enemies on the team. This is my fourth training room in four months. If I don't get better here, I'm probably going to be out of a job. You think you can handle it?"

Kevin gave me a pensive look, but it was only a mask for more sarcasm. "Oh, gee, I don't know. We've never had a guy in here who had an arm that hurt before."

My eyes narrowed on Kevin, who finally dropped his act. He smiled and slapped me on the knee. "Don't worry, tough guy," he said, "we will get you right. And after we do, you can write a book about how awesome we are."

Chapter 32

Rehab was every day of the week, twice a day. I came first thing in the morning and worked for three hours straight. After lunch I came back and worked for three more. It was the most in-depth, rigorous rehab routine I'd ever experienced.

Every morning, Luke met me with a hot pack, stretched me, ran ultrasound, stretched me again, then laid out my work session, complete with written instructions. We'd go through the list, one by one, Kevin and Luke putting me through my paces, making sure I understood exactly what I was supposed to be doing. The devil was in the details, and there were a lot of them. It wasn't simply about the amount of exercises I did, it was how my body was oriented while I did them. The key was to make the shoulder do all the work, not my back or chest or some other big muscle that often tried to step in and compensate.

We always started with the hardest exercises. Manual resistance first. I'd lay on my back or chest and fight the continuously adjusting strength of Luke or Kevin and try to make my arm go places it used to go. Then I'd perch on a Plyoball and, while maintaining perfect posture with my scapula pinched and shoulder isolated, I'd rep out reverse flies and external and internal rotations using resistance bands. I'd rep until my shoulders burned from fatigue, at which point I'd go back to the training table, lie down, and repeat the sequence with hand weights.

When I got tired, I got sloppy. This would prompt Kevin to stand behind me, barking at me to pinch my scapula or relax my neck or adjust my posture. He'd poke me in places where I was supposed to feel the exercises working, and he'd poke me in the stomach or head when I did it wrong.

Poking, smacking, or otherwise whacking people was apparently part of the Andrews Clinic philosophy. They actually had a whole workout system designed around it. Kevin put me in front of a wall and, while having me stand in the oath position, I channeled my inner Karate Kid by doing wax-on/wax-off-style circles with a jelly-filled weighted medicine ball. After so many jelly-ball waxings, I held the ball in the same oath position but rigid, as if the ball, wall, and my arm were one solid piece. At this point, Kevin would whack my arm from every direction to test my shoulder's ability to stabilize. Next I'd push the jelly ball into the wall, with my arm fully stretched out, while Kevin smacked it again. I'd perch on a Plyoball, holding a taut resistance band rigid against more smacks. Finally, I'd balance in the push-up position, on a board balanced on a ball, cantilevered on a workout bench while Kevin straddled me and—you guessed it—smacked the shit out of me.

These were all reactive exercises, meaning they required my muscle groups to react and work together in dealing with stimulus. When I didn't stabilize well, Kevin would poke me in the stomach or armpit. Odd, because when I did stabilize well, Kevin would poke me in the stomach or armpit. I asked him why I got poked good or bad. Depending on the circumstance, he'd say "for screwing it up" or "because it's too easy for you." When I reminded him what would happen if I got hit by any more Andrews Clinic personnel, he'd point at Luke and say, "He's right there, go get him." After the first two weeks of training, I'd been battered so much, I felt like I was rehabbing to become a boxer.

I got the same intense focus every visit, and when my work was done I was stretched, lasered, ultrasounded, stretched again, then iced—every day, twice a day, no exceptions. If Kevin needed to take a phone call, Luke stepped in and took over. If Luke had to set up another patient, Kevin stepped in and took over. In the rare moments when they both were busy, there was someone else in the clinic, like Lenny, who knew every routine and how to keep me moving forward. It was impossible not to get better under their care. After two weeks of working with them, my shoulder was the strongest it had been since my surgery.

Being in the Andrews Clinic was work, but it was also a lot of fun—the kind of fun I'd been missing, the kind that made me feel plugged into something again. The clinic was a hot destination spot for high-profile athletes, and there were several in attendance while I was there. Two notables during my time there were Hot Rob, a compact, muscular, black, and of course injured running back with the Tennessee Titans who spent his days on the training table to my left. To my right, a lanky, head shaven, Mexi-Cali journeyman pitcher with the Yankees who went by Zim. Beyond them, new faces came and went every day. The pro wrestler Ted DiBiase Jr. was there trying to get healthy so he could follow in his dad's footsteps. A couple of guys from overseas basketball teams paid visits, along with various pitchers from major and minor league teams, including guys from the Jays' organization. A former PGA Champion. Some football players. Some collegiate wrestlers. Some track runners. Even J. P. Howell from the Rays showed up to spread the love.

There was no social hierarchy in the Birmingham training room, at least not among the athletes. None of us felt the need to "Big League" each other, tout service time, or hide behind stats. We were all equally useless. If you were a dick, it was because you genuinely *were* a dick, not because you broke team code.

An ego-measuring armistice was in place, mostly because Kevin didn't play favorites. But also because of all the stars we had in the room, he was the most interesting. If crazy looked anything like Kevin, then he made it look awesome.

Kevin was equal parts wild, sarcastic, and brilliant to the point he became bored with some of the personalities he had to work with. He enjoyed the vitriolic exchange of remarks so commonplace to the athletic world, yet also enjoyed being a groundbreaking therapist. Not every athlete who came through the clinic could scale up their mental processes to match Kevin's.

Kevin and I got along well because I think he thought— since I'd written a book—I was smarter than I actually was. This, coupled with the fact that I'd made the firm choice to be myself no matter what, intrigued Kevin. He seemed entertained by my unfiltered thoughts, and quickly became obsessed with testing just how far I would go before putting a filter on things again.

"You're not that cool," Kevin said on an idle Tuesday. He looked down on me while running the end-of-session laser on my shoulder. We were both wearing protective eyewear that looked like a cross between welding goggles and skeet-shooting glasses to shield our retinas from stray beams—no one was cool while wearing them.

"If writing books makes you cool," he continued, "then I'm by far the coolest guy in this room because I've written, oh, gosh, I can't even remember how many."

"You can remember. You bring it up at least once a week,"

Luke said, running the ultrasound wand on Zim's shoulder the next table over.

"Does it make you jealous knowing that you've written more books than me, but don't have a bestseller? Is that why you bring this up?" I asked Kevin.

"Jealous? Jealous! I don't write for fame and fortune, hawking stories about boobs and farts and baseballs like you do. I write for a higher purpose. I write for the benefit of mankind. I'm a healer, Dirk. I don't need fame. I do it because I care." Kevin then took the laser beam away from my shoulder and irradiated my exposed nipples. I slapped a hand over them like a woman who'd been walked in on topless.

"Ask him how much of his books he actually writes," Luke said.

"How much did you write?" I asked. I uncovered my nipples and went back to casually lying on the training table.

"Irrelevant. What matters is I'm helping people. *The greater good.*"

"Ask him who gets flown around the country to lecture at colleges and conventions for top dollar because of the books he's 'authored,' " said Luke.

"Wow, you're a star on the lecture circuit, huh?" I asked, tipping my glasses down my nose. "How much of that lecture money are you giving away to charities, Mr. Philanthropy?"

"It's *Dr.* Philanthropy," corrected Kevin. "And it's unprofessional to ask. Just like it's unprofessional of Luke to bring it up. I suggest Luke give us all the gift of silence or I'll tell everyone here about how he was really born Lucy. I'm sure that would make a great story for a book."

Luke snorted and continued spreading the conductive ultrasound goo across Zim's shoulder.

Hot Rob, sitting at the table across to our right, knee elevated in a self-pumping, continuously circulating hydro-cold pack, whistled skeptically and said, "Listen to y'all nerds fightin' 'bout books. Man, I might have to write a book of my own and out sell all y'all."

"Oh, please, Rob. You can't even read," Kevin said.

"Watchoo talking 'bout 'I can't read,' son? I can read. *Hop on Pop. See Spot Run. Green Eggs and Ham.*" Rob nodded at us. "That's knowledge right there. Best books on earth. Y'all talking bout how hard writing is. *Please.* Dude makes up kids' rhymes about cats and hats and smokes all y'uns. And he was a doctor, Kevin. What now?" Rob crossed his arms across his chest.

"Can't argue with that," I said, smiling at Kevin.

Kevin put the laser on my nipples again. I slapped it away.

"I should write a book," Zim said. "I've seen some shit in my career, shit that would make your head explode." Zim was done with the ultrasound portion of his session and Luke went to fetch an ice pack.

"Like the steroid habits of all your teammates?" Kevin asked. "That always goes over real well."

"Nah, not that. Although, I can tell you after so many years of doing this gig, if pumping some 'roids got me a massive contract and made my shit stop hurting, I'd do it, too."

"I know how you feel, man," I said, looking at Zim from over the rims of my space-laser goggles. "I'm starting to reconsider 'roid use myself. I'm over being in pain. I don't even care about the performance-enhancing part. I just don't want any more pain."

"La-la-la-la-la," Kevin sang. "La-la-la-la, I can't hear you."

"What are you doing?" I said to Kevin, who had the laser covering one ear and his free hand covering the other.

"Absolving myself of guilt, so they can't drag me in front of Congress like they did your brothers, Clemens and Bonds."

"Shit, steroids are old news," said Zim. Luke was back now, trying to lash an ice pack around him, but Zim was too busy adding gestures to his tale. "People don't care if you do them unless you're a famous player. Then they get all pissed off. Firefighters, cops, movie stars, are all doing that shit, too, but no one cares."

"Mmm-hmmm," echoed Rob.

"But I don't need 'roids to write a book. I got way better stuff than 'roids."

"Whatchoo got?" asked Hot Rob.

"When I was with the Dodgers, there was this movie star chick that was a certified cleat-chaser, man. She loved to fuck her some Dodgers, man. But all the guys knew to steer clear of her. Because she was a career wrecker, ya know?"

"Like she was cursed?" asked Luke, still hovering with the pack.

"Like she was a real-life Annie?" I asked, referencing Bull Durham.

"It's like her vagina has teeth or something, ya know?" said the journeyman. "Guys get with her and their careers implode. Plus, you get a little going away present, if you know what I mean."

We all cringed, hands going to our crotches.

"Excuse me." A soft, gentle, and completely out-of-place voice broke into our masculine banter. It was, of all things, the voice of a nun. She was standing at the end of my table, dressed in her coif and habit, hands folded at her waist, prayer beads and cross holstered at her side. She was smiling at us in that way that, without even having to ask, you knew she'd justify with, "I smile because each day is a gift from God."

We all went still and silent, the kind of instant quiet shame brings upon a man caught talking about vaginas in front of a nun. She stared at me specifically, and I felt my temperature rise, as if she was running a holy laser beam right into my soul. The goggles did nothing to protect me.

"Yes, sister, uh, mother, uh . . . your holiness?" I asked.

"I'm sorry to interrupt your treatment," she said with a slight curtsy, "but I understand you're a baseball player who wrote a book about the Gospels?"

There was a collective sniggering from behind me. I looked at the boys from the corner of my space goggles, then back at the nun. "I did, yes, but it's not really what you might think."

"It's even better," Kevin interjected, his tone gravely serious. "As a man who's written several books myself, I can say that his changed my life."

That was bullshit. I hadn't even given Kevin a copy of the book yet. I noticed that behind the nun, on the opposite side of the training room, was one of the other trainers, Lenny, smiling like he'd just pulled off a grand prank. Then it dawned on me that Kevin was the only one not caught off guard by the nun's arrival.

"I'd love to read it. I'm an avid baseball fan," continued the nun, "and of course a fan of the Lord. I lobbied to have Mother Superior let us watch some of the World Series last year, on a television. It was such a treat. When I heard you were the author of a baseball book, and right here in the training room, well, I hoped to get a copy from you and, if it's not a bother, have you sign it."

"Oh, he'd *love* to," Kevin said.

Kevin arranged this encounter. He was testing me. I could not let him win.

I sat up from the table. "Of course," I said. "It would be my pleasure." I reached over to the satchel I used to carry stuff (since I had no pockets in my workout gear), produced a copy of my book, and handed it to her. "Again," I said, "it's not what you think. The Gospels thing can be a little misleading, although Kevin did come to Jesus because of it. He has an amazing testimony. Your classic tale of being bound to Satan by the chains of nymphomania. But now he's been set free."

"Praise God!" said the nun to Kevin. "Do you have a favorite scripture yet?"

"Oh, your holiness, it's so hard to choose. They're all so good," Kevin said.

"Amen. What was your conversion like?"

"I'd love to tell you, but I can't here. You know, HIPAA and all that."

"Some other time, then." She looked back to me. "So, will you sign my copy?"

"I don't have a marker," I said.

"I do," she said, and merrily skipped away to get it.

"Nymphomania?" Kevin held his hands wide as the nun left. "Seriously?" He put the laser on my nipples again, as punishment.

"What? It was a compliment. Now give me my shirt, ya bastard," I said.

"You got two more minutes of laser," Kevin said.

"Just give me my shirt before I lead her into temptation."

"Oh, for Christ's sake," Kevin said, throwing the shirt over my face.

"You keep books in yo purse to sign for people at all times?" Hot Rob asked, still anchored to the table by the robo cold pack. "You think J. K. Rowling does that shit?"

"I try to keep one with me in case I bump into someone famous and want to give them the book and take a picture of them holding it. It's good for business," I said, digging out the book.

"I didn't get a book," Kevin said.

"Exactly," I said.

The nun returned and I signed her book. "I'll read it right away," she said.

"Great," Kevin said. "He loves getting reader feedback."

"Love it," I echoed, not flinching.

The nun thanked us all and teleported away via a beam of divine light. Luke materialized in her place with my ice packs. I held out my arm so Luke could wrap me up.

"Did you arrange that?" I asked Kevin.

He shrugged.

"Did you put that poor nun up to coming over here and asking me for a signed copy of a book that talks about sex with hermaphrodites?"

"She said she loves baseball. You heard her," Kevin said.

"You did, didn't you?"

"Stimulus training, Hayhurst. Gotta see how your body reacts. All part of your rehab." He poked me in the stomach, whacked me in the side of the face, then pointed at Luke and walked away.

Chapter 33

Social stimulus training became a consistent part of my rehab with Kevin. I had to be vigilant because his "stimulus" methods became increasingly more elaborate as time passed. Nuns, fake trainers, prank calls, you never knew how or when he would strike. Oddly, the more intense he got, the more I liked it. He was challenging me, publicly, to react and hold my ground.

Two weeks after the nun I was cleared to start playing light catch again. I'd head up to the American Sports Medicine Institute connected to the clinic for a catch session with Kevin, then come back and do more rehab. On this day Kevin had to go see about another patient, leaving me to throw into a tarp under the watchful supervision of an ASMI intern.

When I arrived back at the training room for my post-throwing routine, I saw an older woman waiting near my training table. She was grandmotherly, dressed like the wife of a pre–Civil War plantation owner. Pearls, gold, white gloves—the whole treatment. Sitting next to her was a black woman dressed in house servant's clothing.

As I walked in, Luke lit up and motioned to the antiquated lady that I, the person of interest, had arrived. Hot Rob's and

Zim's heads popped up like prairie dogs, faces hardly hiding their anticipation of coming entertainment. The plantation wife glanced over at me, but casually, almost as if she wanted me to know she'd looked, but with faint interest. I knew I was walking into something.

Luke, carrying the remains of an extinguished hot pack, slid up beside me and, speaking out of the side of his mouth, said, "She's been asking about you. Lady Chesterfield. One of Kevin's oldest clients."

"You couldn't have radioed up to ASMI and warned me?"

"Kevin wouldn't let me."

"Of course he wouldn't," I mumbled.

"Be nice," Luke said. "She's very proper."

"I can see that," I said.

"She's also rich and well connected. If she likes you, who knows, maybe she could help your book."

"How?"

Luke shrugged. "Kevin said she's very tight with authors."

"Kevin has some interesting friends," I said, doing an armpit sniff check.

I put on a grandiose smile and strode toward Lady Chesterfield. "My dear Lady Chesterfield, I've heard *so* much about you."

"Oh, and the same to you, sir," she said, holding out her white-gloved hand for me to take. "Our mutual friend Dr. Wilk has told me about your, shall we say, *storied* career?" It was a pun, a bad one, but she thought it was very clever and so I acted like it was. Her voice, her mannerisms, the fact they she wore white gloves sixty years after they were fashionable—everything demanded that I behave with all the pomp and pretentiousness of southern high society. She was like an undead Scarlett O'Hara.

"Oh, he is a delightful fellow, isn't he? And such charming

friends," I added with a wink. "I'll have to thank him for once again introducing me to a young lady of taste."

She nearly swooned when I said this. When she recovered, she said, "I'll have you know I've been bragging to all my girls that I've made the acquaintance of yet another bestselling author, though we've only just now met. They get so jealous, I couldn't resist. Now that we've met, I'm released of my fib. You don't think less of me for a little white lie, do you?"

"One can't be expected to be good all the time. Otherwise life would be so terribly boring. Wouldn't you agree?"

"Indeed, sir. Indeed." A devious little smile dimpled her blushing cheeks.

I put my baseball glove down on my training table and rested against it. "Now, my lady, to what do I owe the pleasure of this visit?"

"Well, it would be rude of me to discuss it all here. No, I simply must have you for dinner," she continued. "I can have my woman cook anything that you'd like; all you need do is tell me. I send her to market daily. Her peach pie alone is good enough to warrant a visit."

Being nice to an old lady from the wrong time period—one who kept a servant she referred to as *her woman,* no less—was one thing. Having dinner with her was another. "Ah, but my dear lady, my schedule is so full of medical demands that I fear I shan't have time to enjoy your gracious offer."

"Shan't," I heard Rob echo to Luke. "Muh'fucka just said *shan't.*"

"Surely you have your evenings free?" Lady Chesterfield asked.

"Those hours are precious to me, for they are the ones in which I write."

"Oh yes, your craft, your craft," she recited as if reading a poem about some great lamentation. Then, drifting back into the recesses of her mind, she spoke from memory. "I remember the day I met my first author. I was a girl and my parents had taken me to a fine hotel abroad that had a gambling hall in the lobby. Mother had gone to her room to lie down, while father gallivanted in the gambling hall below. I had nothing better to do, so I went out to explore. I passed an open hotel door and saw the most beautiful man inside, writing away on his typewriter.

"I was fascinated, but first I went back to my room to make myself up. Then, without knocking, I entered his room. I asked him what he was writing, and he told me it was *For Whom the Bell Tolls*. It was Ernest Hemingway! And he wasn't upset that I came. In fact, he offered me a seat on his bed . . ." She stopped, and her eyes seemed to glaze over as she relived that long-ago encounter.

Rob, Luke, Zim, and I all had the same dumbfounded expression. I began to compute her age. *For Whom The Bell Tolls* was published in 1940. That had to place Lady Chesterfield in her middle eighties to have been of legal age then. She was either a liar, or Hemingway was our nation's most prestigious pedophile.

"Mmmm," she said, "he was the most *charismatic* man." She put her hands on her collarbones and slid them, trembling, along her neck. "I was a young girl," she said again. "I didn't know much at the time. But I came to respect writers greatly after meeting him." She was staring at me with a far less proper look on her face. I now understood what that devious smile was all about.

I slowly turned to regard Luke, Rob, and Zim, all frozen in something between disbelief and nausea. Only Lady Chesterfield's woman seemed to be enjoying the moment.

"I find it odd that Hemingway"—I was trying to roll with it, I really was—"would write with his door open. I know, speaking for myself, I need complete focus to write. Seclusion with no interruptions or, uh, temptations."

"Oh, not Ernest. No, he was an attentive man. He preferred to write with his door open because he never knew when life would surprise him with its treasures." She held on to the word "treasures" as if it belonged to her alone. Her hands went back to rubbing her neck.

Rob had rolled over on his side and covered his head with his pillow. Zim was covering his face with his hands. Luke had to leave the scene entirely.

It wasn't just Lady Chesterfield who amused them. It was the look on my face. I simply could not help but cringe at her throes of ecstasy. Maybe she was a lovely woman when she was younger, but that was a long, *long* time ago. The woman before me now was probably just a few years younger than my grandmother, and the thought of this ancient woman doing to me whatever the hell she was mentally doing to Hemingway was enough to turn any man into a scared, flaccid mess.

She snapped out of her Hemingway soft-porn fantasy and zeroed in on me. "You know, I'm quite fond of the restaurant you have in your hotel," she said, referring to the Ruth's Chris Steak House located in the lobby. "I'd be more than happy to meet you there for dinner some night."

"Oh, do that, bro," Rob said, peaking out at me from under his pillow. "Take her back to the hotel, show her how you hold your pencil."

"It would be no trouble at all," continued Lady Chesterfield. "My woman can drive me over and wait in the car while we spend our evening together."

"Dude," Zim said, "think of the book you could write if you . . ." He gagged.

"Uh, why"—I gave an uncomfortable chuckle—"my lady, are you offering to buy me dinner in my own home?"

Ironically, of all that had transpired, Lady Chesterfield found this question very offensive. "I should say not!" she pulled back in outrage. "It's only proper that a gentleman buy a lady dinner after he asks her out."

"But, I . . ." I glanced at Rob for some help on this, but he was near suffocating himself under his pillow. "I didn't ask you out."

"Well, I never," she said.

I looked around for help. There was none. Rob was quivering with silent giggles under the pillow. Zim was dry heaving. Luke was MIA.

"After what we've shared, you'd think a gentleman would at least have the courtesy to buy a woman a respectable meal," continued a spurned Lady Chesterfield.

"What have we shared?" I held my hands out wide, utterly lost.

"Oh, my goodness!" She looked up and away to avoid the sight of me.

Right on time, Kevin, the great architect of embarrassment himself, bounded onto the scene. He was happy as a lark to see Lady Chesterfield, and even happier to see me dazed and confused.

"Ah, Kevin," said Lady Chesterfield, "It's nice to see a man of class here."

"And you as well. I hope these barbarians haven't been bothering you?"

"Well, only one of them." She shot me a cold look.

"Who, Hayhurst? Well, that doesn't surprise me," Kevin smiled. "He's a braggart and a charlatan."

My eyes narrowed on Kevin. "Excuse me, Lady Chesterfield," I said, bowing. "Allow me to apologize for being unavailable for dinner. I can understand how disappointing it is to be denied time with another creative mind. Why, just the other day I asked Kevin out for lunch and he denied me because he also had to write."

"Kevin," said Lady Chesterfield, her intrigue sparked anew, "I did not know you were also a writer."

"Oh, yeesss," I hissed. "An accomplished one. How many articles have you published again?"

"Well, it's not that—"

"One hundred and fifty-five journal articles," Luke interjected. It was as if he materialized from Kevin's shadow. "And ninety-eight book chapters."

"Medical journals and science books," I said, taking hold of Kevin's shoulders and massaging. "Why, he's changed the face of medical rehabilitation with his research." I put my head next to his and stretched my arm out as if portraying some great vision. "Me," I said, now backing away, hands up, "I just write about boobs and farts and baseballs. Kevin is a hero. A real *charismatic* hero. And it just so happens that he loves peach pie."

Chapter 34

Kevin and I were becoming regular performers for the rest of the crew at rehab. It's amazing how different circumstances bring out different sides of people. In Birmingham I was interesting and funny. In Birmingham, being a player/author was a good thing. In Birmingham, I was happy.

Unfortunately the same could not be said for my publishing house. They were rather annoyed that I was stuck in Birmingham while my book was hot. Part of the reason they signed me to a book deal was because I was a major leaguer with all the attendant marketability. They wanted me healthy and pitching, and using the media to goose book sales. And if not healthy, at least around a team of famous somebodies to exploit.

I told them it wasn't like I was trying to be injured, and they told me that I'd have to find another way to strike while the iron was hot. To make up for lost opportunities, they asked me to network both physically and digitally from my current location. I'd mentioned to them how the clinic was full of top-level athletes. In response they sent me a box of books with instructions to press one into the hands of every star that came through the place, begging for pictures, blurbs, tweets, endorsements, and recommendations—anything that would generate buzz.

I asked my literary agent how much I really *had* to do. I'd been paid in full, the royalties were coming in, and the terms of my contract had been met. The publishing house wasn't paying me to tweet, or post, or blog, or proselytize—and all that stuff had a nasty tendency to piss off teammates.

Furthermore, I had made some new friends at the clinic, I wasn't depressed, and my arm was healing. I still had this obnoxious choking feeling, but at least I wasn't surrounded by guys who wanted to choke me for writing. It seemed to me that anything beyond what I'd already done for the book could be a liability. I was enjoying life again. Why press my luck?

"I think the publishers are right," said Jason Yarn, my literary agent, from his Manhattan office. "You should be doing all of it."

"All of it?" I asked, standing on my balcony, watching a group of hotel kitchen employees smoke a joint behind the hotel's giant blue dumpster.

"All of it," confirmed Jason.

"But it pisses all the players off," I said.

"That's not your fault. That's their fault. Twitter is the wave of the future, my man. In two years, everyone will be doing it. They're stupid not to. They could be building their own brand right now. Keep doing it. The first guy through the wall always gets bloody, but there is too much for you to lose here by not doing it."

"I was afraid you'd say that," I said, leaning into the balcony's railing, staring out at the Birmingham hotel parking lot. I felt like I was looking at my future, its ethereal, yet-to-be realized outline blending seamlessly into the humid haze of an Alabama summer, minus the slight contact high.

"Why?" Jason asked. "You've accomplished something so many writers dream of. This is part of you now, and you have to feed it. You're—excuse the pun—a *big league* writer. You're a brand! It would be a waste of money not to keep creating content. The people are hungry for more Dirk Hayhurst."

"No one is hungry for more Dirk Hayhurst. They just want more insider baseball stories," I said.

"Okay, but they want"—he made it sound mystical, breathless—"*Dirk Hayhurst*-style insider baseball stories."

"And what, exactly, is my style?"

"You know, that self-deprecating, nonathlete, uh, not a very good player . . ."

"Diaries of a baseball loser?"

"What? *Nooo.* That's not . . . psshh . . . Come on, that's not"—he laughed nervously—"Are you kidding?"

"My style is being honest about failing in a game that everyone thinks you're a winner in simply by playing."

"Exactly! But, you know, in a good way."

Style, voice, impact, relationships, success, attention: all of these things were good for book sales. But, I'd learned, not rocking the boat was pretty nice too. I shook my head and shifted my feet. The smokers below looked up to regard me for a second, then continued to puff and pass.

"Look. I went through hell to get that book out. We hit all our goals and exceeded the publisher's. Can't I just feel good about that and go back to my regular life as a baseball player? Just, you know, a little more fulfilled?"

"No," Yarn said.

"No?"

"No, you can't go back."

"Why?"

"Because you're a success, baby! Welcome to your new life. People know your story now, and they like it, and it wasn't about vampires or politics or witchcraft—thank God.

Do you know how many manuscripts I get for that stuff? I could wallpaper the Sky Dome with crappy vampire books."

"It's the Rogers Centre now."

"Sure, whatever," Yarn said, undaunted. "Vampires on starships. Vampires from under the sea. Gay vampires who want to seduce the president and get a bill for same-sex, err, monster marriage passed. You wrote a book about baseball and it sold well. You *have* to write again, if only so I feel like I've done something good, as a literary agent, for our culture."

"Why is this always about someone else?"

"That's art in a capitalist society: saying what you want to say in a way other people are willing to buy it from you. You've made your name, and now you have to keep on rolling. Got any more good baseball stories?"

I thought about it for a moment as I watched the guys pass their joint back and forth. I'd never smoked before. They'd probably never gobbled four bottles of sleeping pills before. "I think I'm all baseballed out."

"What about going forward? You know, write as you go?"

"I can't keep making baseball this toxic mess just for the sake of some good material. It's not cost-effective, or sanity-effective. Can I write about something else?"

"What else would you like to write about?"

"I . . . I don't know."

"Hey. *Hey.* I don't mean to push you, but you've got a big payday coming now that your first book is a bestseller. So you should think of something."

"Payday?" I asked, pushing back from the balcony. "From royalties?"

"No. From your next deal. Let me explain this to you in baseball terms—"

"Oh, thank you, because I couldn't possibly understand a concept if it wasn't made in a baseball analogy."

"I know. So, right now you're a free agent coming off a stellar year. Other teams, in this case, publishing houses see you as winning talent. They'll pay a premium to get you. The difference is, you have to pitch a new book to get them interested. Based on the strength of your next pitch, your track record in sales, and the movie buzz, you should be looking at a good payday. Get it? Since you've established yourself as a baseball writer, I think you should at least consider more baseball."

"Wait. Slow down. Did you say 'movie buzz'?"

"Yeah, we've had some people sniffing around about a movie deal. Nothing serious yet, but it's a cyclical thing. Ebbs and flows."

"My book could be made into a movie?" I muttered. I was no longer on a balcony in Birmingham. I had drifted into the land of imagination, where I taught manicured starlets how to talk and act like me so they could portray the mystical and breathy story of Dirk Hayhurst on the silver screen, baby.

"It's a long process," Yarn said, "if it even happens. Don't get your hopes up. Focus more on the task at hand. You need to think of your next book. I can think of around two hundred and fifty to three hundred and fifty thousand reasons why you should."

I needed a moment to compute what he'd just told me: money, plus movie, minus angry teammates, equals—"I think it's pretty fucking obvious I should write about baseball again!"

"But you said you didn't have any more baseball stories."

"Are you kidding me, Yarn?" I spun around on the balcony and marched back into the room as if onto an awards stage. "We're talking about baseball. There is *always* something crazy to write about in baseball. I mean if it wasn't for baseball how else would I have found out there is a cleat-chasing movie star that stalks Dodgers players whose vagina has teeth and Ernest Hemmingway might have been a pedophile."

"Wait, what?"

"It's a long story," I waved it all off though I was alone in the room.

"As interesting as the vaginas of movie stars are, I'm not sure it's a whole book."

"Well"—amazing what a large dollar figure and a chance at a movie can do to your creativity—"I could always write about the year after *The Bullpen Gospels*. You want to talk about diaries of a baseball loser, my first year in the bigs was a catastrophe. More of that loser style the masses are hungry for! What do you think?"

"I'm your agent. If you like it, I like it. Write up a proposal and kick it off to me. It's time to cash in on all your struggles . . . as authored by Dirk Hayhurst, of course."

Chapter 35

"If there is a movie, I'd better get to be in it," Kevin said. He had me facedown on a training table and was putting me through a series of manual resistance pulls. "I'd better be in it, you hear me?" Kevin put me into some kind of restrictive chokehold while twisting my arm as if he might break it off.

"If there is a movie, you can be the team trainer," I gritted out.

"And what about Luke? He needs his big break." More arm twisting.

"Luke can be the . . . the . . . special-needs batboy."

Kevin laughed and released me, saying, "Ha, I love this guy."

Of course I'd told everyone in the training room about the potential movie. Yeah, I knew it was all speculation, but how many people would ever have speculation that their life might be turned into a movie? Besides, the process of getting healthy is all about hope and distraction. In a sense, movie fantasies were part of the recovery process. And, since I wasn't the only one slogging through the monotony of a training room, I invited everyone in the place to skip into the realm of fantasy with me.

"You know how many people I have to find parts for if there is a film?" I said.

"You could use this to make the team love you again," Kevin suggested, releasing me from his negotiation grip.

I sat up on the training table and looked at the crew. "Yeah, but what is that love worth? Love you or hate you, it's out of sight, out of mind with a ball team," I said.

"Fuck 'em, bro. Keep doing your thing," said Rob, knee propped up and swaddled by an ice pack.

"Truth," said Zim, shoulder under a hot pack. "I mean, you're a team, but, you gotta worry about you and yours first."

"Oh, quit whining," said Kevin. "Guy's going to have a movie made about his horseshit baseball career and he's crying over how hard his life is."

"That's it, you're out of the movie!" I said, lying back supine.

"You need to keep your teammates on your side. You get a whole bunch of big names in your pocket as extras and the production houses will jump all over it," Kevin said. "Get Bautista to back you. If he breaks all the home-run records this year, he could endorse anthrax and kids would buy it."

"Well," I said, rolling over on the training table, "I can't do much from here. I can't get the guys back on my side from Birmingham. Hell, I haven't even talked to anyone on the team since I've been here. The publishing house wants me to make new friends. They're sending two more boxes of books here, so I can hand them out to all the famous folks who come and go. I keep praying that more superstars will get hurt and come here so I can get them to endorse my book."

"Well, with Favre coming out of retirement again," Kevin said, "you might get your wish."

"Yeah, man, is Favre coming here or not?" Rob asked,

trying to sit despite the protests of Luke. There was a lone television in the training room, right in front of us athletes, and it was always on ESPN. Brett Favre was said to be making a comeback, but he was also said to be in a lot of pain. Rumors abounded that he was going to see Andrews at the clinic.

"I don't know. He's too good for us," Kevin said. "Does his own program someplace else. That's why he's hurt all the time. Doesn't want to work with the best."

"Damn straight," Rob said.

"What about Tiger Woods?" Zim asked. "He coming this way?"

"I don't know if he gonna have time, bro," Rob answered. "Dude's gonna be in court for the next year or so getting sued by all that pussy he's been running. Plus, you know his wife gonna get half." Rob shook his head in disgust. "Dr. Andrews can't fix that."

"He's going to lose all his endorsements, too," Zim said. My head went back and forth with each interchange in their conversation like I was watching a tennis match.

"Just stupid, man. Just stupid," Rob said. "I mean, you're the richest black man in sports, bro. You ain't getting sponsored by FUBU, you getting sponsored by muh'fucking Wall Street. Investment houses and Buicks and shit. You know they ain't gonna let you stay the face of their brands when you sleeping around with a damn pancake house waitress. You running game with some senator's wife, maybe, but a damn pancake house waitress? Shiiiit."

"Hey man, my wife was a waitress once," Zim joked.

"Better keep her away from Tiger, brother can't help himself. I can just see his next commercial." Rob framed it with his outstretched hands, then his voice climbed into that nerdy, nasally Tiger Woods zone as he delivered the sales pitch: "When it comes to getting a hummer from a pancake house waitress, nothing rivals the spacious backseat and plush interior of the Buick Enclave."

"I don't know if Woods is coming here or not," Kevin said, handing me the end of a resistance band to tug.

"I'll bet Andrews would love to get Tiger as a patient," Rob said. "Dude collects superstars for patients like they Pokémon or something."

"Would you treat us differently if he did?" Zim asked Kevin. "Would you shut down the training room and give Tiger preferential treatment?"

"Do I look like a guy who does preferential treatment, Zim?" Kevin let go of the band and it smacked me in the chest. "I love all my broken children equally." I threw the band back at him. He dodged.

"Don't lie, Kevin," Rob said. "You like them big names." Luke smiled and nodded behind Kevin's back as he picked up the thrown band. "Why else you got all this stuff on your wall made out to you?"

"I'm offended you'd say that, Rob. Why, just yesterday we put Dirk's baseball card on the wall and he's as nobody as it gets." Kevin nodded to my baseball card, crudely taped to the wall only a foot away from Triple H's monster-sized poster.

"But if you must know, big names are good for business," Kevin said. "And that's what we're talking about here: business. We gotta get Dirky some big-name backers, and I just happened to hear that Triple H might be coming in."

I looked upward, to the visage of Triple H staring down at me, muscled, oiled, ensconced in leather pants. "He's kind of a big deal, huh? I suppose I could give him a copy of the book."

"He's a huge deal," Kevin said. "You'd be stupid not to."

"Yeah, but only to wrestling fans," I said. "They don't read."

"Do you have any idea," Kevin responded, "how many wrestling fans are out there?"

"I think your view might be a little skewed since we're in Birmingham, one of the redneck capitals of the world," I said. "I got stuck in traffic yesterday because the confederate flag blew off someone's jacked-up F-150. They had to call an ambulance to make sure it was okay."

"I thought you were smarter than that, Shakespeare," Kevin said. He flipped me over on the table and made me fight him with more manual-resistance exercises. "Wrestle-Mania is one of the biggest television events around the world. These guys are gods. You get your book into the hand of Triple H and you'll be surprised what can happen. He's one of the most popular wrestlers in the business. You get him to endorse your book and you'll never need your teammates to like you again. And who cares if rednecks can't read. They can still buy stuff!"

He had a point: sales were sales. If I wanted a movie to be made, I needed them anyway I could get them. But more than that, it would be nice to not have to pander to the guys in the clubhouse. I wouldn't have to worry about ass-kissing the ruling clubhouse talent if I had stars outside of it selling my stuff.

"Okay," I said. "It's a plan. Will you help me do it?"

"After what you did to me with Lady Chesterfield?"

"You started that. I just finished it."

Kevin looked away.

"Come on, Kev, you're the man around here. The Wow Maker. The guy who knows how to get things done! You gotta help me."

"I just told you he might be coming in. That's more than I'd tell anyone else."

"Can't you connect me to him personally?"

"Totally unprofessional." Kevin threw his hands up. "You

have to do your own dirty work. I'm not going to call up former stars to help you peddle books. If I was going to do that, I'd have them peddle mine!"

"But you can let me know the time and date he's coming. So I can get ready for him. Right?"

Kevin rolled a Plyoball over in front of me, then bounced up and down on it. "I want a role, with lines, and a love scene with a hot starlet."

"One line, as a heckler," I said. "No more than five seconds of face time."

"Two lines, ten seconds," he countered. "And a chair with my name on it."

"One line, five seconds, and the chair."

Kevin looked to the ceiling. Then, suddenly he sprung up into a standing position and clapped his hands. "Deal. Triple H *could* be here next week. *Early* next week. But that's all I can tell you."

Chapter 36

The box of books arrived on the Saturday before Triple H was supposed to show up. I'd wheedled enough information out of Kevin to know that if Triple H came into the treatment room at all, it would be just briefly. He was going to have an operation—a "considerable one," according to Kevin—and if he passed through the rehab section of the place at all, he'd probably be groggy and heavily drugged, like I was when under the pull of sleeping pills and booze.

Since I might not get any time to shake his hand and formally ask him to love on my book, I decided that I would have two books ready for him. Book one was unsigned, in case Triple H was coherent enough to let me sign it in person. Book two was if there was a message on the side of Triple H's face that read, "I'm sorry, Triple H's brain is too fucked up to answer right now. Please sign him a book and he'll get back to you."

The day Triple H was supposed to arrive, I came into the training room at my appointed time. I did my routines, and between each set I asked Luke if there was any word on Triple H. He kept saying he didn't know, "Just like when you asked five minutes ago. Don't worry, I'll let you know."

"I don't think he's going to come down," Kevin said, catching our chat.

"Oh, what? Why not?" I asked.

"I told him not to until you left."

"Why would you do something like that?"

"How's he supposed to get better with fan boys like you down here bothering him, begging him to autograph your Triple H underwear. This is a place of healing, not a fan club. We take our job seriously." From behind Kevin, Luke rolled his eyes. Kevin, without looking, said, "I saw that, Luke."

"You're so full of crap," I said to Kevin.

"You're feeling better, aren't you?"

"Yes, but—"

"Then don't question my methods." Then, addressing himself to anyone within earshot, "They're always ungrateful. All the sacrifices I make for their careers . . ."

Before I had a chance to unleash my quiver of argument arrows, the man of the hour came wheeling through the door: Triple H, looking about as coherent as a tranquilized bear.

All the guys in the know—me, Luke, Kevin, Rob, and Zim—suddenly got quiet. But not quiet like when the nun showed up. This was that silence you get when a person for whom you've been plotting something appears, and you forget how to behave normally so instead you fake it.

Triple H was not as big as I thought he would be. I guess television, specifically television where you play the role of a giant, man-crushing badass, tends to make you look larger than you actually are. He was still huge, bigger than all of us, but he was not an ogre. Triple H looked to be about my height, but sixty to eighty pounds heavier, all muscle. Rob was well put together and I was in good shape, but Triple H was a brick house. He was a bodybuilder on top of an athlete.

He had huge hands that could easily palm a human skull. The rings of his T-shirt sleeves were stretched to capacity by his massive biceps, and his quads challenged the fabric of his jeans even when resting.

Triple H smiled at all of us and said hello as he rolled past, but I think he forgot the words as soon as they came out of his mouth because he was prescription-strength stoned.

Kevin and Luke broke ranks to tend to our new guest. They got Triple H out of his wheelchair and laid him on a training table. Luke fetched a bag of ice and started Triple's rehab routine. Years ago, they would have let him rest for a few weeks. Now, however, they wanted to start flushing out inflammation as soon after the surgery as possible.

Hot Rob and I didn't say much. We kept stealing glances at Triple H, trying to gauge how coherent he was. That question was clearly answered when Triple H fell asleep with the same mile-high smile on his face, about ten minutes into his treatment, ice on and everything.

My only play for a book endorsement now was option 2. I was afraid to deliver the book myself. I feared waking the man, startling him out of a sound sleep only to get a reflex blow from one of his boulder-sized fists. There are a lot of ways to make a bad impression, but one of the worst is to wake up a complete stranger after he's had a major surgery by asking him to endorse your book. I decided to hand the book off to Luke, trusting his judgment on the right time to deliver it, and letting him run the risk of getting punched. It didn't matter who the book came from, everything was written out in the inscription, including an email address, Twitter handle, and website. I handed off the package and left for lunch.

Back at the hotel, I bubbled over thinking of how pleased the publishing house would be at the sharing of my celebrity encounter with my loving Internet followers. I didn't technically meet Triple H, but the folks on the net didn't need to know that. As long as they knew the context in which our paths crossed, they could infer what they wanted. Thus, I tweeted about how I was in the presence of Triple H, how he joined me for rehab after his surgery, that it was cool getting to see him in person, that I gave him a copy of my book, and that when I left him with it he looked very happy.

All I omitted was the part about him being unconscious.

When I came back to the facility for my afternoon treatment, Triple H was gone. Hot Rob didn't show up either—he was slowly slipping into a habit of that—and Zim was done for the day. Kevin and Luke were there, of course, and when I hit the training table, Luke materialized with my hot pack, ready to start round two.

"So, did he like it?" I asked as Luke wrapped the pack onto my shoulder.

"I didn't give it to him," Luke said.

"What! But, that was the whole point of me giving it to you!"

"Relax. I gave it to his driver."

"You gave my *Dear Triple H* book to his damn wheelman!"

"To give to Triple H when he sobers up," finished Luke. "He'll make sure he gets it. Besides, he's probably parked at the hotel right now."

My thumb hit my chest. "My hotel?"

"Yep. Kevin says Triple stays at the Hilton when he comes into town. He gets a room for his staff and then he lives out of his deluxe-custom mobile home because he can watch the matches through a satellite feed."

"He's at my hotel right now?" I envisioned myself walking out to his tour bus and banging on the door. *Excuse me Mr. H-H-H sir, but I wanted to give you this book. Why yes, it is the same book your bus driver seems to be enjoying so much. Yes, I wrote it. Goodness, sir, I'd never thought about writing professional wrestling scripts before, but if you think I have what it takes . . .*

"I don't know," said Luke, "he might be gone. I think they said he was heading back today to work with his rehab team back home."

"Damn." I slammed my left hand on the training table.

"Well, even if he did get it, there's no telling if he'd read it," Luke said.

"Kevin said he would! Kevin said he's a big reader, that he was very well-rounded and cerebral," I insisted.

"Okay, supposing he does read it *and* endorses it, do you think that's going to make wrestling fans want to read it? This is wrestling fans we're talking about."

"Yes, Luke, I do. I did some research and discovered that wrestling fans read if you keep the words small enough and the words in my books are very small. Now stop killing my buzz, dammit. Now what am I going to do to generate attention for this book?"

The answer was back at the hotel, waiting for me. After the door of my room banged shut, I tore free of the medical-grade Saran Wrap that held my ice-bag-to-go to my shoulder. I threw the puffy bags of water, ice, and air into the sink and plopped down in front of my computer.

I refused to check my mail while at the training room. I did this for two reasons. One, a lot of stuff tended to happen during my time in the training room: nuns, doped-up wrestlers, horny old ladies . . . a gold mine for new literary material, stuff you don't want to miss because your head is buried in an inch-wide cell phone screen. Second, I like to relish the publicity, when there is any. And when there is, not being able to respond makes me manic. What if there is an important email about a movie and I want to respond immediately? I can't type a long letter on my cell phone keypad. I'll end up spending my whole time in the training room perseverating on the communiqué, frantic, like a dog chewing on its kennel door. It's better I wait, especially when there is nothing to do for the rest of the night except play video games and throw crap off the balcony to see if it will explode from the fall. This was wisdom.

Tonight? Jackpot. My inbox was overflowing. Way more than usual, a whole night's worth of stuff to reply to and pat myself on the back about. A lot of it was from private email addresses, meaning fan letters, not spam or ads. There was also a grossly wonderful number of Google alerts. I had set them up to tell me whenever my name or my book was mentioned on the web—it was a digital stalker's best friend.

The first site I pulled up was a wrestling site. I deduced it was connected with the Triple H plug I'd put out on Twitter. The second link was also a wrestling fan site. So was the third, and the fourth, and the tenth and . . . on it went. This struck me as odd: Triple H was a big name, but my spotting him seemed to be some viral Internet event. "Jesus, these fan boys are even more ravenous than I thought," I said to myself, lowriding in my hotel easy chair with the laptop on my stomach and my head resting in the chair's lower lumbar spot.

Then I read what the fan boys were talking about. There was an insane amount of speculation on how Triple H hurt himself. Fans were clamoring for details. What did he hurt? Who hurt him? How did it happen and what did it all mean in the Wonderful World of Wrestling?

That's when it hit me: This wasn't fan-boy rabies. My spotting Triple H in a medical center after a surgery was breaking news! No one knew he'd been cut open. It was supposed to be a secret. That's why he wasn't rehabbing in a public facility, that's why he didn't fly, and that's why he didn't stick around afterward.

"Oh shit!" I blurted, struggling to sit up.

I'd just outed the secret of the largest, wealthiest, scariest man I'd ever not really met!

Cold sweat came upon me the instant my mind made the connection. I'd just fucked up real bad. I'd done the one thing all the guys I played with feared I would do: I just screwed up someone's personal life using social media— about a man twice the size and sociopath that TJ Collins was.

His bus! I remembered what Luke said about Triple H staying at the hotel. What if he was still there right now? What if he was on his way to my room right now? *Yes sir, that's my book. Yes sir, that's my name signed on it. Yes, it's highly unlikely another Dirk signed a book for you and tweeted that you just had surgery from the same Twitter account he put in the book. No sir, I don't want to die.*

I ran to the window, but did not fling the curtains open. Instead, I peeked through them, looking for buses that would match the description. There were several out there. There always were. Every goddamn day a family reunion was being held in the place. The pool was always full of kids trying their darnedest to splash all its contents out. Noise, by the busload, coming in fresh every week. Triple H could be in any of them. He was everywhere!

I pulled the curtains tightly shut, picked up the hotel phone, and called down to the front desk. The lady at the desk greeted me.

"Ma'am," I huffed, "has anyone called my room or inquired about me while I was out?" As I spoke, I flung couch cushions at the door, kicking them into place to block the sound from going out this time.

"Not that I'm aware of. Were you expecting any calls, sir?"

"I don't know," I said, frazzled.

Silence on the other end of the line.

I realized that I didn't sound very sane, so I asked her a rational follow-up question to calm her suspicions. "Do you know anything about wrestling?"

"Not really."

"Do you know who Triple H is? Big guy, long hair, massive nose."

"I'm afraid I can't help you."

"Okay. If you see a large man, murderous looking, big nose, don't talk to him."

For some reason, she did not seem calmed by this line of reasoning, so, for her sake, I tried something else. "What name is my room under?"

"Your name, sir, Dirk Hayhurst."

"That's a terrible. We have to change that."

"You want to change your name?"

"Yes, obviously."

"Wh . . . uh . . . what would you like to change it to?"

Optimus Prime and Batman were both excellent options, but, sadly, also dead giveaways. "Edmond Dantes," I said. I spelled it for her, and hung up.

I went back to the Internet and erased all my tweets. I thought that would help take the fuel from the fire, but, an hour later, the sites that were abuzz with my breaking news story were now abuzz that I had pulled all the information regarding the news story from my Twitter feed. This, they declared, was a surefire way to confirm that the story I broke was true, and also that I was probably dead. That's the beauty of the Internet, it's a breeding ground for fantastical speculation. The further I read, the worse it got. It was a terrible time for me to not know anything about wrestling because I couldn't distinguish wild fan-boy fantasy from totally feasible consequence. Many of the wrestling fan sites genuinely believed that the personas the wrestlers portrayed on television were how they actually were in real life, meaning . . . Triple H would kill me.

This was preposterous, of course. Simple logic proved he could not kill me as he was injured, recovering from a major surgery. Jesus, didn't anyone read what I wrote? It was far more likely he'd pay someone else to do it. I mean, if my previous death threats resulting from media exposure taught me anything, it's that the would-be killers always have their connections do it for them. After all, Vince McMahon, an insanely rich delusional psychopath hell-bent on crushing mankind through ruthless corporate domination, was Triple H's father-in-law. He would sue the bejeezus out of me, milk me for everything I had, and *then* he would kill me.

There was no way to stop the damage now, but I did try. I tweeted out into the madness that I was sorry if I'd done anything wrong. I was just excited to see Triple H in person and I didn't mean to cause any drama for him. And then I added, "Please, don't kill me."

Chapter 37

Next morning, I sat in the training room with bloodshot eyes and untamed hair. "You look like hell," Luke said, appearing with the morning hot pack. "Late night?"

I grabbed Luke by the collar. "They can read, Luke. *They can read!*"

I explained the fallout on the net and the sleepless night that followed. I'd employed every technique Dr. Ray had taught me and I was still on the verge of a total anxiety meltdown.

"I don't understand," Luke said, "why you'd run to the Internet to talk about something like that."

"What do you mean you don't understand? That's what social media is for, Luke, to brag about your brushes with people more famous than yourself. I don't get on there and talk about how I hung out with you all day!"

"Why do I always get insulted?"

"Stop making this about you, Luke. I have a serious issue here. I've made a very large, wealthy, sadistic man upset with me and I need to get it fixed."

"Talk to Kevin. He's friends with Triple H. Maybe he'll know what to do."

Luke went off to find Kevin. Meanwhile, I lay on the table

with my shoulder warming, staring up at the poster of Triple H. His eyes seemed to bear down on me more menacingly than usual. Maybe because he knew something I didn't? I wondered who else knew something. Did the Blue Jays know about this? Did they get a call from World Wrestling Entertainment to discuss a lawsuit? Was José Bautista getting interviewed about how hard it was for him to focus when a loose cannon like Hayhurst was waiting in the background, ready to disclose players' secrets on the Internet?

I understood it now, clear and plain. This was what everyone worried about when I was around. That I would take some important piece of personal information and throw it into the hurricane of public opinion. That I would, whether intentional or not, wreck someone's life. This is why I was a toxic teammate.

"What the hell did you do now?" It was Kevin, marching onto the scene. I sat up and spun around to face him.

I re-explained what had happened, adding at the end, "Do you think he'll be pissed off? Do you think he'll sue? Do you think I really inconvenienced him or that this is just"—I laughed nervously—"no big deal and it will blow over?"

"Oh god!" Kevin put both hands to his head. "I don't know if he'll sue, but I'm sure he'll be pissed off. Oh Jesus!"

"R-r-really?" It was hard for me to tell if Kevin was being the sarcastic, needling, I-enjoy-making-you-suffer-while-I-help-you-heal Kevin, or honest Dr. Wilk, the guy who took the Hippocratic oath?

"Of course!" Kevin declared. "They spend months scripting their story lines, developing plots and characters. It's all mapped far in advance. You think they just go out there every night and beat the hell out of each other with steel chairs?"

Actually, that's exactly what I thought.

"Of course not!" I said.

"Everything that happens to them outside the ring has to be explained in their story lines," Kevin continued, pacing around the training-room bench, hands wildly gesturing. "Why they got hurt, who hurt them . . . this upends tons of mapped-out scenarios not only for Triple H, but all his sidekicks and enemies too. That's why they have to keep these things under wraps—they have to work the injury into the story. If the wrestling world thinks he got hurt doing something that isn't part of the script, why, it casts doubt on the whole character. They're not just wrestlers; they're actors in a constantly evolving story."

Kevin chuckled as he finished his explanation, as if to say, *Yeah, it's bizarre and a real strain on the imagination considering the quality of the scripts we're talking about, but you still fucked up in grand style, pal.*

My eyes darted around the room, searching for the nun. I needed her now. I needed her to speak to God on my behalf. But the sister wasn't there. I grabbed my sinking head. I was horrified what would happen to me now—a peculiar kind of horror a person feels when they're in big trouble but can't discount the humor involved. I mean, who looks at wrestling and doesn't realize it's all made up? How could a tweet ruin something that couldn't be taken seriously in the first place?

"I suppose this wouldn't be that big of a deal if it didn't come from you," Kevin said. "But because it came from you, a professional athlete, it's taken as truth. It's ridiculous. I mean, I think all you guys are clowns and jack-offs—you especially—but that's the way it is."

He was right. My voice had power, which is what made me dangerous.

After a lot of frantic confessing, rationalizing, and hair-pulling, Kevin informed me that since I hadn't signed any forms or waivers, I wasn't legally liable for anything that I saw while in the hospital, and couldn't be sued since HIPAA didn't apply to me. That was nice to hear, but I still didn't want my reputation to be ruined. I didn't want the athletic world to think of me as the guy who sent private information to the world via Twitter. Being rumored as a guy who *might* do that was bad enough. I had worked hard to avoid the status of confirmed exposé writer, and this little slip of the digital tongue could make it all moot.

"You can contact him, right, Kevin? You can tell him that it was an accident and that I didn't mean anything by it? I feel terrible. It's really bothering me. I need him to know that I'm sorry. I need to know he's okay." Like a puppy, I stared innocently into Kevin's wise, compassionate healer's eyes . . . only to watch them glaze over and turn into the eyes of the sarcastic needling torturer.

This was the upper hand he'd been waiting for. He was the communications gatekeeper to Triple H. He could do anything he wanted. And, from the way a wicked smile curled up on his face, it was obvious that what he wanted right now was to make me squirm.

"What's in it for me?" he asked.

"I've already given you books and a movie spot."

"What else do you got?"

"Oh, come on, man!"

"I'm serious. These wrestlers, their brains"—he spun his hands around his head like he was winding a tape into a knot—"they don't function like the rest of us. All the body slams, slaps in the face. Isn't that right, Luke?"

"Vicious O did grab my balls," Luke said.

"Whoa!" Kevin threw up his hands. "It wasn't a grab, Luke. There was no cuppage. The hand never closed. Vicious O only flipped your zipper. Just because you had movement doesn't imply cuppage. Stick to the facts." Kevin shook his head. "Now, Dirk. I'm supposed to call Hunter and tell him the reason he's in the middle of a media inquisition is because some blabbermouth Blue Jay outed him in my training room? Come on."

"You don't know that," I protested. "It might be no big deal for him!"

"Dirk, *Dirrrrk*," said Kevin. "I know, okay. Trust me. He'll want to kill you. And you want me to talk him down. I'm saving your life here!" Then, as he was so fond of doing, he started talking about how I'd hurt him with my actions and ruined his professional reputation. "And all this happened in my training room. Do you know how that makes me look? You're lucky I even keep working on you."

Was he joking? Was he serious? God, I hated how hard he was to read! The fog of the unknown, the stress of impending death, the fear of my reputation slandered. My emotions started to race and the pit of my stomach fell. The situation played out the only way it could: "I'm gonna be sick," I said, leaving the table and heading for the bathroom.

Kevin sprang into pursuit. "Alright, I'll call him now," he said. "We'll talk to him about it."

The prospect of confronting Triple H just made me more nauseated. "I can't talk to him," I said, pushing the bathroom door open, hoping to separate myself from Kevin and his scenarios of embarrassment. Undeterred, Kevin followed me in. I went into one of the toilet stalls and locked the door. Kevin stood outside.

"I'm dialing him right now."

"No, you're not!" I shouted. Seeing the toilet bowl made me want to pee, but I also wanted to vomit and cry. Because of all the duress, I couldn't do any of it. "You're screwing up my natural functions, Kevin!"

"It's ringing."

"I hate you! I hate you!"

"Heyyyy, Hunter. It's Kevin Wilk. I'm good . . . yeah . . . How are you feeling? Good . . . Yeah, I know those guys and they'll take good care of you. How's the family? Oh, great. Uh-huh . . . uh-huh . . . Well, isn't that sweet."

I had to decide if I wanted to leave the stall, where Kevin could push the phone off on me, or stay inside and trust him to handle it. I decided to stay put. Triple H was his friend; he'd know what to do. I peeked over the stall door and looked at Kevin, who looked back at me with a casual smile through his reflection on the bathroom mirror.

"Hey, quick question," Kevin said to his phone. "Have you heard anything from the media about your surgery going public because of a baseball player here in my clinic?" As soon as he asked the question, Kevin pulled the phone away from his head indicating the volume had spiked to painfully high levels. Instinctually, I ducked back behind stall door, reduced to watching through a crack between the door and the divider.

"I know, I know," said Kevin. "Yeah, he's kind of stupid. No, he really doesn't think before he says stuff . . . Yeah, I know you would if you were here right now . . . yeah, I told him he was lucky . . . yeah . . . yeah . . . I know you would."

That's right, Kevin, I thought, *let him get all his anger out, then tell him how bad I feel. Tear me down if you must, as long as he knows I'm sorry and didn't mean it!*

"Well you see," said Kevin, "that's just it. He's not sorry about any of it."

My head shot up over the stall door.

"Yeah, he says it's a free country and he can say what he wants."

I attacked the latch of the bathroom stall. I had to get out so I could kill that malicious bastard. But Kevin was on the move; by the time I made it through the door he was back in the training room. I burst from the bathroom in hot pursuit and saw Kevin, moving to the far side of the room, past a confused Luke.

"That's bullshit, Kevin!" I screamed. Patients stopped their treatment and watched me as I streaked across the room. "You tell him I'm sorry. You tell him it was an accident, goddammit! You tell him I want to live!" Having cornered Kevin, I reached to yank the phone from him but, instead of turning away, he held the phone out to me to take. The screen was blank. The phone was off. In fact, it had never been turned on.

"I hate you," I said, again.

"He didn't answer," Kevin shrugged.

"I hate you."

"You love me. I'm the best trainer there is."

My eyes narrowed on him, but before I could say I hated him again, he said, "I'll call him tonight and tell him how bad you feel, that it was an accident and that you're sorry. It was probably going to go public anyway. It always does." He took a big breath and seemed sad, his fun nearly finished. "Geez, relax. This is a place of healing, remember?"

Chapter 38

Kevin letting me relax didn't last for long. Toying with my belief that death would come at the hands of a gargantuan professional wrestler was just too much fun for him to resist. About two hours after the prank phone call he was back to vacillating between how the news *might* send Triple H into the Land of No Biggie . . . or maybe Violent, Death-Dealing Rage. He wasn't sure. Kevin said he was shooting me straight: that while, yes, he was the big man's friend, he also couldn't guarantee my safety and I should be prepared for anything.

It was standard Kevin, and I wanted to call him on it, but he was my only way out of this mess and I needed him to speak well on my behalf. I spent the rest of the day as his dancing puppet, because I knew that by the next day he'd have apologized for me and absolved me of guilt.

It wasn't until I got home that night that I realized Kevin would be out of town for lectures and conferences until the next week. He'd been bullshitting me about calling Triple H. Frazzled, I texted Kevin all through the weekend, asking him if he'd talked to the big man yet. Kevin's response was terse: "Hunter and I had an interesting conversation."

That bastard!

* * *

After a long weekend of trying to keep reinvigorated anxiety and depression symptoms in check, I sat on my training table, anxious to see Kevin.

"Well, I got good news and bad news," Kevin said, flouncing into the room while dribbling a basketball. He dribbled hard into Luke—who stood there, uninterested—did a spin move to a jump shot, missed, cringed as if devastated, then smacked Luke on the ass and said, "Good defense."

Luke took a deep breath and walked away, rubbing his ass.

"Anyway," Kevin said, now sitting on a rolling stool and sliding up next to me, "Good news and bad news."

"Good news first," I said, lying down on the table and letting Kevin take my arm through its morning stretching.

"It's my news. I want to give you the bad first," Kevin said. I rolled my eyes. "Hunter was shocked at how fast the news got out. He seemed pretty pissed, even after I apologized for you."

I tried to sit up but Kevin pushed me back down.

"The good news is, I did apologize for you, and when he comes back in a couple of weeks for his post-op evaluation, you'll probably be gone. Probably."

"That's it?"

"I told you you'd be fine," Kevin said.

"But he's still pissed at me!"

"I can't control that."

"What if I'm still here when he comes back?" I started to think about how much time I had left in the clinic, and how close I was to throwing off a pitcher's mound again. "You think I'll be ready to return to the Jays before he gets back, right?"

"That depends on a lot of things. Mostly on what I tell the Blue Jays about you."

I tried sitting up again and was again pushed back down.

"Hey, Lukey," Kevin shouted in no particular direction, "when does Dirk leave to go back to Dunedin?"

"Four weeks," Luke shouted back.

Kevin froze, clenching my arm in horror. He turned his head slowly toward me. "Goodness, Dirk, that's only a week before Triple H comes back!" He smiled wickedly and began stretching me again. "Oh yeah, I definitely see a one-week setback in your future."

"Come on!" I squealed.

"What?" He held his hands out wide. Then, switching to his doctor-ly voice, he said, "Captain's log: I'm not satisfied with the patient's progress at this juncture. I recommend keeping him for at least another week."

"You're just saying that. You know I've been doing great."

"Everybody does great when they work with me, right Rob?"

Rob, knee in the robo cold pack, didn't budge from the game he was playing on his phone as he responded, "You know it, boss."

Kevin smiled at me. When he saw me frowning though, in a way he hadn't since I'd arrived, he frowned as well and said, "Actually, I talked to George Poulis over the weekend and told him how well you were doing. He said you might as well stay here and build up your throwing routine since you were making such headway. I was going to blame it all on Triple H, but that's what George said. George is the bastard here. Fucking George."

My frown deepened.

"What, you don't like it here? You want to go back and rehab with Jep when you could be here with Luke and Zim and the nun and me?"

"And me, dude," Rob said, still absorbed in his cell phone.

"And of course Rob, how could we forget *Rob*? We love having you here, Dirky! Watching you get hit on by the elderly, insult nuns, and pick fights with pro wrestlers—I can't let you leave! Things just wouldn't be the same. Now roll over so I can laser your nipples some more."

"Do you mean that?" I asked, rolling over and slipping my shirt off.

"Does it make you feel better to think I do?"

"Yeah. Yeah, it kinda does."

"Then I *totally* do, with all my heart." Kevin handed me a pair of space goggles and fired up the laser.

"Seriously, how mad do you think Triple H will be when he sees me?" I asked.

"Hard to tell. He might chew you out but I don't think he'll body-slam you."

"I don't like the sound of that."

"*Mehhh.* What's the big deal? It was an accident. You didn't mean anything by it. So just let him say his piece and then let it go. He probably won't even care by the time he gets here."

"I'm not good with confrontation," I said. "I used to be. I used to be sure and strong. Now, even just thinking about getting into trouble gets me worked up."

"So I've noticed."

"And I've been working on it, you know. I got sent home from the Jays because I had trouble sorting it all out. That's why, even when I know you're just messing with me about stuff, it still bothers me because it's like me versus my brain. I know what I'm supposed to feel, but something just needs to click back into place."

"Wow," said Kevin. "You're more screwed up than I thought." He put the laser on my skull. "Maybe this will help."

"I've been getting that reaction a lot lately, man." I swatted the laser away. "When you confess to people that there is a part of you that you don't understand, they automatically lump you into the crazy pile. But I think a lot of people have stuff about them that isn't exactly 'normal.' They just never get in a situation where they have to confront it. When I got hurt, my life as a baseball player was interrupted. I had to deal with my identity issues and it threw me all out of whack. It's hard to explain that to people who have no questions about how life is going for them. You know what I mean?"

The laser went back to my skull.

"Seriously"—I sat up and made him face me—"the only reason I'm even telling you this is because I finally feel good enough to say it. Kevin, do you know what I mean?"

"Relax. I know what you mean," Kevin said. And whether he really did or not, I felt good hearing him say it. Despite screwing with me nearly every day, he was the best trainer I'd ever had. He didn't baby me, but he didn't ignore me when I needed to talk, either. He treated me like I was normal, even when I felt like a total mess.

I nodded and smiled and lay back down while Kevin ran the laser. Looking around the room I noticed there was a surprising quantity of wrestler posters on the wall, all with appreciative messages to Kevin for his help.

"Triple H isn't your first wrestler rehab, huh?"

"Nope. He's not even the first guy to start a fight in here."

"Really?"

"Yeah." Kevin laughed. "I told you the story never stops running for these guys. Even if they want it to. Over time, the line between the character and the person gets blurred. They come in here and they still have a character to keep up the storyline for. It's like their character got hurt and now that character has to go to rehab. But, at the same time, the real person underneath also has to go to rehab." It sounded crazy, but not too unlike any athlete who, at the professional level, was both a person and a brand.

Kevin giggled at the memories. "Rick Flair was rehabbing an injury, trying to get in shape so he could take on Hulk Hogan. He wasn't around to build it up in the traditional ways, you know, standing in the rings, screaming threats. He was here. So the cameras came in here to shoot his rehab, and we'd have to stage the whole thing out.

"I would be doing manual resistance exercises with him, right, and we'd be like 'ninety-nine, one hundred, one hundred and one,' and Flair would pretend to get tired and I'd have to say to him, 'C'mon, Rick, you gotta get ready for Hogan. *HOGAN*, Rick!' When I'd say Hogan, he'd start shaking like he was possessed. Then he'd fire more reps with super strength. I'd tell him to slow down and he'd throw me off of him. Oh man, it was great stuff."

"That's awesome," I said.

"Yeah. I've had wrestlers bring entire rings in and set them up so they could practice on the ropes. We've had practice matches here. I've even gotten in there with some of them, just for fun."

"Do you think Triple H will bring in a ring and use me as a practice dummy?"

"I hope so. And so should you. That would make a great book."

"Yeah, especially since we've established that wrestling fans read."

"Another bestseller!" Kevin said, flipping off the laser. "If you live to write about it."

He rolled me over and started my own manual resistance program with a series of pulling motions that isolated my lower scapula. I hated this exercise, because Kevin would usually push me until fatigue made me submit to his resistance. After the end of the first set, I lay there facedown, recovering. I thought of how long I'd be in the place and how many more times I'd have to do this exercise. Then I thought of how crazy the last couple days had been and how, in a weird way, I was thankful for it.

I rolled over and looked at Kevin, who stopped, confused. "Alright, from here on, I want to train like Flair did. Every time I get lazy or cranky in here, I want you to yell at me that I have to get ready for Triple H. If I'm going to be here when he shows up, then I at least want to be ready for the rematch."

Kevin smiled down at me. "Alright then," he said, loosening his tie, "C'mon, Hayhurst! Triple H! *You gotta get Triple H!*"

Chapter 39

When I first arrived in Birmingham, my throwing program was modified. That is to say, I wasn't allowed to play catch at all. It was Kevin's call, which was fine. Most MLB teams' rehab programs were based on Kevin's research, anyway. But once I started getting stronger, Kevin would warm me up and take me to the American Sports Medicine Institute to play catch in its high-tech batting cage. When I got too strong for the confinement of the cage, he sent Luke and me to a park across the street for long-tossing. When Luke could no longer bridge the distance between us, a former college baseball player, interning for ASMI, was commissioned for the job.

My improved arm strength indicated that my time in Birmingham was coming to a close. But George wouldn't let me come back to the Blue Jays until I could prove I'd completely turned the corner.

In order to verify beyond a shadow of a doubt that I was back in good pitching shape, I took the college baseball intern to the park across the street from the clinic to throw. After we separated to our assigned throwing distance, I backed up well beyond what was prescribed and let the ball fly. Sometimes I hit the intern on a line, and sometimes the ball flew over his head and into a patch of bushes. The intern was not happy about this, but I was. I was throwing the equivalent of center field to home plate with no pain. Two months ago I couldn't throw across the Cleveland Clinic's parking lot. I was back.

When I got back to the training room, I noticed it was particularly full. Lots more patients than usual. Then I remembered that Dr. Andrews would be making his rounds, conducting checkups and evaluations. I was looking forward to telling him about how far I was able to throw the ball.

I was also anxious to hug Kevin and confirm that he was a miracle worker. I looked around, eager to find him. That's when I spotted HIM: Triple fucking H, parked on *my* training table with his shirt off, joking around with Kevin.

I was wearing my glove on my head when I made visual contact. Slowly, I plucked it off and slid it down over my face until it covered me like a mask, my eyes peeking over the leather fingers. I stared at Kevin like I was on the pitcher's mound, watching a batter dig into the box.

I couldn't hear what Kevin and Triple H were saying, but both seemed happy . . . that is, until Kevin looked my way. He immediately turned back to Triple H and pointed me out. Triple H locked on. The jovial face vanished, replaced by one of hatred incarnate.

"Ohhhh fuck," I said into my glove.

Triple H was on his feet in a snap. Kevin backed away. "Hey!" roared Triple H, pointing a gigantic finger at me. The volume of the word brought the room to a standstill. "You think you can wreck an entire year's worth of work just because you want to run your mouth on the Internet?"

I have no idea why I looked around the room. It was obvious he was talking about me since, even after he delivered his lines, his finger hung in the air, trained on me exclusively. Also, everyone in the training room was staring at me, save for the nun, Sister What's-her-face, who was praying for me thanks to an earlier request I'd made.

Wrestling custom dictated that I posture back. Maybe threaten him a little. Point, rake my thumb across my neck, grab a steel chair and wave it menacingly. I had actually told Kevin, during one of my more boastful days preceding this encounter, that I would come right back at Triple H if something like this present scenario happened.

I could feel Kevin watching me, waiting for me to tear my shirt off and declare, "No man calls out the Garfoose and keeps his balls! What are you gonna do, Triple H, when Dirk-a-mania runs wild over *youuuuu!*"

It seemed, however, that Kevin had finally found my limit.

I unconsciously moved behind a weight machine for protection while Triple H's chest heaved, pumping up and down, bellows of fury. "Do you have any idea how much effort goes into building up our characters? Do you think before you run your mouth, punk?"

The eyes of the room followed me.

"Answer me!" he roared, slamming a hand onto my former training table.

"I am so sorry!" I squealed from behind an exercise bike. "It was all an accident! I swear to God! I take full responsibility for it all!" I dropped my head and locked my eyes on the floor. I tucked my elbows into my sides, engaging full submission mode. I considered dropping to my knees, but thought I'd hold on to that in case he started throwing people and I had to beg for my life. "I felt so bad," I continued. "After it happened and I realized what I'd done, I was so sorry, I wish, I . . . I wish . . ."

Laughter.

I looked up and there was Kevin, leaning into Triple H for support, laughing as hard as he could. Luke, Zim, Rob, Lenny, Sister What's-her-face, all of them. Everyone else in the room, not yet in on the joke, just stood around looking confused.

"Relax man, relax," Triple H said, chuckling. "I'm just playing. Kevin put me up to it. I'm fine. It's no big deal. It never was. I told Kevin that on day one."

I stood there, locked up. A range of emotions came over me. First relief, because I wasn't going to be killed. Then release, because Triple H wasn't really mad. Embarrassment, because a roomful of rehabbers was still staring at me. Finally, remorse. Because Kevin had to die, and I was going to kill him.

Chapter 40

Kevin fled, disappearing like a squid that, instead of a cloud of ink, discharged a basket of rehab tennis balls before escaping to safety. That left me alone with Triple H.

He sat on my usual training table in a pair of frayed jeans and black boots, his shirt off. As strong as some of the athletes were in this place, he was easily the most massive and intimidating. And yet, just like the rest of us broken toys, he sat there on the training table, feet dangling over the edge in boredom, waiting for Dr. Andrews to pronounce him well.

I took a seat on the training table next to Triple H. We had a lot of time to kill, so I took the opportunity to seriously, and under no threat of death, apologize to him. I explained the whole ordeal, how Kevin had been using it to motivate, punish, and embarrass me for the last month and a half. Ironically, Triple H told me that he was the one who felt bad about everything.

"Really? Why?" I asked.

"I got home and my surgery was all over the web. That stuff gets out, it always does, but I was surprised by how fast this time. Then I saw that you'd broken it unknowingly, apologized, and felt bad. I thought, 'Oh boy, this poor guy has no idea what he's in for.'

"I know how wrestling fans can be," he said. "Most are pretty cool, but some of them come up with entire fictional lives built around us and go crazy. Multileveled plots, hidden meanings, wild speculations . . . stuff we couldn't think of in a thousand years. And we write this stuff!"

"So you're saying that there's no truth to the rumors that your father-in-law is sending a WWE swat team that will rappel from helicopters and burst through my hotel-room window?"

Triple shook his head. "Did you get any death threats?" he asked.

"Not *death*, but ass-kicking threats. Some of your fans have gangs dedicated to you, that, uh, take on other gangs dedicated to other wrestlers. They have amazing chat room brawls in your honor. I never knew. Come to think of it, I probably learned more about wrestling in that forty-eight-hour period than ever before in my life."

"Yeah, it's not what people think it is," he said.

We sat silently for a few seconds. That I was talking to one of the sports entertainment industry's biggest names was not lost on me, but neither was the fact that he could say "It's not what people think it is" and I could totally get it. He wasn't just talking about the Internet gang wars or wild fictional subplots. He was talking about what it's like to be a man who does a job where people no longer look at him like a man. A job where people look at the role you play on television and feel they have the right to make up what your life should be like.

"I know there are a lot of people out there who don't take wrestling seriously, but I have a lot of respect for what you guys do," I said. "I'm not a big fan, and if I was, I wouldn't jabber on to you about your job because I know that gets old. It's no fun when people only talk to us about baseball, like that's the only thing we do."

"No, it's fine, ask me anything you want," he said.

"Do people ever treat you like what you do isn't a real sport?"

Triple's eyes narrowed. If there was ever a moment when I thought I was actually seeing the real, genuinely angry Triple H, it was now.

"Those people need to get in a ring and get slammed," he said. "They need to get slapped and punched and then tell me how fake it is. We make real contact. Guys are really hitting that mat and it's not a trampoline like some people think. It's got hardly any give. The abuse to your body is very real."

"How do you take all that abuse? You're getting jumped on, run into, thrown off stuff, I can't imagine the strain on your body. Hell, I got hurt lifting a fucking dumbbell." I smacked myself in the head.

"That's the skill of it," he said. "During some of those moves, you're trusting your life to your partner, and he to you. Your body gets used to it, though. You get calluses in places you never knew you could get them."

I asked him a bunch of other questions, like if the matches were really scripted or not. He said the big ones were, but the little ones were hashed out hours before the match, with only the winner and loser pre-decided. I asked about code words during matches, how they gave each other breathers, how they worked the crowd, who was the biggest douchebag wrestler of all time—all the standard stuff.

After a half an hour or so, I felt like I was being another fan boy even though he was a good sport about everything. Andrews was late, as usual, and I didn't want to tire Triple out by being more of a pest than I already had been. He was a super nice and articulate man, but even super nice men have their limits. I tried to think of something that he didn't get asked all the time.

"Do most guys in your line of work have short careers?"

"Yeah. It's actually a lot like your minor leagues," he said. "There's not a lot of room at the top. Just because you're a big strong guy doesn't mean you have what it takes. You spend a lot of time paying your dues. A lot of guys get hurt trying to make it. Early on, there's very little money. And, of course, a lot of guys who do make it can't handle it when they do, and wreck their careers making bad decisions." Triple H sighed and looked around the room at some of the athlete posters. Then, in no particular connection, he started naming off related vices. "Drugs, partying, and making stupid decisions with their money. We"—he meant the older guys in leadership positions—"try to tell them to be smart, that this isn't going to last forever and you're only one accident away from it all being over. But they don't listen. You'd think they'd have better perspective considering everything they went through to get to the top."

"That doesn't surprise me at all," I said, my voice trailing off into the land of potent memories.

"It happens," he offered. "Guys are going to make their own decisions. They're going to fall in love with themselves. But it seems to me that the guys, at least in my line of work, who believe the hype that surrounds them have the shortest careers. At the end of the day, we're just guys who run around in our underwear and slam into each other."

I laughed at his casualness. He shrugged. "It's hard to take yourself more seriously than you should when you realize what is really going on."

After he said all that, I made a connection in my head that I wished I'd made a long time ago. Professional sports in general were all the same. All the freshly baked analytics argued over daily on cable channels; all the pyrotechnics after home runs and touchdowns; all the mascots, cheerleaders, money, and egos—it was all just the industry trying to distract us from the fact that, at the end of the day, we were just grown men putting on costumes and playing children's games. To take any of it more seriously than that was a mistake.

The doors of the clinic split open and, like a famous pro wrestler himself, Dr. Andrews made his triumphant entrance. His costume was surgical scrubs, with the pants tucked into a pair of white wading boots, and a white surgical mask down around his neck. I couldn't help but picture him covered in blood, or at least carrying a chainsaw. I think it was the boots.

Instead he held a cup of coffee. Flanked by an entourage of doctors in training, men and women who could boast having studied under the rock star of sports surgery, he walked up to a patient to begin his rounds. The entourage carried touch-screen laptops and audio recorders so they could capture all his wisdom in real time.

I sat on my table next to Triple. Dr. Andrews started on the side of the room opposite the pro athletes, and worked his way down toward us. He stopped at every table he came to, his entourage jockeying around him for the best position to witness his greatness.

What was remarkable about Andrews was, even though he sees more patients in a month than some doctors see in a year, he remembered all of us. Once Kevin explained to him where the patient was in his training, Andrews asked questions about family, and jobs, and all the other peripheral stuff. His retention was impressive, plus he was a trailblazer and an innovator. All things considered, if there was one guy in any profession who had the right to think of himself as a badass for doing what he did, it was Andrews. It takes brass balls to cut open some of the planet's highest-profile athletic talent, and he wasn't just good at it, he looked forward to every new chance to expand his résumé. He might have been the most gifted sports surgeon on the planet.

When Andrews got to me, I reached out to shake his hand with some hesitation, wary that I might get smacked at any moment. He took my hand and shook it, asking me how things had gone at the clinic. I relaxed and began to tell him that I was feeling good, but as soon as I let go of his hand he smacked me in the side of the head. *That son of a bitch!*

"Lay down here for me, kid."

I didn't react to his commands as usual. I was still fighting down the urge to go ballistic on him for smacking me again. Luke saw the expression in my eyes and shook his head slightly, but vigorously: *Don't.*

I counted down in my mind and exhaled slowly. I needed the man. As Kevin said, if I ever got hurt, he was the guy to be friends with. I also needed him to give me a clean bill of health if I wanted to play again. Obediently I spun around and lay down for Andrews. With his left hand he flopped my arm around like it was a limp noodle. In his other hand, he held a cup of coffee and talked casually to the entourage who nodded like so many Japanese tourists.

"Looks good," he remarked. "Feel good?"

"Yeah," I said.

"No pain when you throw?"

"Feels a lot better. I think I may have—"

"Good," he said, and that big gold championship ring he got from the Rays cracked me in the crown of my skull, sending a jolt of pain all the way into my molars.

"Take it easy with that thing."

Andrews paid no attention to me. Or just didn't care to acknowledge my reaction. "How's that book of yours doing?" he asked, full speed ahead.

"It's great," I said, careful not to speak too long, and thus drop my guard for another Andrews strike.

"You get anything good to write about while you were here?"

"Yeah," I said. *Boy, did I ever.* Then, recalling a little detail I'd picked up, I said, "But I was really hoping Tiger would be here by now. I heard he was coming." Andrews perked up immediately. This was complete bullshit, of course; Tiger was not coming, but saying he was was my way of slapping Andrews in the head with a championship ring. "Yeah," I continued, "it's all over ESPN."

Andrews looked at his scheduling agent, who shrugged. Then he looked to his entourage, who traded giddy expressions. Composing himself, Andrews said to me, "Now, you can't listen to what the television says about stuff like that. I don't worry about who is coming here until they're coming here."

"Sure," I said, "totally makes sense."

"All the same, let's get a confirmation on that, okay?" Andrews said to his scheduling agent.

I smirked.

"Alright then, you look like you're ready to get back to it," Andrews said.

"Thanks, Doc. Thank for all your—"

He slapped me again.

"Triple! How are you, big fella?" Andrews said, moving right along.

Chapter 41

After Dr. Andrews cleared me, it took less than a week for George to allow me back into the nest. He scheduled a Friday-morning flight so I could get back into Dunedin and get settled in at the Innisbrook resort for the weekend. As good as it felt to know my career was back on track, I was sad to leave the boys in Birmingham. We'd been through our own identity-and-bonding phase, not unlike what I'd missed during spring training as a Blue Jay with a broken wing.

At my last therapy session, I invited Rob, Zim, Luke, Lenny, and a couple of the other trainers from the clinic out to a Birmingham Barons ball game to get shitfaced on Thirsty Thursday beer and celebrate my last night in town. Tickets were on me, as were the beers and whatever else they wanted. I was flush with major league depression money, hoarded from all the days and nights I spent locked in my room. Blowing it on processed carbs, watered-down grog, and cheap baseball felt like the right thing to do.

Rob and Zim passed because they had family in town. I also invited Kevin to join us, but he demurred. When I asked him what could be better than spending an evening out with me, he gushed about how he spent his evenings at home with his wife, grilling exotic fish, drinking exotic wines, and listening to exotic music. We booed him for being a pretentious nerd, to which he responded, "It's called being a refined professional. You should all try it sometime."

Before I left the clinic that day, I paid Dr. Refined Professional a private visit in his office, a humble place with a few family pictures, a few framed degrees, and a horde of books he'd been published in. The door was open but his head was down, buried in email. I knocked twice.

"Dirky," he said, looking up at me, "who did you piss off now?"

"No one that I know of." I pointed at a chair in his office. Kevin nodded. I came in and sat.

"What can I do for you?" Kevin asked.

"I just wanted to come in and pay my respects. Say thank you for getting me better and putting up with all my crap while I was here."

Kevin waved a hand at me. "I didn't treat you any differently than I would have treated anyone else around here."

"You would have set up any other patient with an eighty-year-old woman?"

"No. It's just that I knew you were feeling down, and she was your type. I would have done that for anyone."

I laughed. "Well, that's exactly why I'm thanking you. I'm tired of people treating me differently. I'm glad you treated me normal, even if 'normal' treatment from you borders on medical malpractice."

"Everyone is a critic! My methods work, don't they?"

"They sure do, buddy. They sure do." I smiled and glanced around his room, at all the books and degrees. "Anyway, thanks for all your help. I feel strong and ready to get back to ball. I couldn't have done it without you."

"I know," Kevin said, smiling wryly. He used sarcasm to deflect a lot of genuine emotion, and that was fine. I just wanted him to know how much I appreciated his work.

"You're going to write a book about me now, right? Telling people how great I am?"

"I promise you, Kevin. If I ever get to the point where people care enough about the crap I write, I'll make sure the world knows you're the best trainer in the business. And a pretty good dude, too."

"Good." He looked back at his email. I nodded, got up, and went to the door.

"Dirk."

I stopped and turned around to face him. "Yeah, Boss?"

"You know the reason I'm not going tonight is so all the guys can have a good time out without fear of the boss being around, right?"

"Uh, sure."

"Otherwise I'd go and hang out with you. You made things a lot of fun around here, for all of us. We'll miss ya."

"Thanks. I appreciate that."

"Also, and don't go blabbing this on the Internet, but I hope you don't leave with the impression I'm arrogant. I know I can come off that way sometimes, but really, it's just an act I've developed during my time here. A lot of big names come in and out of this place. Some of them expect a certain . . . *special* treatment from me. As a medical practitioner, I can't do that. I have to be a little tough and cocky in order to make sure I get the respect I need, and so the guys under me respect me as well. I've been doing it so long, sometimes I forget who I am."

"Believe me," I said, "I totally understand what it's like being in an environment where you have to play a role."

Kevin nodded. "Good luck," he said. "That arm's got a lot of innings left in it—if that's what you want."

"Thanks. Take care," I said.

"You too."

"Oh, one more thing."

"What's up?" I asked, holding the door jamb.

"One of your teammates is coming here tomorrow. Brice Jared?"

"Yeah," I squeezed the doorjamb. "What's wrong with him?"

"Don't know. Haven't gone over his file yet."

"Brice is hurt, huh? Interesting . . ."

"I take it you know him, then?"

"Oh, I know him alright."

"How well?"

"Well enough to hope that Andrews smacks the shit out of him."

Chapter 42

I said good-bye to the training room crew boys after the stadium stopped serving beer. Cheap and watered down as it was, Luke still managed to get drunk and hit on some of the Barons' "biggest" fans. With all the abuse he'd taken from Kevin, who was I to stand in his way? I made Lenny promise to record as much of Luke's behavior as he could and show it to the nun. Then I made him promise to record her reaction to Luke and send it to me.

The next morning I went to the airport early, all the while wondering if I'd bump into Brice in transit. After scouring the Internet for details on how he wound up busted I discovered that Brice's problem was, of all things, his shoulder. I won't lie: I smiled when I read it. He was on his way to Birmingham to get a thorough inspection from Andrews before the Blue Jays took their next step. Regardless of what that might be, he'd be spending some time back in Dunedin. It seemed that Brice and I would cross paths again, and soon.

I landed back in Florida in the middle of the day and rented a yellow Volkswagen Bug on the team's dime. I knew I'd get picked on by some of the guys for driving it, but that didn't seem like such a big deal to me anymore. I was a child of the eighties and I'd always wanted to drive a yellow Bug; specifically, one that transformed into a robot and fought Decepticons. Alas, the rental-car company manager said that option was available only on the higher-end models.

Instead of opting for an economy hotel room or a shitty apartment covered in trash and unicorn stickers, I had the team fix me up at the Innisbrook. My room turned out to be a fully furnished apartment on the top floor, with panoramic glass panels that overlooked a manicured par-four fairway. Just knowing life was out there and happy to have me join, should I feel like leaving my apartment, made giving up the housing stipend completely worth it. I pulled the apartment's desk and chair into position to face the view, then kicked my feet up and soaked it in.

That night, Dr. Ray called me to ask me how I was feeling now that I was back in Dunedin again.

"I feel good," I said, feet up and staring out at the sunset.

"Good as in, good right now? Or good as in a more permanent state of good?"

"Jesus, can't a man just feel good without having to qualify it?"

"That's what psychologist do, Dirk; we qualify every emotion! But if you're feeling good, that's *good* enough."

"I'd say a more permanent good, which is surprising because a couple of days ago, I got into what is probably the biggest social mess of my entire baseball-writer career." I told him about Triple H, including my panic for about twenty-four hours afterward.

"I'm surprised you didn't tell me about this sooner," Ray said.

"It was hard," I said, watching the sun draw low and paint the sky orange to purple, "but I wanted to handle it myself. I had to see if I could do it alone. I'd like to eventually get back to a life where I don't have to call you every time I get myself into some debacle or another—I'd be calling you all the time!"

"Yes, and unfortunately I don't get paid by the hour," Ray said, "so I approve. How do you feel you handled it?"

"At first I was really scared. Well, worse then scared. That sick, out-of-control feeling that got me in touch with you in the first place came back with a vengeance. I'd done everything I swore I'd never do. I hurt someone with my writing.

"But, in a way, I'm glad I finally screwed up. I felt bad about it, sure, and I asked for forgiveness. But I also realized that if Triple H didn't want to forgive me, I couldn't force him, and that didn't mean I was a terrible person. I realized I could always offend someone, but that shouldn't paralyze me. And then, you know, when Triple didn't kill me, I realized I was going to be okay. It made me rethink the reaction to the recorder issue. The reaction to the book. All of it."

I stood up and walked across the suite to watch the last of the orange sink behind the distant horizon. "I sure as hell didn't enjoy the trip to getting to this point, but now that I'm here I actually feel like I know me. Like I have a say in my life, as strange as that sounds. Maybe I feel that way because I've finally realized how much of my life I haven't felt that way. How much of me has just been whatever baseball tells me I am."

Ray considered my words. Then, evenly, firmly, he said, "That's great, Dirk. You slowed things down, recognized your behaviors, and made an adjustment. You saw yourself from a different angle, and you didn't run from it. That's great. That's a lot more than most people do. You should be proud of yourself."

"I wish I had known all this earlier, as a young pitcher."

"I would like to point out that I have been preaching this

stuff to organizations you've played for during your entire career. You should try listening."

"Right. Strange how I write down all the boob and fart humor but fail to record anything that might actually help me."

"Good thing you didn't. It wouldn't have earned you a bestseller."

"You know, there is one thing I've been thinking on, and I wanted to talk to you about it. As happy as I am about how the whole Triple H thing went down, I can't help but feel bad about how things went down with TJ Collins."

"What do you think is making you connect these two things?"

"Well, I just wonder, when TJ hears his name, if he thinks of himself as TJ the failing baseball player who everyone wants answers from, or TJ the person? In wrestling, it's easy for the athlete to know they're playing a character. In other sports, like baseball, I don't think people realize what they're doing out on the field is pretty much the same thing: playing a role.

"I always wondered why they don't stop and think about it more. But I suppose when baseball is all you've ever done, when it's all you've ever wanted to do, it's scary to think that there might be something bigger than the game."

"I can certainly understand your analogy, but I don't think it applies to every player," said Ray.

"I don't either. But it applies to some. And it takes only a few guys with the wrong thinking, in the wrong situation, to make life hard for everyone else. Not to mention how miserable it must make things for them."

The faces at rehab had changed since my last visit. Hasher and McGowan were the only ones I still recognized. New bodies had come into town, mostly minor leaguers. Since there are five times as many minor leaguers as major leaguers, it only stood to reason that more of them would be hurt. They were all trying to get healthy as fast as they could since there was less than a month of minor league play left and they wanted to get back on the field before the season ended. It's much easier to find a job for next year when you finish the present one healthy—a luxury I was told upon my return to Dunedin that I would not get.

I would not be cleared for competition in time to get a minor league rehab assignment. The best I could hope for was to spend the next couple of weeks throwing bullpens off a mound, and get strong enough to start the next season fully recovered. Of course, my medical history would always reflect that I was absent all of 2010, but a clean bill of health from Dr. Andrews might convince someone to take a chance on me. Maybe even—if I was a good boy for the rest of the year—the Blue Jays.

Jep seemed happy to see me, and thrilled that I had a list of exercises and routines from Kevin. He said that if the Birmingham regimen was working, there was no reason to change it. Which was code for, "If you can do it without me, do it. I got a ton of shit going on."

Brice returned to Dunedin on Monday. His test results were clean aside from some inflammation. It was just a strain. He'd be shut down until it healed. Assuming he didn't have any setbacks, he'd be competing again before the end of the season. Meanwhile, he and I would attend rehab together.

Fortunately, the injury had sucked the swagger from him. We passed each other like ships in the night, neither of us talking. The days rolled by quietly for our first month. I went to therapy, put my work in, built arm strength, and mixed in some weight training I would have done had I not injured myself—minus the bench press, of course.

Bonnie came to visit and I took her to Universal Studios where we swam with the dolphins. Kevin emailed to check up on me every now and again, sharing stories about how he was torturing Luke. My baseball agent sent me a new pair of cleats, something I hadn't even bothered bringing with me to spring training rehab since I didn't know when I'd need them again.

My book agent called with bad news and good. The bad news was that the movie deal had been squashed. The good was that the buzz had lasted long enough to inspire my publishing house to make a mid-six-figure offer for two more books. I jumped on it. It had taken me my whole life to make that much money in baseball, and even then it wouldn't have happened had I not broken my shoulder. It took only two years, one successful book, and my sanity to match that in the literary world. My agent was right: there was no going back. But at least I had about four hundred thousand reasons to keep moving forward.

I spent my afternoons at the driving range and my evenings putting together my next book, eating out, and playing video games. I was happily checked into Club Med. I didn't feel the slightest bit guilty.

But Brice was getting stronger, too. Two weeks before the season ended for the major league club, he was close to healthy and ready to go.

And as his strength recovered, so did his ego.

There was always a stack of books in my rehab locker. Presents from people who read mine and wanted me to return the favor, along with an endorsement. There was also a slew of copies of my own book sent by fans who wanted them autographed. Seeing so many books pissed Brice off.

It was bad enough that people wanted my attention over his. Worse still that they wanted it from Dirk Hayhurst, Author. Brice hated it, I knew, but he said nothing. He was separated from his power source and could not speak to me as the representative of many against my few, as he had before. But the Blue Jays were soon to play the Tampa Bay Rays at home just a few miles from the Jays' spring Dunedin training and rehab complex. Brice was set to be activated near the end of that road trip. With the return of Brice's health and his entourage, he became emboldened. All he needed now was an opportunity. Which, as fate would have it, I provided him.

When the Blue Jays arrived, the media arrived with them. Barry Davis, the Jays' on-field television correspondent, and I had become friends during the media courtship process I initiated before the launch of the book. He was a nice guy: professional, artistic, and happy to assist me in pushing my book. He interviewed me once already during spring training. Now that the book was a bestseller, he thought a follow-up was in order.

Barry's idea was to document a normal day of rehab for me, show the fans what it's like to be injured. I told him that showing fans what it's like to be injured simply by displaying the rehab exercises we do is hardly scratching the surface. I told him that there is a whole world of mental struggle behind it that exercises couldn't even begin to express. This seemed to intrigue Barry, and he asked if I'd be okay talking about that on camera, filling in all the blanks for the viewers back home. He said he'd drop in some feel-good music, a little B-roll footage highlight package of me pre-injury, and a shot of the book. He said we'd win a Gemini for it.

"Sure," I said. "Why not?"

Why not is because to make it work, we had to film me in the training room—a universally understood no-media zone. But I figured if there was no one but me *in* the training room, it wouldn't be a big deal. I asked Jep, who said it was fine.

The next day, with the training room vacant, the material was shot, the piece was put together, and no one was hurt.

"Thanks for taking the time, Dirk," said Barry, after we finished.

"No, thank *you*," I said. "I appreciate all the publicity I can get."

"You know, if you don't come back from this—and I'm not saying you won't—you should think about going into the broadcasting side of things."

I nodded. "Thanks, Barry. I appreciate that."

Barry shrugged. "Seriously, you never know what your future could bring. You've got a lot of talents. More than the average meathead." He patted me on the side. "Something to think about, eh?"

"I will." And I did think about it. All the way back to my locker. In fact, thinking about it was probably why I didn't notice Brice, sitting at his locker, waiting for me.

Chapter 43

"Media," said Brice, slithering out of the shadows, voice rich with venom.

I looked over at him from my changing stool. "Call me Dirk," I said.

"No reporters in the training room, man."

"No one got hurt. Relax," I said, placing sunglasses in their case.

"Have you gone down to see the team since they've come to town?" he asked.

"No, why?"

"That's kinda shady, bro. Team is in town, you don't go see 'em but you do interviews in the training room for your book."

I thought about his argument. "I guess I can see how you could choose to view that as shady." I shrugged and started taking off my cross trainers and socks.

"It's no guess, bro, it's a fact. Did you ask Jep if that was okay to film?"

"Yep." One shoe off.

"Did you ask Jay Stenhouse if it was okay?" Jay was the team's media rep.

"Nope." The other shoe off.

"Pssh . . . That's shady, man." Brice shook his head.

"I'm sorry you feel that way," I said, pulling my long blue socks down.

"It ain't about how I feel, it's about respecting the team."

"Right," I said, passionless.

"Man," Brice stood up, irritated. "I'm just trying to help you. You go ahead, keep putting guys' careers in danger doing that selfish shit and see how long you stick around."

I sat up, took a deep breath, and turned to him. "Show me your badge."

"What?" Brice tilted his head.

"Show me your badge, officer. You *are* the locker-room police, aren't you?"

"Psssh . . . You always got some smartass comeback for shit, huh? That's why—"

"Nobody likes me," I finished. "Yeah, yeah, I've heard that one already and I'm over it. You got any new material? I mean, come on, Brice. You've had a whole season to think of shit to insult me with and that's your go-to slam?" I finished taking my socks off and slipped into my shower flip-flops, the ones I bought when I moved into the rancid apartment in the spring.

"There it is again, man. You don't even deny it. You only think about yourself. Why don't you try thinking about your team for a change, man?"

"Have you read my book?" I asked, turning on my stool and crossing my legs.

"Hell no, I ain't read your book. Why read a book about a guy that doesn't give a shit about anyone but him?"

"Then how do you know it was a bad thing for me to write and promote?"

"You see anyone else on the team doing it?"

"Oh, so because no one else on the team does it, I shouldn't do it. What is this, high school?"

"It's baseball, dude. It's a game of adjustments," Brice said, pacing around me. "If everyone on the team hates you for the shit you're doing, you make an adjustment."

"Yeah, about that, who is *everyone*?" I asked.

"Everyone. The team, man."

"Everyone on the team has confessed to you that they hate me. You guys all sat down, had a meeting, and it was decided that I was a bastard who deserved your all-encompassing hate?" I crossed my hands behind my head. "Huh." I couldn't help but wonder if this was how Dr. Ray felt when he bombarded players with questions.

"Enough, man. Enough that you should give the team an apology," said Brice

"Who?"

"The Blue Jays."

"No, who. As in, which players are 'enough'?"

"Man, I ain't gonna tell you."

"You want me to apologize to the whole team for something only certain players are upset about, but you won't tell me who. That's kinda *shady,* don't you think?"

"You ain't been 'round the team all year"—Brice gestured from his chest, out to me with both hands—"so you don't know what I know. But trust me, man, guys are not happy with the shit you been doing."

"I haven't been around the team all year, but you expect me to believe they've been thinking about me the whole time?"

"People ain't happy with you, that's all I'm saying."

"That's fine. I don't expect them to be."

"And you're just like, 'fuck 'em,' huh?"

"Look." I dropped my head and sighed. "Brice, you might be worried about what this team thinks of me, but I'm not. I know what I did and I'm fine with it. I've never hurt any of you."

"You take attention from what matters. That hurts all of us."

"You choose to be hurt," I said. "The way I see it, you're the one with the choice to make. Either you're going to suck it up and live with the fact that one of the guys on this team doesn't think like you do, or you're going to let my presence in this clubhouse drive you to the point you can't handle it. I'm not changing for you, or this team. I don't know what else to tell you."

"That's arrogant, bro."

"Maybe."

"It's selfish."

"Whatever." I stood up, turned around, and slid off my shirt in favor of a dry one.

"Selfish motherfucker."

I didn't bite.

"Even the guys up in Birmingham thought you was a selfish motherfucker."

Now *that* made me angry. Not emotional. Not out of control. Angry. The focused, intense kind of anger that had eluded me since I got hurt and felt like I was at the mercy of everyone's opinions.

"That's not true, Brice," I said, pulling my new shirt over my head.

"The fuck it ain't."

"It's not. I know those guys. I talk to them regularly." I turned around. "You're putting words in their mouth and those words are bullshit. Tell me, how much other bullshit have you put in people's mouths this season? How many other guys have you borne a false witness to cut me down with? I must have really hurt your fragile ego if you have to go to such great lengths."

"Keep doing what you're doing and you'll find out for yourself."

"I will," I said. "I'll find out, on my own, when these mysterious voices of the clubhouse confront me. But not until then. Meanwhile, let me tell you something that isn't bullshit. I just signed a contract to deliver two more books for enough money that if I never make it back to the big leagues, I'll be just fine. I'm the real deal, motherfucker. I've gone out of my way to make sure assholes like you don't get hurt and I'm tired of it. I've put my life out there, and shared my mess with the whole world. I got nothing to lose. But *you* do. You confirm it every time you jump me about the choices I make. You had better pray I make a full recovery." I took a step closer and my voice grew soft—a tactic I'd learned in another life, as another kind of player. "You'd better pray I play till the end of time. Because when I'm done and no longer have a career to worry about, I'm gonna burn you to the ground."

"So you're threatening guys now, huh?"

"No, baby, *it's a promise.*"

"Do it, bitch." Brice raised his voice, coming face to face with me. "I don't give a shit what you say."

"Oh, Brice, we both know that isn't true. You're scared to death of me. You don't even know why you are, but you are. Want me to tell you why you're so afraid?"

"Fuck you," shouted Brice. He shoved me with both hands.

"Because baseball is all you got," I said, steadying myself. "You lose this, and you're nothing. But even the meager life you scrape together away from the field? I'll take that from you, too. I'll make you famous, just so I can make you infamous."

Brice wasn't going to swing on me. Oh, he wanted to. He got back in my face again, posturing like he would, but he couldn't. Not here. Not in rehab. Not as a member of a Major League team. He had to use his words.

"And when the team knows you're out to get 'em, what then, bitch?"

"Tell 'em," I said. "Tell them if they fuck with me like you have, that's what's gonna happen. It doesn't matter if they believe you or not. Whether I play again after this year, or not, that's what will happen."

Jep poked his head into the room. The little rage monster I once met living inside of Jep was bubbling out. He must have heard us shouting at one another. His neck was bulging, his eye twitched, and his voice had deepened. "There a problem in here?" he growled.

"No, Jep. We're good," I said. "Just having a talk about the team. Right, Brice?"

Brice smirked and passed a hand over his face, then nodded. "Yeah, Jep. It's cool. We cool."

"I'm ready for some ice, partner," I said, walking toward the training room.

Jep relaxed, morphing back into his normal self. "Oh, sure, uh-huh, you bet," he said, and fell into step behind me, leaving Brice alone to think about all the things I might do to him.

Chapter 44

"Oh, I'm fine," I said to Dr. Ray after he asked me how I felt about my run-in with Brice.

"Have I created a monster?" asked Ray. "Would you actually do all that?"

"Probably not," I said, staring out at the fairway next to my apartment. A hawk was sitting in a tree by itself, observing an elderly foursome turn a par four into a par infinity. A flock of birds circled around the hawk, squawking in irritation of its presence.

"But if Brice thinks I will, that's all I need. It's time he suffered under the weight of his fear-filled perceptions for a while," I said. "He hasn't said a peep to me since."

"Did it feel good to get all of that off your chest?"

"Yes, very much so."

"Are you worried that, by confirming players' fears of what you might do, your playing environment is going to become that much more difficult?"

"You know, I thought my life as a player was going to change this year. Now I realize it was my life as a whole. I can't separate the two, so I might as well quit trying to. This is what I am."

"And if the Jays don't bring you back? Don't you think that will make you regret changing your stance on things?"

"I doubt the Jays are going to bring me back. I think what I said to Brice will have very little to do with that."

"Fine. What if other teams feel the same and you don't get a job next year?"

I walked out of the apartment and put my hands on the railing of the balcony. The hawk was still in his tree, solitary and watching. He was beautiful and lonely and that was his life. Even if he tried his best to fit in with the other birds, he would still be a predator to them.

"Ray, I always wanted to get to the top of baseball because I thought if I did, everyone would agree I was great, and awesome, and I'd finally be respected. Then, when they respected me, I'd respect myself. I thought my accomplishments would make me happy because everyone around me would agree I should be happy. I thought I had something to prove, and now I can't even remember who I was trying to prove it to. Me? Family? An old enemy? I don't know.

"I may not get a job playing next year, but I'm not sure that's a big deal anymore. A lot of the stuff I've done, I've done because I wanted people to respect or appreciate me. I don't feel like I need that as much anymore. I'd miss the game, and the money—assuming I ever made it back to the bigs. But I guess I have to ask myself if I'd be happy doing it. I mean, most of what we do, we do because we think it will create happiness. I don't think I need to keep playing professionally to be happy. In fact, in a lot of ways, not playing might just be better."

"If that's the case, why not just retire?"

"I still like to pitch. I still enjoy the game. It's always going to be a rough environment for me now, I know, but I'd still like to see if I can pitch at the top. For myself. I thought I was going to lose a whole year because of this injury, and that I'd spend all of next year trying to get back everything I'd lost." I chuckled to myself. "You know, Ray, I think I learned more about baseball this year than any season before it, and I didn't throw a single pitch.

When the end of the season came, I handed out gift cards to all the trainers who helped nurse me back to health, and sent a profound thank-you to George. It was the least I could do for all the shit I'd put them through. I harbored no ill feelings toward them, even thought I was still suffering from mysterious choking and pinching issues. It had been a long season for all of us, and now that it was over, there was no use looking back with anything but gratitude. As hard as the journey from injury to health was, I could have been released before any of it happened. The Jays' training staff were consummate professionals; in fact, the organization as a whole was top quality. They did their best, and I appreciated all their help knowing full well I was surely one of the most insufferable patients they'd ever had to deal with. They thanked me for my gifts, I thanked them for their patience, we wished each other well, and that was that.

After I cleaned out my locker, I packed up my apartment at Innisbrook and headed to the airport for the flight home. The Jays didn't send me off with any kind of throwing program, which I took as a telling sign I would not be rejoining them in 2011. I was right. Near the turn of the year, my baseball agent informed me that the Jays had passed on offering me a new contract.

I emailed Alex Anthopoulos and told him I appreciated the opportunities that he'd given me, that I was sorry I hadn't healed up faster, and that I wished him and the Jays well— though not too well, should I wind up facing them. I also told him that the Blue Jays were a fine organization to be a part of and any baseball player who is lucky enough to find their way there should be thankful for the opportunity. Alex thanked me, told me it was a pleasure, and offered me good luck. Just like that, my time as a Toronto Blue Jay came to an end.

Though it was the first off-season I'd ever entered without a job lined up, I trained through the winter like I did before I was injured. I hired Mondo, though I told him that I'd settle for good shape if trying to get into great shape meant falling apart at the seams. He laughed. Then he smacked me in the back and trained me so hard I threw up.

I kept in touch with Dr. Ray. Even though I wasn't technically under his jurisdiction, we'd become good friends. He told me he'd be happy to chat with me anytime I wanted, as long as I agreed to read his screenplay attempts. I happily obliged. It was the least I could do for a guy who'd essentially saved me from myself.

My throwing partner and friend Jason Stephens also had a tough season. His elbow started bothering him again and the Phillies shut him down. He actually had to go to the Andrews clinic shortly after I left. He threw with me at the Kent State Field House, despite the fact that, like me, he had no job lined up. We speculated about what it would be like if we signed with a team as a package deal. I was keen on the idea, but Jason said, since he could hardly stand playing catch with me, the idea of being my teammate for a whole season was enough to make him hope his elbow never recovered. In the end, it didn't matter. His elbow was fine, but his medical track record made teams too wary of offering him a contract and he was forced into retirement.

Two weeks before the start of the 2011 spring training, I began to wonder if things were going to go the same way for me. My baseball agent, despite vigorously shopping my name and services to all possible MLB suitors, had yet to turn up any leads. As the days counted down, I began making peace with the end of my career by inquiring into the possibility of starting others.

During the off-season I finished my college degree and started researching a masters in clinical mental health counseling (Dr. Ray wrote me a letter of recommendation). I was already two hundred pages into writing my next book, *Out Of My League,* and the movie buzz was starting to pick up again. Independent-league baseball teams offered me roster spots, should I choose that route, and some specifically offered permission to write about whatever I wanted.

Then, out of nowhere, I received a letter from the Rogers Corporation, owners of the Toronto Blue Jays. My former employers, in a sense. They wanted to know if I had any interest in television broadcasting. They had heard me on their radio station, and seen the work I did with Barry Davis. They said all the people on the media end of things thought highly of me, and wondered if I'd like to come up and audition.

It was an incredible opportunity. A chance for me to break into a new line of work, at the top, as an expert, all the while allowing me to stay around the game I loved. The work would be handsomely compensated *and* provide a platform from which I could push my writing, with no wear and tear to my body. I already had friends in the business and knew the town. The schedule was flexible and my wife could be with me. And I could openly share my thoughts without a team full of paranoia. All I had to do was say good-bye to my playing career.

With no offers to continue on as a professional baseball player on the table, I said yes to the audition. Then, a few days before I was set to head to Toronto, and two weeks before the start of spring training, I received an offer from the Tampa Bay Rays. A major league camp invite and standard free agent salary in Triple-A. They knew about my writing and depression and were fine with both. They said they made a business of finding undervalued talent and they thought, considering the way I had pitched against them in the past, that I was worth the risk. At least the risk of an invitation and a tryout. After that, there were no guarantees. If I failed to impress, I'd get released. In which case I'd be out of two jobs and back home with nothing.

I took it.

It was a gamble, and, considering how young and talented the arms in their organization were, it wasn't even a good bet. But then again, living is a gamble. We all wind up and deliver our pitch, and what happens after that—strike three, home run, or shoulder injury—is out of our control. We can't go back, but we can go forward with what we've learned. I was a baseball player, and a baseball player takes risks. That's the nature of his work. But I was also a writer, and a writer knows that the risks he takes yield no bad results, just good material.

Epilogue

My locker in the Rays' big league spring training complex was right next to Cory Wade's. He, like me, had come to the Rays after getting let go by his former team; in his case it was the Dodgers, thanks to an injury. Cory explained the whole thing to me, how the Dodgers overused him, how his shoulder didn't hold up to the constant abuse, and how, after he got hurt, they basically rehabbed him and tossed him. I told him that I got released by the Jays because, aside from being hurt, I went insane for a little while and promised to write incriminating things about everyone I came into contact with and sell it to the highest bidder. I smiled, shook Cory's hand, and said, "Nice to meet you. Glad we're locker buddies." Then I offered him a signed copy of my book.

I was just meeting Cory, but I already knew a lot of guys in the Rays' clubhouse. Mike Ekstrom, Cesar Ramos, and Matt Bush were all former Padre teammates of mine. That dude who slept in a bush in Vegas was also back in my life again, which was, uh, *something*. I even had a former college teammate, Andy Sonnanstine. Maybe it was the fact that I'd already shuffled teams before, or that I was older and more experienced, but I felt immediately welcome in the Rays' organization.

I also made a lot of new acquaintances. The Rays were young. More upbeat and socially savvy. Most of the older guys were not the ruling parties in the clubhouse, but hired guns brought in for their experience. Evan Longoria, B. J. Upton, David Price, James Shields, and Ben Zobrist were the core of the team, and I was older or as old as most of them. The older guys like Johnny Damon and Manny Ramirez were brought in not simply because they were talented vets, but also because they had personalities that fit with the team's general persona. I appreciated this and, after only a few days of spring training, it was easy to see the group was much looser than any team I'd been with in the past.

Youth played a factor, but there was also our manager, Joe Maddon. On the first day of camp, Maddon, sporting his white spiked hair, thick-framed glasses, and easy California vibe, greeted us all. He did all the standard manager rah-rah stuff that managers are supposed to do: laying out goals and projections and high expectations. But it was after all the bureaucratic talk was out of the way that Maddon really impressed.

Maddon said he wanted to meet us all individually. He wanted to know us, and us to know him. He wanted to talk to everyone about their strengths and weaknesses, and why they were in camp, and said that he wanted everyone to feel comfortable around him. He hated the cone of silence. He hated walking around the complex, putting players on edge because they were afraid of him. He wanted players to engage him, to know him, and to feel comfortable. With him and with each other. Like a family.

That was the second time I'd heard a coach use the word "family" in my playing career, but in Maddon's usage it took on a completely different feel. Coupled with his charisma, confidence, and penchant for funky-themed travel dress requirements, you couldn't help but believe him. In fact, when he and I had our private meeting, I went in wondering if I was going to be lectured about writing, and instead came out with two lists: great wines and must-read books.

Speaking of books, I was finishing up a chapter in my second book that happened to feature Manny Ramirez. In it, he'd just hit a home run off of me, number 524, effectively putting the last nail in the coffin containing my debut as a Padre. When I asked him if he remembered the homer, he said he remembered because I'd struck him out so many times before. I said, "Manny, that was the first time I ever faced you. You took me out to the opposite field. It's how I made SportsCenter for the first time in my life."

"Oh, sorry, Papi," Manny said.

I didn't believe he was sorry at all. But, after a spring-training game against the Pirates in which I went six up and and six down including two Ks, he met me in the dugout and hugged me, saying, "See, Papi, I'm glad you're on my team now!"

I was glad I was on his team too. Ben Zobrist and I became fast friends through Baseball Chapel. David Price, who had a Twitter account with a zillion followers, told me he'd happily plug any media I produced in the future. Evan Longoria asked me if I could make a Garfoose stuffed animal for a Playboy centerfold model who was into him. Johnny Damon invited me to a team party on his yacht—at last, a real boats-and-hoes party! And Kyle Farnsworth, despite several facts pointing to the contrary, did not tackle me or beat the shit out of me, which I considered as good a sign of friendship as any. The Rays were a good fit.

Four weeks into spring training with the Rays, I was sitting at my locker checking my Twitter feed. Brice, along with a couple of his cronies, had created accounts and were actively engaging the fan base with banal tweets about where they ate, which football teams they liked, and how much they loved fans—the same fans they openly cursed only months earlier for being dipshits who didn't deserve access to anything they did.

I guess we're all hypocrites, because I found myself jealous over how many Twitter followers they had and wanted to get back to the bigs just so I could have more than them. I was pathetic.

I felt a hand tap me on the shoulder. It was Jim Hickey, the big league pitching coach. "I need to talk with you for a second, Digs," he said.

I sighed. If a coach says he has to talk with you in spring training but can't do it in public, it means you're getting sent down. "This isn't going to be a happy chat, is it?" I said, standing up and following him out of the locker room.

"Sorry, pal," he said, leading me down the green mile to a meeting room.

Sitting at a large conference table inside the room were Joe Maddon, general manager Andrew Friedman, bullpen coach Stan Boroski, director of minor league operations Mitch Lukevics, and—seating himself after I entered—Jim Hickey.

I was offered a seat and took it. Friedman was the first to speak, and told me that I was, indeed, getting sent to the minors. I told him I understood. There were a lot of very talented arms in contention for only a few bullpen spots, and most of the arms didn't have a year off before coming to camp.

Maddon went on to say that he thought I was a big leaguer; that based on the way I pitched in spring training, how I carried myself, and my manner around the locker room, I definitely fit with the Tampa Bay Rays. He liked me, which made me giddy because I had come to respect Joe greatly even in the short time we'd spent together.

Friedman asked me if I'd be okay with becoming a starter.

I didn't answer immediately, so he named off why becoming a starter was a good thing: priority innings, bigger workload, high marketability, and, since I had my agent ask for the language in the contract, a better chance of going overseas to pitch. I knew everything he listed already. I was just having trouble reconciling myself to naming a book "The Starting Rotation Gospels." It didn't have the same ring to it.

"Sure. I'd be happy to start," I said.

My response seemed to please the group, even though no one else in the group did any talking; they all just watched me. I wondered if it was for effect or intimidation that they were all present if they weren't going to speak. Maybe they were just there in case I had any questions? I didn't. Go to Triple-A and start, do a really good job, and the future could be bright—same assignment as always.

The meeting wasn't over, though. I should have known things wouldn't be that simple.

"Dirk," said Friedman, "we just want you to know that we respect what you're doing off the field with your writing and the book stuff. However, we just want to make sure that whatever happens in here"—he was referring to closed-door, private meetings—"stays private. We want to be able to control that news. Is that going to be an issue?"

I nodded and said, "I want you all to know that while I do write about my experiences as a player, I go to great lengths to make sure I don't write about people who don't want to be written about. I'm not talented enough to be exposing players and still get a job playing. I think there is more to the game than just the dirty laundry. If there is something you feel uncomfortable about and want me to keep private, that's fine. I want you all to be comfortable around me, and I want to earn your respect."

Everyone in the room nodded to each other, seemingly satisfied with the answer.

"Thank you, Dirk," Friedman said.

Then, before I got up, I added, "Unless you release me. In which case I'll have to burn down every one of you."

Everyone froze.

I smiled. "Nah, I'm just kidding."